Parenting an Only Child

Parenting an Only Child

THE JOYS AND CHALLENGES OF RAISING YOUR ONE AND ONLY

SUSAN NEWMAN, PH.D.

BROADWAY BOOKS
NEW YORK

A previous edition of this book was published by
Main Street Books in 1990.

Broadway Books titles may be purchased for business or promotional use or
for special sales. For information, please write to: Special Markets
Department, Random House, Inc., 1540 Broadway, New York, NY 10036.

BROADWAY BOOKS and its logo, a letter B bisected on the diagonal, are
trademarks of Broadway Books, a division of Random House, Inc.

Visit our website at www.broadwaybooks.com

Library of Congress Cataloging-in-Publication Data

Newman, Susan.
    Parenting an only child: the joys and challenges of raising your one
and only / Susan Newman. — Rev. and updated ed.
        p.   cm.
Includes bibliographical references (p.).
    1. Only child. 2. Parenting—United States. I. Title: Joys and
challenges of raising your one and only.
HQ777.3.N48   2001
649'.142—dc21

2001025119

ISBN 0-7679-0629-2

Designed by Ellen Cipriano

1   3   5   7   9   10   8   6   4   2

FOR ANDREW,
WHO PROVES TO ME EVERY DAY
THAT ONE IS INDEED WONDERFUL

Contents

Introduction xi

PART I: CONSIDERING THE ONLY CHILD

One: The New Traditional Family 3
    The Way It Was   5
    The Trend Toward One   7
    Childbearing Realities   13
    Adoption—A Choice   18
    Why Only One   22
    One Fills the Bill   26

Two: Debunking the Myths 29
    Labeling—Myth Versus Fact   33
    The Leading Edge   48
    One Is Best If . . .   52

Three: The Inner Workings of the Threesome 53
    The Personal Issues   54
    The Practical Issues   69

Four: The Inner Workings of the Twosome 79
    Beware of the Intensity   84
    Set Time Aside for Yourself   86
    Enlarge Your Circle of Support   87
    Once There Was Enough Time   92

PART II: PARENTING AN ONLY CHILD

Five: Working Attitudes 99
    Think Big   100
    Am I Doing It Right?   103
    Moderation Is the Goal   105
    Certain Concerns Are Realistic   109
    Don't Focus on Oneness   110
    Whose Life Is It Anyway?   112

Six: The Specifics 116
    Center Stage: Pros and Cons   116
    Balance Receiving with Giving   120
    Teach Sharing and Respect for Others   122
    Set Boundaries; Define Acceptable
      Behavior   124
    Too Much of a Good Thing   127
    Money Matters   131
    Who's Running the Show?   133
    The Wedge, the Pawn, and Other
      Manipulations   138

Seven: Great Expectations 141
    Warning Signs: Too Much Pressure   144
    Look at Your Child Realistically   145
    The Super-child Syndrome   148
    The Race to Educate   150
    Blinders On   152
    State-of-the-Art Child   155
    Babying the Baby . . . Or, All
       Grown Up at Four   157

Eight: Onlies Need Not Be Lonely 160
    Friends Are Vital   163
    Lessons Friends Teach   167
    The More the Merrier   170
    Alone, but Not Lonely   173

PART III: MAKING THE RIGHT DECISION

Nine: Just One More 179
    Grandparents Are Most Enthusiastic   182
    Keeping Up with the Joneses   184
    Hitting Home   187

Ten: Pressuring Yourselves 197
    Ask Yourselves   198
    Husband Pressures Wife;
       Wife Pressures Husband   201
    The Wrong Reasons   207
    Being a Family Without
       Being Overburdened   213

Eleven: Future Issues Without Siblings 216
    Safeguarding Your Only   219
    Cultivating a Support System   222
    For the Long Haul   224

Twelve: An Only—the Only Way to Go 230
    Master Plan for Minor Pitfalls   230
    Nicholas D'Elia (Age Five):
        Profile of an Only   233
    Only Children Have Their Say   234
    Being an Only Is a Huge Break   236
    The Myth Was . . . The Reality Is . . .   239

Notes 245
Resources .259

Introduction

A dozen years ago, there I was, the mother of an only child, thrilled with the prospect of raising him and enjoying him, yet for the first five years of my son's life people were constantly urging me to have another. But I had too much invested in my career and felt I was too old. I wondered what could possibly be so wrong with only children.

In an earlier marriage I had raised my ex-husband's four children, and from that point of view, rearing one looked like a breeze. As my son advanced to the ripe age of six, and other parents praised his progress, I became more curious about the taboos against the only child.

Today my son is a young adult and I am revisiting the questions, doubts, and facts about only children. I have watched closely as the tide has shifted and swelled in the direction of, and in favor of, the only child. Studies done during the 1990s offer further confirmation, some of it startling, that only children fare extremely well. This new information builds on and strengthens what we knew ten years ago. Yet, in spite of a steadily increasing number of only children and convincing evidence that single-child stereotypes have no validity, people are still conflicted over whether or not to stop at one. They worry, as I once did, that they might be cheating their child.

Unless you know the ramifications of having one child, you may not be content with the decision to limit your family. The overriding questions for me were: Can my only child be truly happy? Is he going to be disadvantaged in any way at any point in his life? At the age of fifteen will he feel he is different because many around him have siblings? At forty-five will he have someone to turn to in a crisis?

Three years past his fifteenth birthday, my son certainly does not feel different because he's an only child. He is part of the trend toward one and, like so many other onlies born in the last two decades, doesn't think much about his siblingless status. Rather, he recognizes the advantages he has had because he is an only child. Hopefully, at forty-five, the support system we have built for him will still be strong and he will have people, sibling substitutes, to lean on if he needs them. After listening to endless stories of sibling conflict, especially in adult years, I'm not entirely convinced that siblings are a sure-fire solution to the need for emotional support or hands-on assistance in situations that may arise in later years when an only "child" must care for or help his parents in some way.

But what of the stereotypes that have adhered to the only child for more than a hundred years? The more publicized traits—selfishness, shyness, loneliness—neither fit my son as a young child, nor do they fit him as a young adult. I had feared, as most parents of onlies do, that the effects of being without siblings would become evident as he aged. More than a decade ago I decided to find out whether the lengthy list of stereotypes had any basis in fact, and even though I happily discovered they did not, myths still die hard and slowly. During the ensuing ten years I found much more evidence of the ridiculousness of such myths, and I have included it in this new edition.

With the myths surrounding the only child dispelled and the inordinate advantages clarified, the ultimate trick for me was and remains not to undermine my son's chances for success in life. Like every parent, whether she has one child or several, I want to raise him "right." I want him to flourish and grow into a well-rounded, contented human being.

If you have one child or are thinking about having only one child, you undoubtedly have some of the same questions I had: Should my one be my only? Is it fair? Is it possible to raise a great only child? And if so, how do I do it?

This book sorts out these issues for couples and single parents who seesaw between wanting a single child and wanting to, or thinking that they *should,* add to their family. It will help you determine what the best solution is for you. Since the first edition of this book was published, the Internet has blossomed into an incredible network of information and support for parents of only children. Internet web sites as well as other pertinent parenting sources are listed in a new, comprehensive resource section.

For those who choose to stop at one or have already done so, for those who are forced to limit their family because of secondary infertility or other health-related reasons, for those who find the complexity and expense of adoption too difficult or impossible, and for those who are still deciding, this is a sourcebook of insights and tips for parenting an only child. You will find easy solutions for the day-to-day dilemmas and unique pressures only children and their parents face. It also examines the difficulty of accepting a single-child family when that was not your choice. If nothing else, you will have a better understanding of what it's like to raise an only child *and* to *be* an only child.

We have been programmed for so long to think only children are unhappy and difficult to raise that it's hard to believe otherwise. This close look at social change and the only child will help you evaluate your personal situation, consider your own needs, and respond truthfully to the questions you find troublesome. You will learn the sources of the pressure to have another child and be able to better cope with a barrage of well-meaning but unnecessary, and at times out-of-line, hints from those, including your spouse, who advise you to have one more. A lone thought could be the morsel you need to end your wavering.

More and more women are in the workforce than ever before, either out of necessity or choice, but many remain plagued by the conflict of whether or not to work when their children are young. In these pages you will enter a discussion of the effects and considerations surrounding this decision in light of having a single child—a complex issue for any parent. In response to the increase in the number of single parents over the past ten years, the resources for single parents with single children have been greatly expanded.

In search of insights and answers I turned to the experts— parents who had reared or were rearing only children, and to the only children themselves. As you read, you will be introduced to many of these people. In an effort to get to the core of the only-child phenomenon, I gave interviewees the option of anonymity. Names and places have been changed for those who exercised that option; however, their comments have not been altered.

My sample group started small, with a dozen of my colleagues in the Northeast. As word got out, the sample group mushroomed and spread across the country into small cities and towns as well as into major metropolitan areas. I had tackled a subject about which people—from the ages of seven to seventy-nine—wanted to talk and share advice.

At this point, after having been immersed in this subject for so many years, upwards of three hundred people openly discussed or wrote to me about the joys and resentments, pitfalls and tactics of raising or being a single child. They voiced their predicaments, suggested solutions, and shared their glee, and in doing so have turned *Parenting an Only Child* into an extensive and rich study of only children and their families. Together, they reveal a complete range of views and further unravel the myths and mysteries. Only children explained their special needs, aired their complaints, and praised their oneness. Their personal responses reflect how it feels to grow up as an only child and, later in life, to be an adult only child. Their honesty exposes the few and very manageable stumbling blocks in rearing the only child.

In addition to my own research, psychiatrists, other psychologists, researchers, and educators gave me valuable insights into the single-child family and provided tested techniques parents can use. Are you doing too much for your only? Too little? As a parent, have you adopted a realistic and healthy attitude? Collectively, the advice of these professionals may assuage your guilt or give you a constructive method for putting your only back on track, if she's gone astray.

In this survey, numbers and statistics are few; opinions and emotions are plentiful. Individual comments, I came to understand, are far more illuminating than formal numerical conclusions. Some recent statistical findings, however, are enlightening and have been included for that reason. The only children and parents who speak throughout this book are concentrated in middle- and upper-middle-income families, those most able to do something about the quality of their lives as affected by family size.

Surprisingly, a marked number of the only children interviewed had only children or were married to only children. I repeatedly came across cases of third-generation singletons who chose to continue the tradition of bearing one child—a strong testimonial in itself. Coupled with the enthusiasm for being an only child, these "repeat performances" firmly indicate that being an only child is a far more positive circumstance than we have been led to expect.

Although I am not an only child, my life as a parent allows me to bring a unique and broad perspective to the subject. I am constantly enamored of and amazed by my only son. From a parenting point of view, this experience is no less exciting or rewarding than the one I had as the stepmother of four. It is different. One is truly wonderful, and I am not only convinced, but also reassured, that my son is not missing out. We have found ways to compensate for or duplicate the advantages offered by a larger family.

As the pros and cons of parenting and being an only child were fully explored and revisited a decade later, two things have become very obvious: First, there is a definite change in attitude toward the only child, and second, the singleton has become a desirable choice. In fact, the one-child family unit is well on its way to becoming our next traditional family, a projection I made when I originally wrote this book and a reality as we proceed through the new millennium.

So when you ask yourself, as I did, "Is it wise to have an only child?" your response can be resoundingly in the affirmative. Throughout your life *and* your child's life, there should be no second thoughts, no recriminations. There certainly don't have to be.

Parenting an Only Child

PART ONE

Considering the Only Child

1

The New Traditional Family

Is it a factor of economic restraints, more complex lives, increased infertility, pure good sense, or something else that is changing the makeup of the family unit?

When you were growing up, you probably knew or knew of a family with four or five, even eight, children. In those days, raising a station wagon–size family neither attracted attention nor caused alarm. But mention a family with five or six children today and someone is certain to groan, "How do they do it?" "Why do they do it?" "There must be a better way." There seems to be.

Never before have there been so many choices in family type or size. Our ever-evolving definition of family is broadening and diversifying to encompass blended families, biracial families, homosexual-parent families, and single-parent families. Even though family policy and laws are slow in catching up to current lifestyles, different choices are widely accepted, especially those revolving around single, or gay and lesbian parenting and adoption. Families are getting smaller and the only-child option is becoming increasingly popular.

The preference for smaller families is evident. In 1972, 56 percent of those asked in a large national opinion study thought that three or more children were ideal; in a similar study done in 1998 that percentage had dropped to 39.[1] Although both men and women may still state a preference for two or three children, the number of women who have one child mounts steadily.

According to the U.S. Census Bureau, in 1972 there were between 8 and 9 million only children. By 1985 the number had grown to 13 million, and by the beginning of the new millennium it approached the 16 million mark, confirming psychologist Sandra Scarr's claim in the mid-eighties that "many serious parents . . . are planning to invest their best efforts in one or at the most two children."[2]

Those who study demographics agree that the one-child household is the fastest-growing family unit. It surprises many people to learn that one-child families outnumber families with two children and have for more than a decade. "Fertility rates in many places are dropping rapidly, especially in the richest countries, where, to put it simply, any two people are not producing two more people."[3] There are a number of explanations for this trend. People marry later, leaving them fewer childbearing years and a greater chance of facing infertility or secondary infertility; more and more people opt to have and raise a child as single parents and one is realistically all they can handle; one out of almost every two marriages ends in divorce, often before a second child is considered or born, and predictions are that divorce rates will not change much in the foreseeable future.

But probably one of the greatest influences on the changing family is the influx of women into the workforce. Over 77 percent of women with children work, many with young children. By 1998, 67 percent of parents both held jobs outside the home.[4] Beyond the stresses of working, many feel a second child is more of a financial strain than they can, or want to, undertake.

Long gone is what we once called the typical or "average" family that was made up of two children, a father who worked, and a mother who stayed home to raise her children. Today, that family as we knew it, of *Ozzie and Harriet* fame, makes up barely 3 percent of American families.[5] Whether women work outside the home or devote themselves to their families full-time, the family is smaller. Over one-fifth—and climbing—of all families with children has one child. Between 1980 and 1990, there was an increase of 76 percent in the number of women ages forty to forty-four with one child, who, because of their ages, were unlikely to bear a second. If changes in childbearing patterns and family styles continue, which they are more than likely to do, it's safe to predict that more and more families will have one child.

The Way It Was

Forty, thirty, or even twenty years ago an only child was not the desired lot. Although there were exceptions, in most cases if a couple had an only child, something had intervened to prevent them from adding to their family.

What we view as normal in the childbearing arena has a lot to do with what was considered normal as we were growing up. Decisions about how many children to have are equally affected by what is accepted at the time we are deciding. "I had two children because at the time [thirty years ago] it was the American thing to do," explains Betty Plumlee.

Susan Leites talks about the childbearing milieu thirty years ago. "Many women admitted they were afraid to take care of themselves. They married and had the obligatory two or three children whether or not they wanted them. It was the 'right' thing to do. Having one was easy for me because I was a painter committed to my career. I had rebelled anyway; I didn't feel constrained to follow the norm. I don't think the number of children a woman had then corresponded to how she felt about having children. Women followed the conventions of the time."

Says Jamie Laughridge, a former editor of *Woman's Day Specials: Bridal Magazine,* "It was so much easier for our grandparents and parents. They didn't know what we know or have the career opportunities we have. Women's lives were mapped out: You fell in love, got married, had children. No concern over options or how many children to have. No fears of being trapped in the house or of losing your job if you took too many or too lengthy maternity leaves because mothers weren't supposed to have jobs. It seems women may have been better off. We simply know too much."

In the past there were many reasons why people felt the need to have more than one child. For one thing, children were more isolated. Parents feared the spread of disease. A child with strep throat or chicken pox stayed home for two or three weeks. Swimming in public pools was avoided during the polio scare.

Today children are immunized against most childhood diseases and given antibiotics for the less serious illnesses. Usually they return to school and their normal routines within days. "The absence of 'health isolation' was one of the factors that made me feel having only one was okay," admits Susan Leites.

Higher mortality rates were also a factor early in the previous century. Today's parents are not faced with the threat of smallpox, influenza, and many other diseases that took young lives. Unless you need extra bodies to harvest the crops and milk the cows as families did in colonial America, more than one offers no economic gain.

"Around the world there is a pattern of one man and one woman raising one baby for about four years, that is through infancy," theorizes Helen Fisher, Ph.D., author of *The Sex Contract: The Evolution of Human Behavior.* "Similarly, around the world there is a pattern of couples divorcing after about four years of marriage. About 25 percent of worldwide divorces occur with one dependent child. So we are going back to that trend which is quite suitable.

"In hunting and gathering societies a woman bore four to five children, but only one to two lived. Women tended to bear their children four years apart," explains Dr. Fisher. "For four years each child was an only child, nursed and nurtured by his mother within a large social group. After about four years the child became more independent of the mother, actively joining the huge social network on which he depended. This natural four-year cycle of childbearing parallels the universal divorce peak that comes in the fourth year of marriage."

Based on her findings, Dr. Fisher believes that "being an only child is a common incident in human family life that has probably been going on forever."

The Trend Toward One

During the baby boom years, when the parenting tune was, "A boy for me, a girl for you," the percentage of families with one child ranged between 10 and 13 percent. Today that percentage pushes toward 30. The same phenomenon can be seen in European countries, which were the first to see slower birth rates. Italy has the lowest birth rate per woman at 1.2; Spain and Germany follow at 1.3 children per woman; and Ireland's is 1.8, dropping from 3.5 children in 1975.[6] America appears to be following Europe in the reduced bearing of children as well as in the diversity of family structure. In China, one child per family was the national goal and a public mandate was enforced in an effort to control population. From 1979 until recently, China's strict one-child policy included steep fines for bearing a second child, forced abortions, and sterilization.

This book is neither a plea for zero population growth, nor an extended argument centered on preserving our natural resources and Social Security reserves by limiting families to one child. Rather it looks at societal and personal attitudes toward bearing children and the realities that surround those feelings and decisions. Having babies is too private and too irrevocable to be determined by dated ideals and social pressure or by legal standards and threats, as the Chinese government finally recognized. Japan, a country with one of the lowest birthrates in the world, is attempting to use government and business influences to increase the number of births. Japan's strategy is the reverse of China's—companies are offering bonus dollars and the government is providing monthly subsidies to parents who have second, third, and more children.[7]

In theory, Americans can still have or adopt all the babies they would like, but parents, especially mothers, are pulled in many directions, presented with other options beyond having large families, and concerned about how to meet the demands and needs of the child they have.

Roughly twenty-seven years ago Maggie Tripp delineated what would eventually become one of the underlying motivations for keeping families small. How right she was! In the book *Woman in the Year 2000,* she wrote, ". . . there are literally thousands of people testing a new kind of marriage. It is a marriage changed primarily by a new breed of woman—and by men who accept, desire, prefer her. She is the *un*-dependent woman. She knows what she wants and what she wants includes her own development as a self-contained entity. By the year 2000, all women of intelligence will emulate her."[8]

Now into the millennium, women no longer muse and mumble over what might have been. They take action. On average, over 50 percent of women are likely to start or continue some form of higher education,[9] enter law or medical school, or pursue graduate work in fields once controlled by men.

Women head major corporations, hold key government and executive positions, run their own successful businesses, and match their male counterparts in training, performance, and technical skills in myriad fields. A comparison between women in 1983 and today is striking. In 1983, 7 percent of dentists were women versus today's 17 percent; among female lawyers the jump during the same years was from 15 percent to 29 percent. Today there are more policewomen and female security guards than in the 80s—13 percent were women in 1983; today the figure is 29 percent.[10] Similar inroads can be seen in the accounting, computer programming, and medical professions, among many others.

The influx of women into the workforce has greatly altered

childbearing patterns. Whether or not women hold jobs outside the home, they have a new purpose beyond making babies, as Maggie Tripp predicted. To them, bearing two children no longer seems as compelling as it did to their mothers. Women do not bear children—especially second children—without seriously examining the effects on their family.

Lisa Turk's analysis is germane to many women today. "I know some people think when you have one child that you are not very maternal or think you like your job better than you do your child, but I love everything about being a mother. Work is not more important to me, but it is part of my life, a big part of who I am. I know I would have to give up a lot professionally and economically if I had a second child."

Since the mid-1960s young men have been less able to support families on their own.[11] We've known for a long time that working mothers are also good mothers and that work does not put their children's development or well-being in jeopardy. The difference now is that many mothers work as an economic necessity and/or to provide more for their children, especially better education. To working mothers, the juggling and the stress are worth it.

"One doesn't simply 'have kids' anymore, as a part of the natural course of life's events," Cheryl Merser aptly states in her 1987 book about thirty-year-olds, *"Grown-Ups": A Generation in Search of Adulthood.*[12]

The number of married couples with children under 18 declined sharply between 1960 and the year 2000, from 45 percent to 23.5 percent. In fact, fewer people are marrying and they are marrying later; marriage among 35–44-year-old women increased 78 percent in the last decade.[13] In real numbers, the marriage statistic is the lowest it's been since 1958—8.3 out of every 1,000 Americans marry. In major cities like New York, the marriage rate fell 30 percent during the late nineties; Houston saw a drop of 23 percent between 1995 and 1999.[14]

This doesn't mean that women are giving up their maternal rights for careers and personal adventures. Quite the contrary.

"Very few women get to their late thirties," Dr. Daniel Levinson, psychologist and authority on the stages of life, told a *New York Times* reporter, "without strongly wanting to have children." But as his eight-year study of women in the United States makes perfectly clear, women cannot depend on marriage lasting forever.[15]

Arden Holmes, married briefly during her twenties and a successful computer stock analyst, could have been part of Levinson's study. "It suddenly struck me at the age of forty-seven that work was not everything. A desire to have a child seemed more important to me. I was so amazed by the change in my thinking, I asked a psychiatrist friend if she thought I had lost my mind. Her response was, 'No, you've found it.' "

Linda Marsh fits the Levinson profile, too. "I wasn't planning on having children, then around my thirtieth birthday, I felt the urge. We just did it," thirty-five-year-old Ms. Marsh explains. "We felt another would be emotionally impossible for us, thank goodness." The Marshes have divorced.

No matter how in love you are at the moment or how "forever" you feel your marriage will be, there's a distinct possibility that one partner could wind up raising the children by him- or herself. Single parenthood is a reality in this country. Certainly food for thought during childbearing years and a compelling reason to have second thoughts about a second child. By all accounts, parenting one child alone is far more manageable than parenting multiples. The current divorce statistics are not surprising to Dr. Fisher, who adds, "I think the human animal was designed for a series of peer bonds." Marriage predictions for the twenty-first century strongly support Fisher's thinking—most divorced people will remarry, but there will be a longer period of time between marriages.[16]

Divorce is only one factor in the trend toward smaller families. Social norms are changing in response to the reality of women working. As beauty corporation executive Nancy Coleman, pregnant at thirty-eight, sees it, "One child is the only way today. Two's the maximum, but that won't be us. If you have three or four kids, people think your outlook is from the 1950s or you're plain strange. Very few people have four children anymore. It's not socially acceptable." That said, Coleman went on to start a family. Like many who begin their families in their mid- and late thirties, she and her husband had to turn to fertility specialists. Ironically, this strong advocate of the only child bore triplets and is blissfully happy despite her original reservations.

Thirty-two-year-old Candice Crummley's views are stronger than Coleman's. "Everyone I know who works and has one child is going crazy. None of them would ever admit that she wanted another. If you're in the workforce today, people view you as a little bit off center if you have children." In fact, more and more are choosing to remain childless and those who have children are stopping at one.

Single women are deciding to have or adopt children in significant numbers because they hold sound jobs, making it economically feasible to support a child. In general, one is all they can handle financially, emotionally, and physically without feeling spread too thin. Financially independent women are also a significant proportion of only-child advocates.

Single parents are not the only families that feel that way. "I gave up my corporate job when my daughter was born. It's been a real struggle to make it on one income; we've had to cut back, but it's been worth it. I've started working part-time to supplement our income," Miranda Davidson explains.

"A lot of people who come from larger families are being pressed by their ages and faced with the only-child situation themselves. They must deal with their thinking that only children are weird," states Mary Kelly Selover, thirty-two, an only child who grew up surrounded by many cousins and enormous neighborhood families.

Miranda Davidson is the oldest of five. "I have a wonderful daughter who is all I could ever want or expect from a child. She's creative, kind, and intelligent. I'm so happy with her, but I come from a big family. My siblings all have large families. We're one of those families in which it's natural to have a lot of children around. I figure if I am meant to have a second child, it will happen. I won't be devastated if I don't have another child. As every year goes by I'm having mixed feelings about becoming a parent again in my mid-forties. I don't think we'll continue trying much longer."

Dawn Childs and her husband echo Davidson's concern. "We fleetingly considered adopting a second; at forty-six, it's kind of too late and neither of us has a traditional nine-to-five job or a predictable income. We're always in a mad rush to earn a living."

The final factor leading to today's small families is that women are adopting and having their babies later. Birth rates among women between the ages of thirty and thirty-nine are the highest they have been in the past three decades. Likewise, the rate for women between the ages of forty and forty-four jumped by two thirds during the 1990s and is higher than any year since 1970.[17] It's safe to conclude that more babies will be born to "older" women.

Dawn Childs, who had her son at the age of forty-one, is one of them: "I've had an unplanned life. I was married once in my twenties and again in my thirties, but knew they were wrong relationships from the start and never felt I wanted children with either of these men. In spite of the occasional urge that would at times come up, my photography and travel were really important to me. At thirty-nine I decided I liked my life; I liked my friends and I loved being alone. Then I met my husband and we had our son almost immediately. Now I think back on when I wanted no children, and say, I almost missed it. By the skin of my teeth I had Trent. Life without him is unimaginable."

Men, too, start families later and worry about missing out. Many in their mid-thirties and early forties feel time is running out. They want to be agile and fit for their offspring. Some, like Rick Marin, feel parenthood is a measure of success, a statement of manhood, and a "reprieve from the self-absorption of our 'Seinfeldian' lives, a more worthwhile time investment." Approaching age thirty-eight, Marin notes, "I, too, have longed for the pitter-patter of little feet. If my biological clock were ticking any louder, they'd have to bring in Tom Cruise to defuse it."[18]

Childbearing Realities

Although personal reasons and circumstances vary greatly, the trend to one is firmly fixed. Men and women alike are postponing having babies during the years previous generations were most reproductive.[19] Sheldon Weinstein, Dallas obstetrician/gynecologist and president of the Society for Gynecological Surgeons, documents this from his practice: "The average obstetrical patient I see today is at least five to ten years older than the ones I was seeing twenty years ago."

It's no longer unusual for men to begin first or second families in their late forties, fifties, and even sixties. As baby boomers age and fertility technology improves, we see more middle-aged mothers and fathers. However, because most women and men focus on careers before childbearing, the number of children they have is limited by their age, whether they are bearing or adopting them.

Dr. Miguel Damien of East Coast Infertility and IVF in Little Silver, New Jersey, notes that the slope of problems is always going up. "I have patients in their mid-thirties—sometimes younger—with clear-cut problems that may be tubular or hormonal. Specific disorders can be related to the thyroid, ovulation, or sperm. But, of course, as you get into your forties, problems related to poor ovarian reserve will be more likely."

Very often postponing pregnancy until the middle or late thirties or later leaves little time and sometimes no opportunity for expanding the family, as the Thompsons and Ferlingers learned, each in their own way. The Thompsons' situation contains many of the elements that are causing couples to stop at one child.

Lila Thompson, who is forty-three, explains: "We waited until what I felt was the last possible moment. Our lifestyle was incredibly seductive. We both had fabulous jobs with incredible perks, a combined income that gave us money to travel and buy whatever we wanted. We had the freedom to come and go as we pleased. I don't think I cooked more than once a month. A baby, we both knew, would change all that and we weren't sure we wanted to give up our high living. I wanted to have children in the abstract sense. By the time we got around to having Kristen it was too late to give her a brother."

Indecision for indefinite periods turns many firstborns into onlies. "We circled the issue for years," recalls Suzanne Ferlinger. "As Alissa crossed each milestone, we said, 'Not yet.' If one of us said, 'Now,' the other said, 'The timing's off. Something big is happening at the office.' We played out this charade until I was forty and then our excuse was that a pregnancy at forty was too chancy. I guess what it boils down to is that we didn't want a second child. If we did, we certainly blew it."

"Because you had a baby at age twenty-five doesn't necessarily mean you can have one at age forty-five," says Weinstein. As women get older, the risks must be considered. "The older mother is over thirty-five," Weinstein explains, "and the incidence of having an abnormal baby increases each year. For example, the possibility of having a Down's syndrome baby begins to accelerate at age thirty-five. We see 1 out of 350 at age thirty-five; 1 in 40 at age forty. Thirty-five is the age we commonly recommend amniocentesis, which tests for this abnormality, but there are also simple maternal blood tests to indicate increased risk and targeted ultrasounds that will reveal any congenital anomalies, all of which can—and should—be performed on a pregnant woman of any age."

All the eggs a woman has are present at birth. As she ages, Dr. Damien points out, "the quality of the eggs and their ability to perform the cellular functions to produce a healthy baby lessen."

"The aging uterus complicates the process further," says Dr. Weinstein, "because it becomes increasingly less flexible, inhibiting a woman's ability to carry the fetus." Miscarriages increase sharply after age thirty-five because of abnormalities in the fetus and/or rejection of the fetus by the aging uterus.

This holds, of course, if the "older" woman can conceive in the first place. Limits on family size are compounded by the fact that older women have more trouble conceiving.

"It never entered my mind that I would have a problem getting pregnant," says Jeannine McGraw. "I just assumed you wanted a baby, you had it, so I wasn't in a hurry. I planned to have a baby at thirty-five and another as soon as the first was out of diapers. How wrong I was. I could not conceive and we endured every imaginable test and invasion of our privacy before I became pregnant four years after we saw the first of several fertility experts. The doctor who delivered Victoria informed us that we would probably face the same problems if we tried again. I could not go through the tests and indignities. Vicki is it. We feel fortunate to have her."

In *The New Yorker* magazine, playwright Wendy Wasserstein described her trials as an "older woman" trying to get pregnant. Many women say they endured a similar plight: "For the next eight years I progressed from artificial inseminations to egg-stimulating Clomid pills and on to daily injections of Pergonal . . . As my failure rate accelerated, I moved into high-tech reproductive territory: I tried in-vitro fertilization, GIFT (gamete intra-fallopian-tube transfer)." Having investigated surrogacy and adoption, and at the point of almost giving up, Ms. Wasserstein at last became pregnant with sperm donated by a friend. She noted, "[F]ertility treatments, even more than high school dances, are a regular confirmation of negative femininity, with every disappointment underscored by megadoses of hormones."[20] At age forty-eight, Wasserstein delivered what will probably be her one and only.

"The delay in having children is probably the biggest cause of fertility problems," states Weinstein. "The more periods a woman has had, the greater her chances of developing endometriosis." Endometriosis occurs when a section of the uterine lining is outside the uterus, around the ovaries, fallopian tubes, or in the abdominal cavity, obstructing the fertilization process. "Additionally," adds

Weinstein, "the older you are, the more likely you will have had more sexual partners, thus increasing the chances of infection."

"I had no problems getting pregnant the first time, but we've been trying for the past five years," explains Miranda Davidson. "I've had cysts removed and a laparoscopy for endometriosis and still have not been able to conceive. I discovered during the basic tests for infertility that I had a thyroid imbalance. My thyroid was out of whack for several years, which helped contribute to the infertility. Having had the surgery, having gotten my thyroid in check, I'm assuming it's my age at this point. I look in the mirror; I look like I should be able to have another child. I don't look forty-five, but that's how old my body is."

Secondary infertility, having had one child but being unable to conceive a second, affects younger women as well. Lorraine Brewer had her first child at the age of twenty-five. "We tried everything, and I mean everything," she notes. "I would have loved my child to have a sibling."

Women who experience infertility wonder why their bodies fail them. The miscarriages, the testing, treatments, and technology that consume infertile couples range from being stressful to heart-breaking, from embarrassing to detrimental to a marriage. In short, says Davidson, "Trying to get pregnant is a horrible struggle."

Fitness trainer Amanda Locke tells her story. "My husband didn't feel ready to have children when we first got married. He wanted his career to be lucrative . . . wanted to wait until he had enough money to support a child. I started trying to have a baby when I turned forty; that's when my husband and I thought we would begin. I'm one of those healthy people who assumes it will be easy to get pregnant. I eat properly, work out constantly. It took seven, almost eight years for me to get pregnant, just about the time we decided to adopt." Amanda describes the rigorous testing she and her husband went through as "devastating when they couldn't find anything wrong with either of us. Ultimately, I think it was the age factor, being well over forty and having used most of my eggs. With an egg donor, I eventually conceived."

Surrogate mothers, sperm, and healthy eggs are hot commodities today. The combination of available fertility "essentials" and specialists in the field has allowed lesbians and heterosexual women who choose not to marry or live with a man, as well as couples who start late, to become parents. "Heterosexual women in the thirties and lesbian partnerships account for a large increase in the sperm demand."[21] Because of the legalities and often the high cost involved, most who take advantage of the technology tend to stop after one.

"When women start having babies after thirty, two is usually the maximum number of babies. Over thirty-five, it's one." In Dr. Weinstein's opinion, older patients feel because of their age and their husband's age, one is all they want to raise. "They're glad if they can conceive and not miscarry. Many feel they got lucky with one: 'I had a normal baby; I'm not going to try for a second.' "

About his patients who have fertility problems, Dr. Damien adds, "It takes a lot of work to become pregnant. The majority of people I see come in for one baby. They are delighted to have that one child and don't want to go through all the work again."

In today's accelerated world, time slips away, circumstances interfere. "My husband was moved around in his job a lot, so we were separated for long stretches," explains Patty Wellden. "I had gestational diabetes and was on insulin during my pregnancy and there was a serious complication at birth that required an emergency C-section. It was so many things, seemingly working against a second child. By the time our heads cleared our son was six years old."

Having a second child can present serious, life-threatening health risks for certain women. Dr. Frank Boehm, professor of obstetrics and gynecology and director of obstetrics at Vanderbilt Medical Center in Nashville, says, "I have had chronically ill patients, who, having finally struggled through the hazards of having one child, without question will plan the second merely because their concept of family includes more than one child. They ignore the argument that there is nothing wrong with raising a single child."

If parents have been advised against a second pregnancy, like many who battle infertility or had complicated pregnancies, there's a sadness for both mother and partner, but as one mother says, "It's no contest. I want to be sure my child has a mother. You live with the hand you've been dealt. I can't have another baby, but the one I have is perfection, so I focus on the positives of what we accomplished and think about our good fortune."

Some couples, Kathleen Wheeler and Doug Werner among them, decide they want to be parents in their late thirties or forties and don't want the risks of a pregnancy. Says Kathleen, "At forty-six, I thought I was at peace with not having children. Over the years I had wrestled with the reality of finding myself in a life where circumstances never quite led in that direction." Doug and Kathleen were concerned about, in their words, the "chances and chancy-ness" of Kathleen's giving birth in her middle forties. When they both felt ready to be parents, they adopted one of the estimated 4 million baby girls in orphanages throughout China. The Wheeler-Werners were expecting a three-year-old because of their age, but to Kathleen's delight, their baby girl, Joy, was given to them when she was only ten months old.

Adoption—A Choice

For the growing number of couples and single women who postpone starting their families until they are older, and for gay and lesbian couples, adoption has become a viable choice, quite frequently it's the perfect, and for some, like the Wheeler-Werners, the preferred, solution. After thirteen years of marriage, Henrietta Eakins never got pregnant. She says. "I really had no burning interest in being pregnant. Our main desire was having a child. My husband and I chose adoption over infertility treatments and high-tech methods to get the child we wanted."

In a sense, Jill Shu felt the same way. "I never thought I would get married or have children. I got married and we felt our family unit of two was very important. We had our work and felt we'd never be bored. We raise show dogs, so when we got home from the office there was plenty to do. When I was diagnosed with breast cancer—what I call the best kind to have in that it's the most curable—we started to rethink what we wanted. Neither one of us felt we had to have our genes in the pool."

Jana Wolff, author of *Secret Thoughts of an Adoptive Mother,* explains how she ended up watching Martie, an eighteen-year-old girl, deliver the multiracial baby who became Jana's son: "I loved Martie for the gift that was coming, and I utterly resented her for doing what I couldn't. Our female bodies had all the same parts . . . but hers worked and mine didn't. Recompense for the needles, the pills and the bills, the cold examination rooms, the gloved fingers up my cervix, the waiting—month after endless month—for my chemically confused body to follow orders. Unfortunately, I took too long to meet and marry my husband—by that time, my eggs and his sperm were middle-aged."[22]

Although national adoptions outnumber inter-country adoptions, international adoptions have been escalating steadily, more than doubling since 1990, according to the Evan B. Donaldson Adoption Institute. In 1999, for example, Russia and China, followed by South Korea, were the major sources for Americans seeking to become parents.[23] The number of children available from any given country is politically sensitive and open to change.

Sandy Ripberger of Spence-Chapin, a private adoption agency in New York City, reports that within a given country the rules, like the availability of children, change in relation to the health status of children permitted to leave a country, ages of adoptive parents, and whether or not the country is open to single-parent adoptions. Like so many today who bear a child, adoptive parents are limiting the number to one for assorted and well-founded reasons.

Ken Woodmere was a grandfather of three when he and his second wife, Vanessa, decided to adopt from Eastern Europe. "Foreign countries seem much more open to giving children to older parents," Vanessa explains. "We were told because of our ages we were unlikely to be chosen for a domestic adoption. The woman from the agency was quite frank about it. Because of open adoption laws in this country, the birth mother looks through a book of possible parents and she said, 'You're probably her parents' age or older and it doesn't matter whether or not you can offer her child the most fabulous lifestyle and advantages.'

"I saw adoption as a good alternative," continues Vanessa Woodmere, who was forty-one when she adopted Zack. "My husband had his vasectomy reversed and when that didn't work, we decided to stop. I didn't feel good about going to elaborate and extraordinary extremes with fertility. At some point, I asked myself, what is my aim? Is it to have a family or to create a carbon copy of me? I realize people will disagree with me, but that's how we felt. And we're delighted. You do have to be a little more accepting, more open to a child with a developmental delay or nutritional problem when you adopt."

In some countries the child must have a diagnosis in order to leave the country. As it turns out, more often than not, the diagnoses are or quickly become invalid, say both adoption agencies and adoptive parents. Theresa Galinsky confirms the experience: "My son was delayed only in the sense that he hadn't been stimulated; he had been on his back in a crib for almost a year. The pediatrician at the orphanage in Russia said, 'He'll be fine; you just have to get him home and feed him and interact.' The doctor was right. The delays were so minor; we had early intervention for six months, and by age two he tested with the best of them."

Arden Holmes, a single mother, has a different, but remarkable story to tell. "My daughter was eighteen months old when she was given to me. There were no cries, no smiles; it was as if I had been given a robot. It was scary. She looked malnourished and I was worried about post-institutional adjustment, given her total emotional shutdown. I envisioned years of therapy and special help for this child.

"I was on my own, with no one to confer with about keeping

this child. For several days I hugged, I kissed, I sang, I carried her incessantly. Three days later, this huggy, kissy, adorable child emerged who was thrilled to have a mommy. I saw a personality, a curious person.

"When we got home, I realized she was not underweight because of orphanage neglect or malnourishment, but because she's a terribly picky eater. The Chinese government is fairly accurate when they say a child is healthy; they are rarely wrong."

Adoption is similar to giving birth; there are no guarantees and both require a major commitment. Whether it's a national or international adoption, the process can be long and arduous, involving months of criminal checks, home studies, reams of paperwork, and often lengthy travel. For many, single or married, money is a crucial factor in forgoing a second adoption as it is for those who bring their own babies into the world.

China and Vietnam, in particular, solve the problem for childless couples, singles, and those who are older, but the upper-end age limits change periodically in different countries. China is especially single-friendly. Arden Holmes looks back: "Things came together when I saw an article on adoption from China and noted that China valued single parents and had gorgeous kids. Because of care-giving problems with my own parents, I wasn't able to pursue adoption until I was fifty. To my delight I discovered I wasn't too old."

But, as Arden Holmes is quick to tell you, she was lucky, but not with the first referral. The emotional strain of adoption is no less for married couples who are eager to adopt, who dream and plan, only to have their hopes shattered. "When the agency sent me a picture of the child I was adopting, I was thrilled and immediately began all the shopping I had been afraid to do. When the agency called to tell me my daughter had been adopted by someone else, I grieved as if I had miscarried. I felt such a terrible loss. I fell so in love with that child that I didn't want to see the second referral when it came within a matter of days. I thought it was the ugliest child I had ever seen.

"Although she's only five, she's turning into a strikingly beautiful child," says Arden, "but I would not open myself again to the heartache and disappointment of being given a child only to have it taken away."

Why Only One

When one combines the obstacles to bearing or adopting with women's desire to achieve and consequently putting off pregnancy, the high divorce rate, and the potential complications of second marriages and blended families, it's easy to understand the swift increase in the number of only children in our society.

Unlike preceding generations, couples today—whether they are young or older—are making the choice to have one, for reasons both personal and practical, from outside child-care obstacles to a preference for a tranquil, organized home.

"We decided to have a child when it looked like time was running out, and when we felt we had enough financial security. We had enjoyed the freedom of a childless life for a long time and we wanted to experience parenthood," explains Doug Werner, who with his wife adopted their daughter when they were both forty-six.

Laura Dixon was twenty-nine when her son was born. "We talk about Luke as being our only child and being happy with that decision. Having Luke is a complete delight and a very rewarding experience, but it's also an enormous time commitment. Nine months being pregnant, a responsibility for the rest of your life, and Jim and I have a lot of things we want to do. We'll enjoy doing them with Luke, but if we have more children, we would be restricted in the things we can accomplish. We need quite a bit of time for ourselves."

Both Laura and Jim come from large families. "I know how much time a large family takes," notes Laura. "I saw it in my family with four children. My mother was trying to have a career at the same time she was raising us. Everytime she wanted to do something on her own, she was strapped to the household."

Tess Berkley concurs, but for a slightly different reason. "I'm the oldest girl of three and I always thought it would be wonderful to be an only. I didn't have wonderful, big-family feelings growing up. I always thought I couldn't live up to my brother, and my mother couldn't live up to her responsibilities. I think the third child, my younger sister, tipped her over; she was more than my mother could handle and as the oldest she took it out on me. I know that factored into my decision to have just one."

Conversely, Henrietta Eakins and her husband thought about going back to Korea for a second child, but only briefly. "We are older parents. I'm an only and my husband was essentially an only, his brother is ten years older than he is. We decided we really want to concentrate on one child and not more. I'm not sure we would have adopted another child even if we were younger, because we both came from families in which our experiences as only children were very positive."

Belinda Nehman, a Wall Street analyst and executive vice president of her firm, says, "I, not my husband, was very firm that one was the limit. My job is too important to my identity. I was not giving up the cachet and prestige I had worked so hard to earn. I love my daughter, but I also know that she will grow up and not need me anymore. If I don't have my career, I'm afraid I will need her too much."

Jody Cohen, thirty-one, registrar for the Dallas Museum and mother of a sixteen-month-old confirmed only, had a rude awakening. "Since Jordan was born and I've been in the throes of it, I've realized that motherhood is not my sole career. I'm a perfectionist and one made me realize my limits."

After fourteen years of marriage, Gail Duncan, thirty-eight, whose husband John calls her brutally honest, is quite firm about her intentions. "I adore my child, but I don't want to go through that again. I had the easiest pregnancy imaginable and I still hated every minute of it. I am not a mother. Having Phoebe was a temporary lapse of sanity. She's a terrific kid; I'm not sorry I did it, but why should I risk what I've got?"

Gail's husband, John, has practical reasons for keeping Phoebe a singleton. "We both have careers; we want to travel. When we renovated our apartment, we designed it to accommodate one child. It works. One child is just very manageable," John Duncan comments, showing no signs of vacillating.

Debbie Diehl-Camp, thirty-six, and her husband have made the same choice: "We are not having another. Our reasons are partially financial, but primarily, I am a bookbinder and a photographer and I want to do my work. Now that Cameron is getting older, I feel that I will be able to start working again. If I begin with a new baby, I will have to give my full attention and energy to that child. I feel one is all I can do."

"Children test your patience in a whole new way and I'm not a particularly patient person," admits travel writer, Katy Koontz. "I know I'm a better mother to Samantha than I could be to Samantha and a sibling. I view having one child as a luxury in that I'm able to devote myself to her. With more, I know I would be frustrated and impatient. I don't want to parent beyond my ability and I think I know what that is."

Gloria Sloves, twenty-eight, who married a man with three grown children, feels lucky to have her child. "It took me a year to convince Tom that we should have a baby. He had had it with raising children. I could not imagine existing without Tom, but I also felt my life would be incomplete without a child. It wasn't an easy task to win Tom over to my side. I got my baby, but knew there was no chance of his agreeing to more, even though I am young enough to have them."

In the world of the formerly married, few men with children from their first marriage are willing to have more than one more. The men who have raised or partially raised children must weigh their advancing age when contemplating having children during a second marriage. Said one second husband, "I would be in my seventies by the time our second child reached the age of eighteen. It's bad enough that I'll be in my sixties at that point in our daughter's life. My age was the major reason we stopped at one."

Virginia homebuilder Duff Badgley, the son of an only and the father of an eighteen-month-old only, readily declares that he prefers a small family. The thing he remembers most about growing up was the quiet in his house. "I do chafe at having my wife's family around. They're like an octopus; it's never ending. She has five brothers and sisters. It's not the way I want to live my life."

Their own poor relationships with siblings or parents is another reason people have only one child. Lori Karmazin is a case in point. "I don't like an environment with sibling rivalry. I don't think it's healthy. Reflecting back on my brother and myself, we are total strangers to each other. Yes, there is a bond there, more from spending twelve to eighteen years with each other than from anything else . . . I don't believe a person needs a sibling so that he or she will always have a friend. The theory doesn't hold true."

The choice to have one is increasingly a very determined, rational one, and one with an unexpected benefit: You may actually be doing your child a favor by not providing a sibling. A translator and guide to foreign dignitaries, Helen Umbretino is a forty-year-old mother of a four-year-old. "I work, yet I manage to spend three hours a day during the week and the entire weekend with Joey, but they are 'perfect hours,'" as she calls them. "I rarely lose my temper with him. We read, we go out and do things. With more children, I would have to sacrifice those 'perfect hours.'"

"At the witching hour, when my wife was thirty-nine, we decided to stop with one," says Steve Katz, whose daughter is twelve. "We stopped basically because of the quality of life we wanted for ourselves and for our daughter. The decision was financial to some degree, but that was the smallest issue. We were both deciding what we wanted to do with our lives and didn't want a little one around at that point."

Older and younger parents alike are steadfast in their decision to have one. The Elerbees, who are in their mid-twenties and have a two-year-old, realize they have plenty of time to have another, but are firm in their decision to have one because "when he's college age, we'll still be young and have time to do whatever we want."

"Having more children isn't a great need for us," says Barbara DeMarco-Barrett, forty-six. "We're happy with Travis, our six-year-old. We're happy with our lives, and we don't feel there's a hole we need to fill with another child. We don't really talk about it at length. It's just never been important to have another child."

Unlike the DeMarco-Barretts, you may not be as confident about your decision—that's natural and not unusual. You may be unsure and may be considering having a second child. Before you do, think about yourself and ask yourself these questions: What's best for me? Is it harder or easier to raise an only child? Will it be less complicated down the road if there are two children—for them or for me? If I have one already, how frightening can another be? Can I cope with the additional responsibility? How will another child affect my marriage? How will more children affect my career? My sense of self? Will we need to move to larger quarters? Do we want to change our lives again?

As irrevocable as the decision to have one is, the decision to have another will again alter the direction of your lives—permanently. Before you plunge more deeply into parenthood with a second child, study the only child, examine the many sources of pressure to have another, reexamine what you want for your child, and think about what you want to do with your own life.

One Fills the Bill

Consider the reasons why you want a child in the first place. What will a second child offer you that one can't? You may be afraid that you will raise a spoiled, selfish, precocious, demanding only child. For decades, the only child label was a stigma for parent and child alike. The bad rap that onlies have taken for centuries is finally becoming obsolete. Savvy parents are turning out fabulous only children with no or very few hang-ups. It is crystal clear, as you will see, that being an only child is advantageous, desirable, and beneficial.

However, pressures to deliver more offspring remain in the

forefront with good reason. The favorable attitude toward larger families, a residue of former generations, is a pervasive undercurrent. Admits Meg Reese, an only whose singleton is twenty-eight, "I felt it made more of a family to have two children. Perhaps it was the fantasy of two children, white picket fence. The description was never 'big yard, white picket fence, and *one* child.' "

Nor do you hear the question phrased, "Do you have a child?" People ask, "Do you have children?" Or "How many children do you have?" The wording alone is highly suggestive of the underlying assumption. However, the current crop of onlies don't take these questions too seriously. Detroit thirteen-year-old Jill Vince believes people ask out of curiosity more than for any other reason. "Whenever you meet someone new, the question often comes up casually, 'Do you have any brothers or sisters?' It's no big deal."

The question should be, "How many loving people are there?" "In retrospect, being an only myself," Meg Reese reconsiders, "I don't think being a single child has nearly the significance I thought it did when I was planning my family. A child learns from everything around him, not just from his home environment. If a child is loved and feels warm and secure, it just doesn't matter."

In the business world as well as in many academic fields, there is an unspoken law that says essentially, "Produce and you'll go far. You'll be rewarded and respected." Within the family structure, however, there are no promotions, no raises, no accolades or awards for productivity. You rank as high with one child as you do with two or three. Four hundred college students—our next generation of parents—were asked their opinions of mothers with no children, one child, two children, and eight or more children. One- and two-child parents were rated about the same. And interestingly, the undergraduates no longer "glorified" mothers of eight or felt that being childless would lead to a less gratifying life.[24] With one you can still be president of the PTA. You can be a Cub Scout leader or Little League coach. You can bake cookies for the class Halloween party or chaperon the senior prom. Another baby will not add to your parenthood credentials, improve your résumé, make you more stable, or magically turn you into better parents.

The nuclear family has changed dramatically in the last decade alone. The typical family you may have grown up in has been replaced by new and more diverse models: single parents, unmarried cohabiting parents, remarried parents, and gay and lesbian parents, among others. Whatever the makeup of that family and whatever archaic stereotypes remain, the single-child family has taken hold as the new traditional family size.

One child offers what most parents claim are the reasons they have children in the first place: someone to love, to teach, to explore the world with, to have fun with, to cherish.

Today's onlies have a supreme advantage over only children from past generations. They have company. "When I grew up," comments Richard Dewshurst, a thirty-seven-year-old television and motion picture writer whose wife gave birth at forty to their only child, "I was the only only child I knew. I felt different. Divorce was unusual and most people had three kids."

That's all changed. Sixteen-year-old Samuel Barron says, "It's not rare to be an only child. My best friend is an only child, as are many of my classmates."

The reasons why so many people are having only one child are tightly intertwined with their choices about parenting and lifestyles. It's not self-indulgence, but rational thinking and concern that causes more and more people to decide one is best for them.

Family therapist Fredda Bruckner-Gordon acknowledges that for her, one child is more than satisfying. She speaks for an entire new generation of parents when she says, "I wasn't too driven to have another. I find the experience of one fulfilling and enough."

But wait, your only child just refused to share his new deluxe set of Crayolas. He swatted his friend with the container after pouring sixty-four crayons over his unsuspecting guest's head. That's it, you're convinced: He needs a sibling. You'll nip this selfish, spoiled brat problem—the so-deemed "only child syndrome"—in the bud.

2

Debunking the Myths

"When I was growing up, the automatic assumption was you're spoiled, you don't know how to share, you are certainly a monster," reports only child Ruth Hague, an employees' assistance counselor in her forties.

These stereotypes and others have formed many of our notions about only children. Enlightened information about onlies exists, but it has been slow to penetrate society. Sue Astley, an Atlanta mother of a fifteen-year-old only, says, "I am constantly amazed by how many people seem to think that there is something wrong with having an only child. I always took it as the ultimate compliment when I was told that Christopher didn't act like an only child—whatever that's supposed to mean."

Even today, with family structure so diverse, parents of only children remain concerned about the same issues primarily because attitudes about family are cemented in *Brady Bunch/Partridge Family* notions. For such a progressive society, too many of its members choose to ignore what decades of research have proven.

The personality defects attributed to the only child don't stand up when they are put to the test. As a group only children are not overprotected, domineering, lonely, or self-centered. Yet in his book *To Listen to a Child*, well-known pediatrician T. Berry

Brazelton made it clear that many still cling to obsolete ideas without taking into account the variations among people in any group. "With the increasing pressure on parents to limit their families, there is a parallel feeling that an only child may be 'spoiled' or may 'suffer.' "[1]

Stereotypes are nothing more than a set of beliefs; and in the case of only children they are the result of faulty thinking that leads to incorrect and unjustified generalizations.[2] Frank Sulloway, who studied birth order for twenty-six years, points out that only children are the "least predictable subgroup." "In addition, singletons tend to be more variable than individuals with siblings."[3] In other words, you can't peg an only this way or that.

Dr. Toni Falbo, one of the country's leading authorities on only children and a professor of educational psychology at the University of Texas in Austin, cites one reason why stereotypes linger. "Human beings don't like to think too deeply. When we think about other people, there's too much information, too much variation. In order to cut down on the mental work, we tend to categorize and ignore parts of the information. We assume we know more than we actually do. We say, 'Oh, only children are like that. Women are like this. Blacks are like that.' "

It's much easier to label people than to look at them as individuals. Most people stereotype because it's quick and convenient. Less than twenty years ago, people looked at the only child and surmised that there was something wrong with him, something wrong in the marriage, or something physically wrong with the mother or father. In 1977 Dr. Judith Blake, a premiere researcher on the impact of family size, found that 67 percent of the people in her study believed the only child was disadvantaged.[4] Bearing only one was considered the act of selfish adults who were unconcerned about the harm that would be done to their child. People worried that the only child would grow up to be an oddball and psychologically unbalanced.

There is no question that views are changing. Gail Duncan, whose only child is three, believes that "the stigma attached to only children is a generational and suburban problem. It's less prevalent in urban areas and among Yuppies and Generation X-ers."

Even so, eliminating the folklore is tough because, as adult only Barbara Friedman puts it, "Too many people still don't assume oneness as a positive, which I generally think it is." Rather, they tend to agree with the 1896 assessment of psychologist Dr. G. Stanley Hall, who said that "being an only child is a disease in itself."[5] Only children have been living down this and similar unflattering characterizations ever since.

Our long-held views about only children date back to the late 1800s. If you were planning your family at the turn of the century, you had reason to worry about having an only child. The propaganda against onlies was intense, and virtually everyone believed it.

In 1898 the *Journal of Genetic Psychology* published E. W. Bohannon's study, "The Only Child in a Family." The summary of its main points reads like an armed attack: Only children are not as healthy or vital as children with siblings; only children do not do as well academically ("Their success in school work is below the average") or socially ("Their social relations are . . . more frequently characterized by friction"); only children compensate socially by forming imaginary friendships more often than do non-onlies. The study concluded: "Peculiarities in these children seem to be more pronounced than in others."[6]

This distorted judgment was reinforced and intensified for decades by prominent psychologists, psychiatrists, and scientists. The list of flaws and faults assigned to the only child grew to include: The only child walks and talks late; the only child is jealous, domineering, egotistical, selfish, overly dependent, anxious, and maladjusted. More than a century later we are still battling these very unscientific findings, which at the very least state or strongly imply that only children are abnormal and essentially handicapped. In the year 2000, a California talk show host and the mother of two talked with me on air about an only child who had come to play with her daughter. The host remarked that as soon as her son joined the daughter and her guest, problems started. She wrongly concluded that the only child's inability to share the toys was because he lacked the experience of interacting at home with siblings. What she failed to take into account were the children's young ages and the fact that threesomes rarely play harmoniously until they are late into elementary school—if then.

She held fast to her conviction about only children, even after I presented hard evidence to the contrary. It occurred to me while I waited to explain and defend only children that this parent was using a story to justify her position as the mother of two. Like many, she believes only those facts and actions that confirm the stereotype. This kind of stereotyping becomes automatic when people's positions are threatened; it's more comforting to lapse into stereotyping than to think about or notice what makes others unique.

China, with its one-child policy, has given us fertile ground to explore the only child. When second- and fourth-graders, with and without siblings, were assessed and compared, no significant differences were found in social behavior, peer acceptance and relationships, or social competence.[7] In the areas of popularity and sociability, according to the results of a social competence study done with Korean children in 1999, almost a hundred years after G. Stanley Hall, only children scored similarly to other twelve-year-olds with siblings.[8]

Many men and women of childbearing age who have been raised to think of only children as difficult, demanding, and emotionally unstable must update their thinking after being exposed to the facts. Jonathan Cheek, professor of psychology at Wellesley College, is quick to warn those who embrace dated attitudes. "What people don't realize when they look at old research is what you think is the truth is really the truth for a given cohort in a specific time and place. Being an only child had a different status forty years ago than it does now. Only children who were born forty years ago had growing-up experiences that were so much different from the only child growing up today. Our whole culture has changed."

The truest picture of only children today comes from the people who have lived as or with onlies. They adamantly refute the labels and validate adult only Dale Schlein's belief that "the stereotype is blown so out of proportion, that it's just a silliness."

Labeling—Myth Versus Fact

The myth of misfortune that surrounds the only child is, by all current accounts, erroneous. Eliminating stereotyping is a process—a slow one at best because stereotyping stems from oversimplified views of, in this case, only children that are rarely based on facts. The opinions that colored attitudes toward only children for generations are nothing more than generalizations and prejudgments that do not stand up to intense investigation.

Myth 1: Only children are shy; only children are aggressive and bossy.

Fact: Since shy people are generally retiring and aggressive people are normally outgoing, it's difficult for one person to be both. The contradiction in this dual assignment alone is sufficient to render it useless.

An examination of young children who were either extremely inhibited or uninhibited concluded that there is a biological base, a predisposition for childhood shyness. Some of the factors that contribute to shyness in both children and adults are inherited. Only children were found to be the same in this respect as their peers who had siblings.[9]

"At age three, my son is already very outgoing," says Debbie Diehl-Camp. "He has learned to interact and makes friends easily. He sees another child and walks right up to him. Children from large families don't have to go out and break through to another child, so they can afford to be more shy. In that regard, I think being an only child is an advantage. I had three sisters to play with so I've always been bad about going out and meeting other people."

Of course, outside events, such as the prolonged absence, illness, or hospitalization of a parent can trigger any predisposition toward shyness that a child may have. However, the only child who is withdrawn as a result of isolation from his peers is most unusual. Society has geared up for the only child. Today parents make play dates for children as young as six months old. Attendance in day care or nursery school is almost universal. Facilities for socialization are no longer scarce and their use is rarely interpreted as a shirking of parental responsibility.

The "shy" label may have emerged from a perceived inability to stand up for one's rights. While onlies have no at-home experience fighting with other children, they have another skill that siblings may not have. Onlies learn to fight with their parents and consequently have excellent verbal skills.

"In day care and nursery school," explains Dr. Roger Zeeman, psychologist and a director of pupil services for a school district, "young children learn how to compete, to share, to stand up for themselves. These preschool lessons accomplish the same thing as interaction with siblings. Nursery school isn't twenty-four hours a day, but six hours is enough to learn how to get along with other children."

"I don't feel that he's being raised as an only child who won't know how to socially integrate," says Jody Cohen of her son. "He's with other children from first thing in the morning until late afternoon. He thrives on it."

"The Leader of the Laundromat" is the title given to four-year-old Zoe Steadham by her mother when discussing her daughter's adjustment to nursery school. Linda Marsh's daughter, also four, is the leader of her class. "The children flock to her," claims Linda. And Jennifer Walsh will proudly tell you that she is more of a trendsetter than a follower. Her mother unhappily complains that Jennifer has too many friends, especially after all twelve of them have spent the night. Yet none of these children was described as aggressive or domineering.

Only children learn quickly that attempting to run the show, a ploy which they may get away with at home, doesn't work with friends. Onlies realize that a bossy, aggressive attitude is a quick ticket to ostracism from the group. Lacking siblings, only children want to be included and well liked. Domineering behavior on the part of young onlies, if tried at all, tends to disappear after a few attempts.

Judith Blake's findings regarding the social skills of only children back up claims of parents and onlies like Steadham, Marsh, Walsh, and the hundreds of other mothers and fathers who were part of the research for this book. Dr. Blake reports that "only children may actually be more outgoing and have more friends than kids from larger families."[10]

Myth 2: Only children prefer more solitary, noncompetitive amusements because they are alone a great deal of the time.

Fact: This preference has a basis in fact, but it has more to do with social class than family size. Some only children actually would rather read, build model trains, or listen to music than play football or be a cheerleader. These interests stem from parental values and the home environment of middle- and upper-middle-class families, which are more likely to have a single child. Working-class families tend to be larger and lean toward competitive team sports and group activities.

One father of three, who is himself an only child, feels his time alone was so valuable in developing his imagination that he insists each of his children play by themselves from time to time. "There's developmental value in private time that's self-initiated and not necessarily noticed and commented upon," notes Dr. Sharon Ramey, a child-development researcher.

Children with one sibling show only a slightly greater inclination than onlies toward group activities and team sports. The decision to swim, jog, collect butterflies, or catalog coins rather than to be on the baseball team doesn't exclude a social life. Most onlies have both.

Myth 3: Only children are antisocial and, therefore, lonely.

Fact: Today's singletons are hardly asocial and scarcely have the chance to be lonely. Among those interviewed for this book, a handful said they had been lonely as a child. They were onlies who are now adult and had parents who were either unaware of the importance of involving their children socially or were unable, because of the times, to do so.

Physicist Frank Owens, an only with an only, analyzes the difference between his childhood and that of his eight-year-old son. "Twenty-five or thirty years ago an only child didn't learn to deal with his contemporaries as well. The give-and-take between children your own age wasn't there if you were an only child. In my day, you went outside after school and, if there was someone to play with, great; if not, it was too bad. Now there is so much organized community activity—soccer leagues, baseball leagues, afterschool clubs, library reading groups—that my son is not going through what I went through."

Linda Wegner, whose son is sixteen, assesses the current situation. "Only children want lots of friends. They never want to be in a situation in which they have something to do and no one to do it with."

Herself an only and the mother of a teenage only, Susan Barron stifles the myth further. "I know a lot of children who are not onlies who are miserable and lonely because they are not socially successful."

Researcher Judith Blake found nothing in children in small families or families with one child to indicate "isolation, sadness, or hopelessness."[11] What's more, in any given peer group, few pay attention to whether or not someone has siblings. High school senior Scott Scranton says, "None of my friends care whether or not I'm an only child. We don't even think about it."

Myth 4: Only children are four-eyed intellectuals and eccentric child prodigies.

Fact: Only children do have "higher academic skills and higher need to achieve."[12] However, when only children are compared with children with siblings on social adjustment, indicators of eccentricity and/or superior intellectualism that would set them apart, "they have no obvious character or personality defects."[13]

A gifted youth who scores highest on whatever test is in front of him, Gary Inge is an intellectually-advanced only child who at age fifteen takes college-level courses. "Until seventh grade Gary was a misfit; he had terrible problems with his peers," his mother explains candidly. "But one must weigh the facts. Physically, he is long, lean, overly thin. Not your typical All-American boy running off to baseball practice. The reaction by his peers might have happened to this particular child no matter how many siblings he had."

There are many other only children who do as well as Gary on an academic level, yet have no factors working against them that alienate them from friends or isolate them from social activities. In a grouping of similar people, any peculiarity will be singled out. More often than not, the obese child will be tormented; the unathletic one, ridiculed; the smart one, teased—with no attention paid to his sibling status.

Myth 5: All only children have imaginary companions to compensate for their loneliness.

Fact: Studies and books written about the prevalence of pretend playmates and companions confirm that onlies don't have any more or less pretend playmates than other children and that these imaginative creations can be useful in certain situations.

Seven-year-old only Brandon Maynard enlisted a fictional brother as his protector for about a year. "My brother will get you," he screamed at friends who taunted him.

" 'The brother' was short-lived," says Brandon's mother, Wynne Maynard. "His 'brother' got him over the transition from nursery to elementary school. We didn't have to set a place at the table or put food out for Brandon's 'brother,' so we weren't worried." The only time there might be cause for concern is if your child favors his pretend friends to the exclusion of other playmates.

Marjorie Taylor, author of *Imaginary Companions and the Children Who Create Them,* explodes this myth: "It is not solely children who are firstborn or who have no siblings who create imaginary companions, and the appearance of an imaginary companion in the lives of these children is not necessarily a sign of loneliness or psychological distress." Some parents recognize the presence of imaginary friends after the birth of a second child, generally a period in which the first or other children in the family receive less parental time.[14]

On this subject Dr. Falbo is adamant. "Anyone who says only children have more fantasy friends than children with siblings has no basis for making that statement. There is no scientific evidence. People think, 'If a child is alone, he is going to need to come up with some friends; he will imagine them,' but a lot of only children spend their time with other people. They are not so isolated that they have a greater need than anyone else to conjure up mental friends."

"My daughter never made up friends, but my brother drove the family crazy," recalls Lisa Palmateer. " 'Charlie' stories are revived every holiday when the family gets together. Somebody asks my brother how Charlie enjoyed his plane ride or tells my brother that Charlie isn't eating his vegetables. It's very funny. When we were kids, we had to wait for Charlie—he couldn't walk very fast, you know. My brother would insist there wasn't enough cereal in Charlie's bowl or enough toothpaste on Charlie's toothbrush. My mother says that she had seriously considered getting my brother psychiatric help."

Jerome Singer, Ph.D., professor of psychology and child study at Yale University, confirms that the imagination required to create make-believe friends "is not the exclusive property of the 'only' child, the isolated, the ill, or the handicapped. Imaginary friends serve a purpose of meeting a need—to confront loneliness, to combat a fear, or to compensate for feelings of weakness in relation to adults or older children." For that reason, if your child creates one, view it as a positive. Adding to the positive are the results of Singer's studies that counter the notions that imaginary companions indicate social maladjustment.[15] Typically, children with imaginary friends are "more independent, cooperative with teachers and peers, generally happier and less aggressive than their peers, and have a richer vocabulary."[16]

Pretend playmates and spurned child prodigies were just two more concerns in a lengthy litany of negatives that *could*—and some felt surely did—affect the only child.

Myth 6: Only children are spoiled.

Fact: Dr. Zeeman is a firm believer—and has lots of company among other psychologists and sociologists—that being spoiled is a reflection of our society. "Expecting that things are coming to you, that you're entitled to a lot, is a syndrome of well-to-do middle- and upper-class children. We give them the latest toys and computers, we take them from place to place, act as their chauffeurs and pay for their activities. What we need to do is balance the giving by making them earn some of the things they get and by giving them responsibilities. This applies to all children, not just only children."

Only children themselves unconditionally pounce on the term "spoiled" when it is applied to them. "I wasn't indulged particularly," says Kathryn Joyce, who was raised in a family of modest means. "I did have more than my friends because there was only one of me. But I was formed by the depth and goodness of my father's personality, not by the extra toys I received at Christmas."

Twenty-one-year-old only Amy Sommer, who was raised in a financially advantaged home, laughs when this issue is raised.

"I find it amusing when people call only children spoiled and selfish because a lot of American culture is based on self-actualization."

Dale Schlein would surely agree with Ms. Sommer. Dale notes, "I grew up in an upper-middle-class neighborhood. We were all spoiled—my friends with siblings and those without."

The Chinese feared they were raising a generation of "little emperors" as a result of their one-child policy. After twenty years of studying only children, the conclusion is that only children are not particularly spoiled.[17] In fact, no differences were found in relationships with peers.[18] Only children have been evaluated extensively in this country as well with the same result and shown to be as generous as children with siblings.[19]

Terry Maloney, whose only daughter is fifteen, admits she harps on the subject. "I have bent over backwards to be sure Robin is not a spoiled only child who is unwilling to share. I tell her in those words when she gives me a hard time about doing things. In fact, she says, 'I wish I had a brother or sister so that I didn't have to listen to that line.' "

Myth 7: Only children are selfish.

Fact: "Selfish means you are thinking of yourself as opposed to others," explains Michael Lewis, professor of pediatrics and psychiatry at the Robert Wood Johnson Medical School in New Brunswick, New Jersey. "Selfish behavior is predicated on the fact that you are able to think about others, how they might feel, or how they might act and decide not to take that into account. The youngster who is unable to take the view of another, who cannot be empathetic, is going to appear selfish. This intellectual ability to take the perspective of others is not completely developed until the age of six."

"I get furious when someone implies that my child is selfish. Caitlin's only three. Every young child is selfish. Being selfish and possessive is not limited to only children," Holly Gavigan, Caitlin's mother states vehemently. She is correct in her assessment.

Discussing the toddler years in *Dr. Balter's Child Sense*, Dr. Lawrence Balter writes, "Toddlerhood is a definition-of-self stage: 'Whatever I want is mine; whatever I have my hands on belongs to me.' . . . forcing a child to share what is his can be experienced as a violation of his integrity and will affect his sense of well-being."[20]

"The concept that the world revolves around you is one almost every young child, with or without siblings, believes," says Sandy MacDonald, author of *The Toys 'R Us Guide to Choosing the Right Toys for Your Child*. "A child gets disabused of that notion when she starts hanging out with the other egomaniacs." The self-centeredness gets balanced pretty quickly when a child is involved regularly with other children.

As a child matures, he begins to understand the concepts of borrowing and lending and sharing. Parents should be able to relax their concern until adolescence. A teenager's preoccupation with himself is often interpreted as the result of being spoiled and selfish when, in fact, his self-absorption has nothing to do with his being indulged or being without siblings.

There is a period of adolescent egocentrism during which teens are very concerned with themselves, with their physical appearance, their developing sexuality, and with their identity. They see things from their own point of view. This nearly universal stage affects most teenagers.

Terry Maloney, like many parents of teenage onlies, was worried unnecessarily when her only daughter did an about-face during her preteen years. "I used to feel that Robin was very generous and reaching out to people. She used to be very kind and sympathetic and had empathy for other kids until she turned twelve."

According to Dr. Lewis, altruism calls not only for the ability to stop focusing on oneself, but also for what he calls "psychic" energy to act on that capacity. "There are points in people's lives, one of them being adolescence, when the energy is withdrawn.

Hormonal changes and physical growth during that time may be particularly harsh and the energy to focus on others just isn't there. A good talking-to or a severe punishment will not bring back the needed psychic energy."

When parents cultivate the tools of sharing and feeling for others during preadolescent years, onlies easily wipe out our preconceived ideas. In the absence of siblings, parents are the best early teachers because of the trust and faith inherent in the relationship.

Sheila Beckmann, whose daughter is ten, started early with good results: "When Cynthia was about eighteen months old I began sharing my food with her. All mothers share their food, but I made a point of telling her we were sharing. When she played, I asked for a turn at pushing the buttons on whatever the toy happened to be. I continued this practice well into the second grade. Other adults were surprised by Cynthia's willingness to share even during those terribly selfish years when others were crying if a child came within five feet of a favored possession."

Myth 8: Only children must have their way.

Fact: "Children with siblings, who are constantly forced to share their toys, their parents, and their television time, are often more difficult than those children who are not in day-to-day combat for the possessions or attention they want," notes Dr. Laurie Levinson, a New York child analyst.

Psychiatric secretary Carla Vozios provides a mother's point of view. "I think single children respond better because they are not in constant competition." Like other myths examined in this chapter, only children score as high as children in other family sizes on being cooperative,[21] and some feel they are more cooperative.

Deejay Schwartz, a highly respected and experienced kindergarten teacher, shares this view. "It's the ones who have been jostled and have had to compete who are always trying to push someone down, to be first in line or yell louder in order to be heard." Her evaluation is the antithesis of the tantrum-throwing image of only children. "Onlies have always been heard and therefore function in a very calm way. They are very easy to deal with in a group because they feel confident that their turn will come because it always has. They wait and will even explain to someone else why she should wait for her turn. When they come in at the beginning of the kindergarten year, they are really modeling very good behavior for the others."

Myth 9: Only children are dependent.

Fact: The abundance of attention and time spent by parents answering questions and giving onlies "their say" leaves the impression that only children are very tied to their parents. "In the early part of their lives only children will have a tendency to be either more dependent or more independent because they have had a lot more to do with adults," says Boston child analyst Ava Bry Penman. The same child may exhibit a tendency in each direction. As he matures, he will lean predominantly in one direction.

Linda Cartee, an adult only with a fourteen-year-old only, spent five years living in California before settling back in the small Georgia town in which she grew up. Still, she feels she is very independent because she was accustomed to taking herself places and doing things on her own. "But I have known only children who were very dependent, who are afraid to go away from home, who didn't like to spend the night away from their parents."

As with other stereotypical traits, the variations between individuals must be taken into account. "At the age of seven," says Henry Wallman, a professor of psychology in Chicago, "I went to sleep-away camp for the first time and continued to attend into my early teen years, never once yearning for home."

As a whole, only children are more self-reliant because of adult guidance and because they don't have siblings to lean on or to help solve their problems. However, viewed individually, onlies are not necessarily more or less independent than children with siblings. The reports are mixed. Many had no fear of leaving their parents and were quite content with their experiences: One girl, age sixteen, said, "I never minded going to overnight camp." The parents of an eleven-year-old reported, "The first time she went away—never having slept over at anyone's house—she got on a plane, stayed with a friend's family, and didn't call home once in four days."

Others admitted to being unhappy or homesick when sent off to camp or to visit distant relatives. "He was mortified at the mere idea of going to sleep-away camp," said the mother of one boy, age ten. Similarly, while some onlies remained in their hometowns or close to them for college to keep their parents happy, most went away to college. Kathryn Joyce describes her family as "closed and quiet. I had such strong bonds that the ties provided security. I felt certain of that home life so leaving was not difficult."

Aware parents of onlies strive for independence in their children. "I encourage her to be as independent as she can be at age eleven," says social worker Diane Kass. "You need that to fulfill yourself and reach your potential."

Overprotectiveness feeds dependency by limiting the child's thoughts, actions, and ability to make decisions. Most young children are sent off early in life to play at a friend's house or to spend the night. The child who has not slept over at a friend's home by the end of second grade is considered pampered and protected. Excessively close contact with parents makes it far more difficult to become independent because it slows down the separation and growing-up processes.

"Being independent," says Joe Michalcewicz, whose only child is seventeen, "is an important issue today, since peer pressure is not always a positive vector. My daughter is clear about what she wants and who she is."

Myth 10: Only children become too mature too quickly.

Fact: Whatever their dependent/independent status, onlies, it is true, do seem more grown up. From day one of their lives, onlies are dealing mainly with adults, not other children. "For her," comments Linda Marsh, speaking of her four-year-old, "there's no difference between talking to an adult or to another child." Being comfortable with adults and acting mature enough so they do not mind having a child around opens vast opportunities for learning to the only child.

Children with siblings relate and talk to their peers rather than their parents. The only child's primary role models are parents, not other children. The result is that only children copy adult behavior as well as their speech patterns. Giving up baby talk or skipping it altogether can't possibly harm the only child, who because of time spent with adults will, in most cases, have an increased and advanced vocabulary.

Says Professor Henry Wallman of his teenage only, "His interests are more adult and that's because he is an only child. We can pay more attention to him and foster those interests. His environment at home is adult."

"With an only you talk things out a lot more; you explain more so they learn about reasoning. I do find with my own child and among my patients who are only children, onlies are more reasonable," says Dr. Sylvia Saltzstein, a clinical psychologist.

Teacher Deejay Schwartz sees the rational side of onlies early on. "Onlies are more interested in listening to the reason. If I say to a kindergarten class, 'We can't go to the library today because the librarian is ill,' the only children are more likely to draw a conclusion, such as we should make get-well cards for the librarian or we should keep our books for an extra week."

This type of mature reasoning permits only children to react in more responsible and adult ways. They are better equipped to recognize and handle problems without going into juvenile tailspins and resorting to childish behavior—a quality that wins the admiration of adults. This facet of maturity, rather than being detrimental, actually helps ease many of the ups and downs children encounter.

Barbara Friedman suggests another benefit of early maturity: "You start out being an adult sooner than your peers; by the time you really are an adult, you're better adjusted."

Myth 11: Only children have more emotional problems; they are maladjusted, anxious, and unhappy.

Fact: Many studies conducted to assess the mental health of only children indicate that being an only child is not related to anxiety and emotional problems. Five studies between 1927 and 1967 show that only children are under-represented among psychiatric clients.

According to Dr. Toni Falbo, "There are no differences in emotional health among only and non-only children." Although onlies are "more likely to be referred for clinical help and to repeat visits to the clinic," Dr. Falbo points out the "investigators suggested that the major reason for this relatively high referral and repeat rate was the overprotective attitude of the parents."[22]

It is important to underscore that the closeness of the only child to his parents allows them to be in touch and notice if something is amiss. "If something is wrong or bothering your child," observes Elizabeth Harrison, the mother of a six-year-old, "you will pick it up sooner because you are not distracted by the demands of other children."

Even in single-parent families with only children, where one would expect a higher incidence of emotional problems—especially soon after a divorce—it was not found. In one study, only children from married as well as the divorced groups displayed very positive traits: "bright, mature, independent, and comfortable in adult company."[23]

Dr. Saltzstein pinpoints the matter: "Onlies don't necessarily have more problems than children or adults who have siblings; onlies simply have different types of problems." Not one of the professionals questioned during this research could claim that they had more only children than children with siblings in their practices, and most responded that they had none or one.

There is little to justify a century of accusations that only children are mentally unbalanced, spoiled, selfish, shy, lonely, difficult, dependent, and intellectually overdeveloped. In his book, *Perfect Parenting & Other Myths,* Dr. Frank Main, associate professor of counseling at the University of South Dakota, shows how negative traits can be assigned to non-only children as well as to onlies: "Like it or not, oldest children have a propensity for excess. They are generally too task-oriented, bossy, serious, rigid, and right. Middle children are truly unique; some say outright strange . . ." His description of the youngest is not so glowing either: "The youngest is truly the crown prince or princess. This child, by some fluke of fate, is cute, charming, charismatic and helpless."[24]

These descriptions are no less flattering and no more desirable than many of the ones that have been used to label only children. The reality is that an only child *could* develop any of the often attributed stereotypical personality traits, but so could an oldest, youngest, or middle child.

All these social stereotypes exist without any grounding in reality. Unfortunately, simply because they exist, some people continue to believe them. For those who still believe, Dr. Main sets the record straight. "What you tend to believe is stereotypical of onlies is truer of the youngest. Onlies tend not to be pampered, materialistic, and spoiled. They tend to be more like oldest: task-oriented, responsible achievers. In fact, only children wind up not being what you expect them to be. They wind up being productive and upwardly mobile."

What it comes down to is that people prefer to pigeonhole

others, especially advocates of birth-order effects. But, even Frank Sulloway, author of *Born to Rebel: Birth Order, Family Dynamics, and Creative Lives,* had to admit that because only children do not have sibling rivalry and therefore do not have to fight for parental attention and a particular place in the family, they vary considerably in personality.[25]

The Leading Edge

"I can't think of one only child who as an adult is not successful," says Nancy Coleman, who is married to an extroverted advertising executive only. "The ones I know are dynamic and outgoing. They're business leaders, doctors, or have very prestigious jobs. That doesn't fit with what I always thought about only children. Until I was out on my own, living alone and working, I was under the impression that only children were shy and retiring, not very forceful, probably because that's what I heard from my parents."

Ross Yearwood, a thirty-two-year-old marketing director for a large group of magazines, claims that "the onlies I know have good jobs, are mature and extroverted. They are not necessarily overachievers, but certainly people like me who want to reach their potential."

Studies support Mr. Yearwood's claims. Onlies, like oldest children, crop up disproportionately among Merit Scholars, college students, graduate students, and in the professions. Onlies score higher on aptitude tests and get better grades. They are better educated and more ambitious. They exhibit leadership and tend to be more career-oriented and more creative than peers with siblings.

Like leadership, which can be seen in nursery school, creativity shows up early. Deejay Schwartz explains it this way: "Onlies are fairly inner-directed. They attract friends because they have good ideas. They are used to spending time alone and thinking up play situations. They have formed a habit of making things by themselves. Left to their own devices with blocks, they will create a structure that is quite complex. If a child approaches them, the onlies will be able and happy to tell a lot about what they have built."

One of the most extensive studies ever undertaken tracked more than three thousand high school students—half were only-borns, half had one sibling—for a twenty-year period. This study, conducted by three psychologists from the American Institutes for Research in California, concluded that only children from two-parent homes exhibited higher intelligence than peers with one sibling.[26] Whether the studies were conducted in the 1960s or today, the conclusions are the same: "Only children scored significantly better than other groups in achievement motivation and personal adjustment and were in all other respects indistinguishable from children with brothers and sisters."[27]

Linda Cartee, who teaches gifted students in grades three through seven, has a concise explanation. "These children [only children and children with one sibling] are advantaged because of exposure to cultural events, because their parents read to them when they were younger, and because of the extra insights they have culled from being around adults more than children with many siblings. They have support from their family for their school life and generally their parents expect a lot of them. Other children often don't have the push that comes from the extra caring and concern."

"If I ever needed their help, they were always there for me," says Jennifer Walsh, sixteen, who has been at or near the very top of her class since first grade. "My parents spent considerable time with me on current events and cultural topics, and when we went on day trips, they explained sooooo much, too much," she adds with both pained inflection and jest in her voice.

Jennifer Walsh's experiences are not unique to her. Tenth-grade boys were asked about forty-six experiences ranging from dancing to attending a sports event, from flying in an airplane to acting in a play, and the results demonstrated that only children had "richer and more varied lives," and "experienced more socially stimulating and 'upbeat' home environments."[28]

The extra attention the only child receives manifests itself in many areas from a strong sense of security to the desire to achieve. Onlies seem to thrive on keeping busy. Nancy Armour is a prime example. "I'm a self-starter; I don't like to do badly in anything; I like to be on top of whatever I'm doing! I don't get upset about little things. I'm a tremendous achiever." Her son is following suit.

John Armour, a high school student with an excellent grade average, says, "I stretch myself thin sometimes. I'm on the school paper, one of the literary magazines; I dive in the winter; I have a job as a gofer for a tiny computer company. I'm a dog walker and babysitter. I have jobs around the house—raking leaves and mowing the lawn—for my allowance. I love everything I do."

Larry Brand, an only from another generation, illustrates what seems to be true for a good number of single children: They are motivated. "I saw myself as being able to do everything. I went out for several sports in high school. I was also in glee club and very conscientious about my academic work. I'm very structured, a trait I enjoy."

Later in life, as a whole, only children do achieve more. You may not like or even approve of some of the achievements of people on the following list, but you would have to agree that these only children are highly accomplished individuals who have maximized the positive factors—especially creativity—of being an only child: Jean-Paul Sartre, John Updike, Hans Christian Andersen, Edward Albee, Ezra Pound, Truman Capote, Leonardo Da Vinci, C. Everett Koop, Albert Einstein, Charles Lindbergh, Frank Sinatra, Elvis Presley, Beatle John Lennon, songwriter Burt Bacharach, photographer Ansel Adams, and actresses Lauren Bacall, Candice Bergen, Brooke Shields, actor Cary Grant, comedian and actor Robin Williams, football great Joe Montana, golfer Tiger Woods, political leaders Josef Stalin and Indira Gandhi, business success Carl Icahn, and the Clinton's daughter Chelsea. Three onlies—Frank Borman, William Anders, and James Lovell, Jr.—

were on the first Apollo crew to orbit the moon in 1968. These are just a few of the successful people pursuing diverse endeavors who are or have been in the public eye and who also are only children.

One lengthy examination of only children as adults shows a slight income advantage for onlies. The study also demonstrates that onlies have fewer children, that they are no more likely to divorce than children with siblings, and that male onlies choose more educated spouses than do males with siblings.[29]

As parents, we want our children to have self-direction and motivation and to be responsible, happy adults. Giving your child a brother or sister appears to have no effect on obtaining these goals. In fact, many are convinced that a sibling may impair the leading edge that only children have. Says only child Dewhurst, "I was a year ahead in school; I could read the newspaper by the time I was three. I don't think I would have been able to do that in a larger family."

Terze Gluck, the mother of an only, argues for singletons. "I was so influenced by my sister. I would watch to see what she was doing, then fall back in line behind her. The sibling relationship has a lot of humiliation built into it. Without a sibling, who would be sure to humiliate, an only child will have tremendous self-esteem, assuming the parents don't humiliate her."

On most issues that relate to general well-being, psychologist Dr. John Claudy, the principal investigator in the American Institutes for Research study, found that the only children were very much like the children from two-child families. In fact, there were no differences in key areas: self-confidence, vigor, calmness, impulsiveness, health, or age of marriage.[30] In referring to his study, Dr. Claudy summarizes his findings: "The differences were small; the similarities, striking. Onlies are much more like other children than they are different."

One Is Best If . . .

Although the evidence shows that only children excel, not every only child will make noteworthy achievements or be an academic star. "Other things are more important," notes Katie Crosby. "My husband, who is a second child and comes from a less culturally enriched family than mine, was an academic genius. He graduated from high school, college, and medical school with honors. To my parents, being happy and well adjusted were more important than whether I got good grades or eventually earned a lot of money. My husband's parents were very concerned that their son earn money and did not care so much about whether or not he would be happy. I'm much more content than he is."

"What is more important than to excel in academia or sports," says therapist Fredda Bruckner-Gordon, author of *Making Therapy Work: Choosing, Using and Ending Therapy,* "is the ability to function and have a lot of friends and that goes counter to putting the emphasis on competition."

On self-evaluation, only children were either as happy and satisfied or happier and more satisfied with their lives than children who had one or two siblings.[31] Surely, this is the most significant discovery to come out of the scrutiny of the only child.

We know that each child within a family sees the family from a different perspective; each is in a unique position and sees it that way. Rearing molds the child. When the question is posed, "Does the only child need a sibling?" the answer is unconditionally "No." One is best if you conclude that you want to raise one child.

3

The Inner Workings of the Threesome

Parents who choose to have only one child have discovered, as you will, that singletons do not suffer, that in fact, children flourish if they remain without siblings. One child brings most of the pleasures of multiple children with very few of the negatives. One child also offers a substantial number of the benefits gained by couples who remain childless. In short, one son or one daughter offers the best of both worlds.

"Every once in a while," admits Suzanne Coburn, mother of a singleton, "a large family seems like a wonderful idea, then I come to my senses."

What's right for Ms. Coburn is working for more and more couples. Almost three decades ago, Dr. Jessie Bernard, a sociologist at Penn State University, projected the point we have now reached: In her book, *The Future of Motherhood,* she wrote, "The future calls for an end to the glorification of the large family. . . .'[1]

Before you reach a final decision, consider the issues that seriously affect life as family size increases. The subtle interpersonal relationships of your threesome need investigating before you decide whether to expand your family or to stop at one.

The Personal Issues

Issue 1: How will more children affect my marriage?

You may love your spouse deeply and want to have time to be together. When parents of one were studied in the early eighties, the quality of the marital relationship—specifically, less time with one's spouse—was one of the most important reasons for not wanting more children. Less free time and increased restriction, hence reduced job opportunity, were also important considerations as they are today.[2]

It is well documented that with each added child marital relations become less ideal. With one child, intimacy has a chance. There is a real end to one child's demands and requirements. Someone is not always awake, barging in, or insisting you pay attention. You can deposit one child with her grandparents, another willing relative, or a friend for a much-needed vacation.

When your child sleeps at a friend's, the entire night belongs to you, not to another sibling, who will undoubtedly want a special treat that makes up for his sibling's privilege. "When our daughter spends the night at a friend's, we seize the opportunity. We're alone; we treasure that time. We do something special," says Diane Kass.

Even when both parents work, you can find time for each other. There is space in each day or a few times a week for sitting down together quietly. Couples schedule regular "talks" to prevent time and commitments from slipping between them. Gabi and Charles Longi, both marketing executives in Indiana, have a nightly cup of coffee after they have put their seven-year-old daughter to bed. "This time is set aside to tell each other what we did that day, to discuss any problems or share happy events. Without it, we would miss so much of each other's life," says Gabi.

The Daniels of San Diego, whose son is twelve, go out for an early dinner alone every Thursday evening. They have been meeting after work since Brent was five. "We retain some of the romance of courting, but can be home before Brent goes to bed," Tricia Daniels explains.

"It's really what a child gets used to," she continues. "Brent accepts our Thursday dinner as fact. I admit, I have been very lucky in that I have had little trouble with sitters. We did go through short periods of sitter problems, but we never completely abandoned our ritual. I don't think you can devote weekday evenings to your spouse if you have more than one child. Children have too many needs that cannot be met properly if parents are out of the house too often on school nights."

Palma Anthony looks beyond the school years. "This is my second marriage and I feel totally blessed to have found Larry. Neither of us is young and if we start over again with another baby it will seem like forever before we are just us again. I adore my son, but I want to give my husband my love and attention, too, and having two children would pull me too far away from him."

"We've been able to give to ourselves earlier in life and our happiness benefits our child," Diane Kass says with conviction. "Our daughter has derived all possible benefits that can come from a family of three. We don't feel guilty about not giving her a sibling."

Issue 2: Will our personal freedom be curtailed by another child?

"One is civilized," remarked Jolie-Ann Johnston, thirty-eight, and in the early stages of her "only" pregnancy. When you drop your only child off to play at a friend's, the rest of the afternoon is yours. There is a hiatus between homework, haircuts, reading books, planning birthday parties, and applying Band-Aids. Once your singleton passes through infancy, unlike parents with a "fullhouse," you can take relaxing baths, read the newspaper, or actually do the work you cart home from the office.

As Gin Choa, the mother of a four-year-old, sees it, "When

you have two, one of them needs you and the other needs the other of you. You can't give each other a break."

One child allows a couple and the individuals within it to retain a substantial amount of freedom and flexibility. It's feasible that either spouse will enjoy or surely not object to being in charge of one child for an evening, a day, a weekend, or the duration of a business trip.

The Cardonsky-Steins spend two nights a week out, but separately; each parent has one evening free to see business associates or friends. Sharon Stein, a busy New York matrimonial attorney, occasionally spends hers alone, shopping, seeing a movie, or catching up on work. Says Stein, "Lauren is thirteen and I haven't missed too many of my nights out. I enjoy being by myself or having dinner with a friend I know my husband is not crazy to see."

"Having a second child would prevent both my husband and me from accomplishing things we want to do," explains Lori Karmazin. "Perhaps they are selfish reasons, but I feel that I'm a better person, I'm not frustrated, and my attitude is better. I don't resent my child. One child does not prevent me from returning to school. I love being a mother, but just the mother of one."

Before determining family size, parents must decide individually how they want to parcel their available hours among child care, work, and leisure. Marjorie Pratt, home-based working mother of thirteen-year-old Billy, analyzes her decision: "I knew the way I wanted to rear my child was going to take a great deal of my time and it was something I did not want to do more than once. I think that Billy has gotten the message that I did exactly what I wanted to do. The time I put in has given him a great deal of self-esteem."

Issue 3: How will family life change if we have more than one child?

With one it's easy to keep tabs on who is doing what, when. Neither parent feels so overwhelmed by lessons and practice schedules that he or she consciously or unconsciously bows out at the slightest opportunity.

Few would argue with Arlene Cardoza, founder and director of "Woman at Home" workshops in Minnesota and author of *Women at Home,* when she discusses the importance of private time with children. "Every child craves attention from, and interaction with, each parent; and conversely, each parent needs a personal relationship with each child. Regardless of how the recognition of these needs is implemented—whether private time is a quiet conversation, a busy activity, or an errand turned special—it's essential that within the constellation of active family life, each parent finds a means of maintaining an individual relationship with each child. Those are the building blocks of future relationships, and so, too, the building blocks of successful total family life."[3]

"The threesome," notes Ann York, an executive for a health and beauty aids company whose only son is in ninth grade, "is more open than the relationships in multichild families. Parents talk to the only child in a more adult manner earlier and he is included in more adult events than children with siblings."

Under normal circumstances parents of onlies have a greater choice in how they spend time with their children. An only can relish—and not be rushed in—the time spent with a parent. He does not have to worry about how soon it will be "baby brother's" turn or that he will be forced into an activity selected by a sibling that he does not find particularly fun or interesting. He will not be swept away from an engrossing game and into the car because his older sister has a piano lesson and he's too young to stay home alone.

"It's their schedule, *not mine,* that makes it impossible for me to spend time alone with each of my children," protests Lydia Weber, a bewildered part-time education consultant and mother of a six-year-old and a three-year-old. But is it? "Arianne is never alone with me; my son is always with us. To avoid spending my entire afternoon in the car, I must schedule their activities at the same time. Arianne is suffering from a lack of individual attention. I'm a consultant; I recognize the problem daily. Yet since the birth of my son, there has been no sensible, convenient way to solve this dilemma that I know is detrimental to my oldest child." (Arianne has been in therapy to overcome her discipline problems in school and at home.)

When children of working parents were asked what they want from their parents, they replied they did not want more time with their parents, but rather parents who were less stressed and less exhausted from their jobs. They wanted their parents to focus on them and give them their undivided attention.[4] Not so easily accomplished when you have several children and work long hours.

Guilt levels run high when time is at a premium. With one child, private time is almost a certainty. With two or more, it's questionable. Now a mother, Denise Montgomery remembers an inordinate amount of parental time spent with her when she was growing up as an only child. "I can see with my three children, time is very limited. I don't have time to go over each one's homework; the interruptions are constant."

Susan Ginsberg, Ed.D., author of *Family Wisdom* and editor and publisher of *Work and Family Life,* a newsletter devoted to balancing job and personal responsibilities, views the situation thusly: "With one child, being employed is doable, but still a balancing act. With two or three children, it becomes very, very difficult to be with your children and be at work in a way you believe best satisfies both demands. With two, and more frequently with three children," adds Dr. Ginsberg, "the economics of going to work often don't work out; it could be cheaper to stay home."

Parents who work at demanding jobs are spending more hours at their endeavors, seriously reducing time and energy left over for children. A working frenzy pervades American society, making it harder than ever before to find balance between work and family. In the years between 1995 and 1998, the number of people who spent more than fifty hours a week at work almost doubled;[5] the average workweek is roughly forty-seven hours.[6] Not many waking hours remain for family life.

"I function in a constant state of guilt," says Shirley Blacker, forty-one, a sales executive for a toy company. "I feel terrible when I have to be at a meeting and my husband takes Lizzie to the dentist. I'm old-world enough to consider doctors' appointments a mother's job. I feel worse when Lizzie wants to go to a friend's house and neither of us can take her. How do mothers bear the guilt of not being available or able to please several children? I couldn't handle it."

Even for masterful planners like Rosemary Simmons, one more is too many. "When we decided to have a child, we moved into a vacant apartment in my mother's building so that she would be right there to fill in. I have a baby-sitter from nine to two and my mother takes him until one of us gets home from work. We're into the next phase, our son will be going to school in the fall, we will be closing on a house this summer, again near my mother. Some people can manage two children, but I don't know how they do it. We're very organized people."

In an article for parents considering or about to have a second child, writer Louise Lague spells out genuine changes you can expect. "With two children, home becomes your anchor more than ever; you are less likely, for a while, to see the inside of restaurants, movie theaters, and airplanes. You start buying the large economy sizes at the grocery store, and the fridge now contains more than two steaks, a bottle of champagne, and a container of yogurt. As soon as baby food is over, family meals begin.

"If your two children are the same sex, the older one starts getting fewer, better, sturdier clothes. You get a VCR, you start to cocoon." In short, Lague concludes, ". . . you are no longer just a couple with one little darling tagging along."[7]

There was a time when women wore themselves out being A-plus mothers. Today couples are stressed out simply arranging who is going to do what and figuring out how to squeeze it all in. The kind of spontaneity, which belongs primarily to childless couples, is still attainable with one child. With more, spur-of-the-moment decisions to visit friends, go out to dinner, or take a weekend trip are less likely to be a part of family life. One child, on the other hand, tags along quite manageably, especially if she has a good disposition.

Says Carla Vozios, "You have more mobility with one. You can take him to other people's homes for the weekend. If you have more, the honest hostess says, 'Oh my God, they're coming with the children.' The polite hostess grits her teeth and stashes the breakables."

Issue 4: Are you prepared to give up your love affair with your firstborn?

Below the surface of practicality and everyday nitty-gritty are unexpected forces that can impair the happiness of a family when you add to it.

"It's hard to see how you could love another baby as much as you love the first one," says thirty-three-year-old Bob Parlapiano, who is considering a second child. "I'm sure you can, but it is hard to imagine."

"The anguish with which parents face this question of giving up the love affair with their first child in order to share it with a second is surprisingly painful," writes pediatrician T. Berry Brazelton in *To Listen to a Child.*[8] If it is so painful, why do it?

It is perfectly acceptable to feed your strong feelings for your firstborn and to continue to bond and cement that relationship. Parents should not feel obligated to spread their love just because, until recent years, having more than one was the "thing" to do. Projected changes in your attitude and most importantly in your relationship with your firstborn are in many ways more important than how you solve child care, financial, and career problems.

"Nobody tells you that the hardest thing about having a new baby is kicking the old baby out of the nest of your heart," writes Kate Moses, a Salon.com editor. " 'I love you both equally'—the age-old answer sputtered by querulous, stammering parents to their querulous, suspicious children—is a myth we would like to believe . . . As much as it saddens me, the truth is that my heart did not simply 'expand' to accommodate my second child. Though I do, unequivocally, love both my children deeply, it is also true that I have been more connected to my baby than to my son since the baby's birth."[9]

Janet Spencer King, former editor of *Working Parents* magazine and the mother of two, says, "Second and subsequent children have almost as great an impact on the adjustment process as do firstborns."

With the addition of a child, not only does the chaos of infancy return, but a reshuffling of relationships also takes place. For a while at least, everything will seem as out of control and overwhelming as it did the first time around. Your family, in essence, experiences a complete overhaul. Each relationship—you and your spouse, you and your child, the three of you and relatives—is dramatically and suddenly changed. Moses notes of the changes and her love for her firstborn, "Like anything vital, it changes. And grows. And perhaps this change, which feels like such a loss, is also necessary and healthy. Perhaps we are now forging the relationship that will carry us, connected and yet separate, not just loving each other but with enough distance to like each other, into Zachary's adulthood."[10]

Debbie Diehl-Camp is aware of the difference family size makes. "I have given Cameron almost undivided attention. I make conscious decisions about the toys he plays with, the friends he has. From the minute he wakes up until the minute he goes to bed, we're interacting with him. When I was growing up, I had three sisters and I don't feel as if I knew my parents very well. My mother says, 'I never played with all of you; I never held you the way you hold Cameron.' "

"There's an intimacy there I can't imagine could have developed if I had two and certainly not eight children," claims a very satisfied Joe Michalcewicz, who was raised in a three-child family. "We do more things together. Our daughter has allowed us to be part of her growing up. There's more sharing and better parent/child communication than I remember in my home growing up."

"In a world in which each of us has to fight for attention every waking minute, my daughter has the advantage in one place—home," comments Sandra Steadham, who is the oldest of six children. "In my house there was always a new show on the road that I had to compete with. Zoe doesn't have to fight for my affection, time, or attention and that gives her a jump on self-esteem. If everyone tells her she's not important that day, she still knows she's important to me. We all need that." Where else but in the only-child family can you get a one-on-one that is so intense and so character-forming?

Issue 5: What happens to the inner workings of the threesome if it becomes a foursome?

The chemistry changes when a sibling is added. Having a sibling can be wonderful, horrible, or a bit of both. There's no possible way to know in advance. However, when you have two or more children who are close in age, you are more likely to have a division, a "we" and "they" relationship that clearly separates children from parents. "Face it. When you're an only child, you can't be put aside. You're one of the group right from the beginning," says Larry Brand.

"My mother was and is my greatest fan," boasts Duff Badgley. "I suspect if I had a sibling, it would not have been that way."

Sibling rivalry is a divisive force. In many families with only two children, the rivalry and emotional battle begins even before the children have language. Often there are angry feelings before they can identify them, understand them, or verbalize them.

"A new sibling is always a shock," declares Dr. Betty Wilson, who teaches psychology at the College of St. Elizabeth in New Jersey. "The blow can be quite powerful and is often long-lasting. In so many ways, the arrival of a brother or sister is at the core of sibling rivalry."

Patty Wellden, mother of six-year-old Jay, believes "siblings go into confrontational relationships all their lives. We don't want that for our son."

On meeting a new sister or brother, firstborns are well known for speaking from the heart: "Can we send her back if I don't like her?" "When we move, does he have to come with us?" "I wish you could put her in the garbage." Such charming "terms of endearment" from the child you've adored and lived for are most distressing.

Only children, on the other hand, don't get displaced, diminished, or dethroned. Achievements are applauded. Without a sibling who talked at eight months or was valedictorian of his high school class, the only is recognized whenever he walks or whatever his slot in the graduating class.

Says fifteen-year-old Daniel Saltzstein, "I'm glad I don't have sibling rivalry in my family. I can't think of a reason why I would want a sibling. I'm never lonesome and am always doing something. It's also easier to be close to your parents because you are not competing for their affection."

In his studies of family dynamics and birth order Frank Sulloway found that "offspring strive to maximize parental investment, adapting their strategies to their own particular family niche. Ultimately, sibling rivalry is about surviving childhood."[11] With one, you don't have to worry about the effects of birth order and children's vying for parental attention and favor.

As an only child you have a more indulgent relationship with parents because they are not spending their time arbitrating between children or soothing hurt feelings. Kathy Coers, who teaches philosophy at a Georgia university, believes "the extra time and sensitivity the only child receives have given her son an inner core of strength that children with siblings are less likely to develop."

"People romanticize siblings; they think siblings will love each other. As a therapist I see more siblings who hate each other than siblings who love each other," reports Dr. Sandra Leiblum, psychologist and professor of clinical psychiatry at the Robert Woods

Johnson Medical School in New Jersey. "There are forces that mitigate against siblings having a wonderful relationship. There is always competition, always a favored child."

In contrast, thirteen-year-old Billy Pratt assesses his family life: "I think I have a better relationship with my parents than most kids do. I talk with them. My friends are rebellious and go against what their parents say. My parents give me plenty of attention so that I don't have to act out to get it."

As many mothers of two or more discover, you can throw out thoughts of time management and be sure you will have less time to be with your spouse. When your children are young, you're likely to spend more time "maintaining them" and monitoring their disagreements than nurturing their growing minds.

Issue 6: Can partiality be avoided when there is more than one child?

No parent sets out to treat one child more lovingly than another, but it happens in the most sophisticated and educated families, and very often the parents are unaware of their actions. The damage may be done before anyone realizes the cause. "You love him more than you love me." "It's not fair, he got a new bicycle when I needed one." While on the surface, such comments seem typically "sibling," they are emotional reactions that can have permanent effects on a child.

A mother of four considers favoritism a major concern in her home: "My husband clearly prefers our oldest daughter. I put a lot of time and energy into smoothing over his obvious leaning. When I suggest to him that he is spending more time with Caroline, he tells me it's my imagination. When I pursue the subject, he tells me I do the same thing with Zachery. I adore Zachery, but I never let it be seen by the other children. I try hard to give them equal time."

Victoria Bedford, a behavioral researcher at the University of Indianapolis, found that "the psychological requirements for parents to be fair are formidable." Even when parents go out of their way not to compare their children, the children perceive comparison nonetheless. It is quite impossible for parents to be fair at all times when age differences, abilities, and needs are bound to be unique for each child and are constantly changing. Violating the fairness ethic with the resulting consequence of believed favoritism is inevitable.[12]

It is extremely difficult for parents to equalize praise and encouragement. When one child excels, it is near impossible. Even if parents appear to be successful, the other child will feel slighted in spite of their efforts. Suppose for the moment you have two children close enough in age to be on the same baseball team. Number-one son has a great throwing arm, is a stellar batter, and hasn't missed a fly ball in the last six games. Number-two son couldn't catch a fly ball or stop a grounder if he wore two mitts; his hitting is no better.

After a game, you naturally congratulate your star and so do other parents. You are quietly proud, but no matter how you hide your delight, number-two son will view your broad smile or pat on his brother's back as favoritism. Because of sibling rivalry, parents cannot avoid perceived partiality. If you spend more time shopping, reading a book, or building a treehouse with one child, the sibling will notice. She may balk, feel less loved, or feel as if she were being treated unfairly.

It is often argued that growing up with siblings is good preparation for the real world. Many like Deejay Schwartz disagree. "The world is a tough place," she says. "It is very difficult to give too much confidence. The child who is sure that people want him and like him is better off than the child who is not so sure. The child who feels treasured and listened to has a big advantage."

Issue 7: What if there are personality clashes within the threesome?

John Armour is a strong testimonial to the success of a well-matched threesome. "I think my parents are fair; they give me a good amount of freedom. There are things they don't want me doing, but I don't want to do those things anyway. What I'm saying is that we agree on a lot of things. Now that I think about it, we rarely disagree. I rarely get upset with my parents. We have a great relationship."

John Armour has what is called a temperamental match with his parents. Psychology professor Henry Wallman details the harmony. "A lot of the success has to do with the natural endowments of the child and the particular match between parents and child. The temperamental match—the innate predisposition—is probably more important when you have an only child." If you're very social and your child is not, for example, pushing her to have social contact will probably cause your child to withdraw.

Unfortunately some parents, whether their child is their natural offspring or adopted, have personality clashes with a child that can be spotted during the first few months of the child's life, become problematic by the end of the second or third year, and intensify during adolescence. "Let your spouse take over whenever possible," advises Professor Wallman. Or a close friend, companion, or relative if you are a single parent.

On the other hand, personalities can be too well matched. The parallels in the personalities of Elizabeth Harrison and her six-year-old daughter have created a situation comparable to a mismatch. "My husband would say that we are the same in every way: She is intense, has a low frustration tolerance, and has a temper like mine. The similarities often make it more difficult for me to deal with her because we lock horns regularly."

When the personalities don't mesh or mesh too well, the threesome can be excruciating for the only child unless the compatible parent spells the incompatible one. "My father made my life bearable," recalls adult only Jerome Ettinger, who is the father of three. "My mother was overbearing, overprotective, and plain difficult. We did not get along or see eye-to-eye on anything. She resorted to bizarre and extreme measures to control me. To get me back into the house from playing ball, she would invent nonexistent telephone calls."

A mismatch can happen, but all parties aren't necessarily miserable. Twelve-year-old Carol Pappin readily announces, "My mother and I fight all the time because we are so alike. But my mother is happy and so am I. We know why we fight."

It can also happen that both parents are one way and the child is another. As your child begins to enter his or her teen years, conflicting personalities will become more pronounced. In the Patterson family, for example, Adam's parents are both highly motivated overachievers and sixteen-year-old Adam is laid back, easygoing, not interested in setting the world on fire. The differences in their attitudes and dispositions, says Adam, "make it feel as if they are united against me. They are constantly bugging me—both of them. I know what will happen when I don't do something, and if I do it, it won't be well enough or fast enough for them. They don't get that I'm not like them. Whenever I can, I don't tell them what's going on—what paper is due at school, what I did with my friends, what's going on in my life. It's easier. If they don't know, they can't be all over me."

You may, for instance, be raising an introvert who needs quiet time and space. If you're overscheduling him or smothering him with attention, you may need to respect his personality type and learn to step back.

When personalities clash in the one-child family, there must be a greater effort on the part of the parents to control frustrations and eliminate the conflicts. Recognize the similarities and differences and do your best to accept them.

Even the only with a "perfect match" needs someone close, understanding, and ideally nonjudgmental when your adult world leaves no time for him or when he has a problem he can't or doesn't want to discuss with you. "It's difficult for me to talk to my parents about girls," explains Victor Smythe, eighteen.

Family problems will present the same obstacle. With no sibling sounding board to hear a child's anger or frustration, it's a good idea to cultivate a warm communicative bond with someone less personally involved: a friend, a parent's friend, an aunt, an uncle, a cousin, or a neighbor you know and trust.

More than any other family size, the threesome is the most apt to run smoothly without internal friction, with little need for strong disciplinary measures. Many parents voiced statements comparable to this one: "We have virtually no discipline problems. My daughter [age twelve] is so reachable; we discuss what might turn into a problem. I'm more inclined to behave badly than she is."

Because the only child's parents are less harried and stressed, they are more likely to listen to every detail of their child's dream, be enthusiastic about an inning-by-inning playback of baseball practice, and be happy to read every word of his compositions and term papers. The end result, more often than not, is contentment on all fronts, especially when parents respect natural differences in their temperaments and their child's.

Issue 8: What does the only child think is the perfect family size?

"I only see an ideal," says teenager Samuel Barron. "I would want a brother. But I suppose if I had a brother, I would wish I were an only child."

Richard Dewhurst hones in on the issue. "When I was younger, I was envious of kids that had brothers and sisters and conversely they would always tell me that they would prefer to be an only child. The grass is always greener."

Kathy Coers recalls one reservation she had about being an only child. "I envied people who had hand-me-down clothes. That seemed like a warm and snugly thing to me. Used toys seemed already loved while my new things seemed cold and hard." But talk to the child who is the unwilling recipient of hand-me-downs from an older sibling . . . To cover all bases, if you can, find a friend or cousin with an older child who can pass a few items on to your only.

Be it cars or clothing, more independence or less, siblings or none, Jane Rinzler discovered in a study of teenage thoughts, hopes, and feelings, ". . . somebody always wants what somebody on the other side of the street wants to get rid of." In response to the question "If there were one thing about your life that you could change at home, what would it be?" one person wanted to get "some siblings," while another said, "Get rid of my little sister—*seriously!*"[13]

The gist of this concern is that parents must review their own circumstances to determine what is possible and what is comfortable for them. "We were never undecided," says Lois Angel, whose only son is seventeen. "Having Dan was such a wonderful experience that we felt we could not duplicate it; nor did we want to try. The emotional involvement and economic commitment would have been too great for us."

Lucas Saunders, a psychiatrist, the father of an only and an only himself, worried that his son would feel deprived without a sibling. "You want more for your kids than you do for yourself. I did not feel deprived as an only child. But was I cheating my son out of an important experience? I was never concerned to the point I thought I was doing irreparable damage by not providing a sibling. My concern never reached the point of saying to my wife, 'Let's have another child.' "

The Practical Issues

"If I won the lottery tomorrow, I'd have another," reports Carla Vozios. "I have to work. A second child would have been too financially stressful for us."

Most parents of onlies have many more options than parents with several offspring in the lifestyle they choose for themselves and for their children. The cost of most six-week summer programs for young children or teens, from a tour of Western America, a trip to Israel and Italy, or a summer camp, start at around $5,000, not including transportation. One six-week summer tour of this country for twelve- to fourteen-year-olds had a price tag of $10,500! The money available for educational trips, luxury family vacations, or private training in the field of your child's choice is a key factor mentioned by parents as the reason why they *prefer* one child.

Issue 9: What are the cost implications—big and small—of one versus two or more children?

Although money isn't the sole factor in decisions about childbearing, it is impossible to ignore cost implications. For instance, treatment for infertile couples averages $8,000 for each attempt at pregnancy. Couples spend as much as $50,000 and more trying to have a child. Sperm banks have become big business and charge accordingly—if you're willing to pay the price you can buy Ph.D., medical, and professional school student sperm.

Depending on insurance coverage and including prenatal visits, it costs between $2,800 and $6,400 to bring a child into the world today in a hospital; the average Caesarean comes in at $11,000. Those figures apply to normal prenatal care with no pre- or post-delivery complications for mother or baby. A premature baby requiring neonatal intensive care or a child with any after-delivery problems will increase the costs substantially.[14] Adoption, too, whether national or international, carries a considerable price tag in spite of any tax credit.

By year three, if not long before, the majority of parents will want or need to add day care or in-home childcare and nursery school to their expenses, which vary greatly depending on family income. "Day care has become one of the most pressing issues—and serious expenses—for young families."[15] Plus, you'll probably spend an additional $98,000 or close to it "to live in safe, leafy neighborhoods with good schools" with one child.[16] If you live in an area with poor schools, you may want to send your child to private schools throughout his elementary and high school years. Add thousands more to the tab.

There are good reasons to worry about the choice of schools and the quality of education. With so many mothers working full-time, our schools, especially the kindergarten and early elementary grades, are preparing children for the world. Busy career parents should consider how much time they have left over for filling in the learning gaps for more than one child.

Without including private school and without being extravagant, to get a middle-class child to college age requires a minimum of $228,000—a very conservative figure—if your family income is about $60,000 before taxes.[17] Other estimates are steeper. According to the United States Department of Agriculture, a middle-class family who gives birth to an only child in 1997 can expect to spend $301,000 until the child reaches age eighteen. The same report claims with a family income over $60,000, parents will spend well over $437,000—of that, almost $55,000 goes toward food.

College education has become almost mandatory in our specialized and technological world. Allowing for inflation, secondary education in a state school as an in-state student, including room and board, inflates the total to close to $600,000, depending on the college's prestige and ranking. If you send your child to a top private college, you're looking at well over $800,000; some estimate over $900,000.[18] Complicating the financial picture in many cases is the fact that so many people are starting families when they are older and/or starting second families. Not surprisingly, saving for children's education can compete with saving for retirement. Fortunately, state-sponsored savings plans, which vary by state but are open to parents from other states, offer tax breaks as you save for your child's college expenses. State-trust savings plans are just one way to stay ahead of the costs of raising your child.[19]

Perhaps most distressing to parents is not the long-range cost but the routine needs of children that become magnified by their seemingly constant requests for more. The "must-haves" begin early with computer games played at a friend's house and grow to state-of-the-art sound systems and complex electronic equipment during the teen years.

The available dollars permit the only child to explore any and all special interests she may have. "We didn't have much money," adult only Henrietta Eakins explains, "but my parents were able to offer me opportunities they simply would not have been able to provide had there been more children. I had expensive interests like horseback riding and skiing. I was able to do that and I want my child to have those advantages. In terms of sheer finances, we've been able to travel extensively with our daughter and would not have been able to do so if we had another one."

Gail Shore feels that way, too. "My husband and I both work so we're not poor, but we're not rich either. Lia can go to camp in the summer and have all the lessons she wants for the most part." Providing such opportunities is something parents of onlies are good at because they often have extra money to spend on luxuries.

The demands and necessities are noteworthy in larger families. They seem endless when you have more than one child. Mothers like Vivian Loomis, an aerobics instructor, complain, "As soon as I give Wendy lunch money, Jessica decides she wants to buy lunch, too. No sooner does Jessica hear that Wendy is getting socks with stars than she has to have them. I know it sounds petty, but the small things add up."

The incidentals for two or more are like ocean waves; they wash up on shore relentlessly. After the essentials of food and clothing, there are school pictures, notebooks, backpacks, Halloween costumes, and of course, at least one of the latest toys being advertised on television or the Internet. There are footballs and baseball cards, stuffed animals and doll accessories, followed by updated computers and cell phones a few years later. There are birthday gifts for friends, gifts for the teachers, and special attire for recitals, graduations, and performances.

Issue 10: Is your "house sense" attuned to your taste, your needs, and the times?

If you have a second child, the need for more space can have tremendous financial ramifications. A mother of an adopted girl reluctantly admitted that she and her husband took their names off the waiting list for a second baby because they simply could not afford to move to a larger home.

Single-family dwellings in the United States carry an average price of almost $180,000 nationally and around $240,000 on the West Coast. You can expect to pay much more if you move to metropolitan cities such as Boston, New York, Honolulu, San Francisco, or Los Angeles. Tack on thousands more if you plan to live in one of the "most desirable" locations.[20] But when you start house hunting, the house you love, the one with enough space for another child and land for a tiny bed of roses or six rows of vegetables, never seems to be anywhere near the median or average price.

With only one, you can be content with living quarters that at first may seem too cramped. Until children reach their teen years, most prefer to play and be near adults. Onlies are even less likely to go off by themselves. So if you think you need more space, you probably don't, unless it's another bedroom for a second child. The only, given a bedroom of his own, will make do happily for many years in the same square feet that meet your adult needs.

"We have a playroom downstairs and my son has a huge bedroom," says Meredith Gable. "My son played smack in the middle of the living room until he was almost eight years old. I felt as if I had the only living room in America that was decorated in vintage Lego. It was the setting for his castles, cars, books, and works of art. Whenever I went on a rampage and moved his toys back into his room, they and he resurfaced in no time right in the middle of whatever I was doing."

A parent of two college-age children had a similar complaint.

"When we felt our children were old enough to sleep alone on the main floor of the house, we turned our old bedroom into a den for them and built a very expensive addition over the garage for us. Until they left for college, where do you think they watched television? In our part of the house! So much for privacy—we couldn't get it and they didn't want it."

Buying a new home or financing an addition to accommodate a second child seems minor when compared with the complexities of maternity leave, job security, child care assistance, and daily logistics. These realities have far-reaching, long-term effects on the family.

Issue 11: Can you "afford" a second maternity leave?

One of the fastest growing segments of the work force is women with children under age three. In fact, 62 percent of women with infants and toddlers and 68 percent of mothers with preschoolers hold jobs. If you expand the age group to include school-age children the percentage of employed mothers rises to seventy-seven.[21] For those mothers who work outside the home, repeat motherhood is neither easy to negotiate nor practical because maternity leaves in this country are far from ideal.

Corporate benefits make being away and being relaxed extremely difficult. The Family and Medical Leave Act, passed in 1993, grants parents extended periods of time with their children away from their jobs; however, this time, most often twelve weeks, is usually unpaid. Those larger corporations offering paid leaves limit them to six to eight weeks. The United States is one of only a handful of countries that does not require paid maternity leaves. Without any other source of income, the financial strain can be felt for a long time, especially in single-parent families.

In contrast, a woman is paid her salary while caring for her newborn in Sudan, Cameroon, and Nepal according to a United Nations survey of 152 countries.[22] Those on parental leave in Norway are entitled to a one-year leave and are paid at 80 percent of their earnings or 100 percent if they take 42 weeks. Finland and Germany, likewise, offer benefits that far exceed America's: Finland provides full-time leave for twenty-six weeks with pay that ranges in percentage according to earnings; in Germany, full-time leave is possible until a child is three years old with a standardized payment until the child reaches his second birthday. Italy, too, outstrips the United States by giving ten months that can be taken any time until a child's eighth birthday. Italy pays its workers on parental leave approximately 30 percent of their salaries.[23] Sweden's first paid parental leave law dates back to 1891![24] The United States doesn't come close in monetary support, time, or job security.

The Family and Medical Leave Act was designed to encourage fathers to take leaves to be with their newborns as well. One poll indicates that almost three-quarters of the people asked could not think of a man—friend or relative—who had exercised this option.[25] This is hardly surprising, since most leaves are unpaid. That said, it's difficult to justify in the face of evidence that shows that men who spend considerable time with their children early in the children's lives become more involved parents throughout their lives.[26] But men, perhaps more so than women, worry about how their competency at work will be perceived if they choose to take care of their babies.

Almost three-quarters of women taking maternity leave feel their bosses think they are less committed and worry when and if they will return to work. Even more disturbing: Many find themselves overlooked for promotions and those who take more than one leave are "more heavily penalized."[27] This is not a new reality.

Attitudes toward motherhood and prolonged absence from the job are improving, but at a snail's pace and at a price. In segments of the law profession, for example, women have made great strides, receiving good maternity leaves and flexible hours among other benefits. In 1988 the *New York Times* reported, "Women who take advantage of them often find themselves left behind when it comes to partnerships, choice assignments, and stature. Intended to foster sexual equality, these measures also have created a new category of law firm associates who work with no prospects of advancement in what some lawyers call 'the mommy track.' "[28]

Six years later, the same newspaper ran a story with the sub-heading, "No matter how short the child-care detour, many women pay a high price to return to the corporate road."[29] Although there are exceptions, it seems to matter little how well a woman does her job. When she leaves to have a baby or spend time caring for her family, she is "still perceived as less dedicated [than men] to the job or the company."[30] University of Maryland sociologist Harriet B. Presser summed up the reality for women: "What we call opportunity costs of having a child are greater now . . . you're losing more in the labor marketing by dropping out, even temporarily."[31]

Jobs that allow you to care for successive babies and continue to advance without being torn apart are few and far between. It takes overtime and "face time" to get ahead, according to David Gould, a teacher of leisure studies at the University of Iowa.[32] Patty Wellden knew that. "I gave up my management job and took a less demanding one in the same company so I could work fewer hours and travel less. I wanted more time with my son." Other women start their own businesses or settle for less money in less demanding jobs, as Wellden did.

Surely, more women would have more babies if job security and re-entry were not so difficult. To ease you back into a full-time schedule, part-time employment is usually a transitional and negotiable choice when maternity leaves run out. However, it is a rare new mother who is welcomed back on a permanent, three-day-a-week schedule.

Some companies have added flextime (the option to select your hours—for instance, starting later and working later—as long as they equal the required number of hours in the organization's workweek). Others allow a compressed week (you work more hours per day, but fewer days) or allow you to telecommute a day or two a week. Job sharing is also possible in certain lines of work, but you will probably earn half your salary. And you just may need the missing half to help support that second baby.

Issue 12: Can you juggle the logistics—and aggravation—of more child care?

Child care is one of the most nerve-racking conditions of parenthood, closely paralleling a persistent back pain or headache. Unlike most European countries, the U.S. government, although with increasing exceptions, believes it's the parents' personal responsibility to provide and pay for child care. Corporations, however, have woken up on the child-care front and often bend to meet parental needs. The state of government and corporate assistance in this department is somewhat better than in the realm of maternity leave policies.

Family benefits in the workplace are increasing as corporations begin to acknowledge the difficulty and expense in lost time and in training women to replace those who are forced to abandon their jobs to care for their children. Thousands of organizations—government departments, schools, hospitals, and corporations—have instituted child-care referral services and/or child-care centers, and projections indicate more new centers will open each year. Still, child care is expensive even if your company offers some financial assistance. The cost is often a substantial chunk of your income, and the best child-care arrangements fail from time to time.

Despite more lenient schedules and corporate support, most care arrangements are tenuous at best. Libby Fantina, a merchandise manager for a large department store, refers to her child-care arrangements as a "house of cards." She says nervously, "If just one card slips, the entire structure crumbles. I either have to race home from work or remain in the store stewing until I know my son is safely home or at a friend's. The frantic phone calls, the waiting for word . . . sometimes it's just too much." Some women cannot abide the tension.

Family support—a willing mother or a sister who is at home taking care of her own children—is rare these days. When possible, such arrangements are usually suitable for a year or two at best. A frightening shortage of trained personnel exists for home care, day care, and after-school supervision. The lack of adequate support is one of the major impetuses for women who can afford it to stop working.

If arrangements can be made and you are happier working, it is evident that children have more respect for parents who don't compromise their dreams. "My daughter says that a lot of what she achieved was because she used me as a role model. I always worked and was successful at what I did," relates Rita Graham, the second only in a four-generation line of female onlies.

Getting help, be it for a few days, a week, or full-time, is less of a hassle when you have an only child. An only child gives parents a substantial edge in the household help department. Most baby-sitters—students or otherwise—prefer to watch fewer children. Women who provide child care in homes with siblings become disenchanted more quickly. Because society has not yet fully solved the predicaments of child care, parental leaves, or the extraordinarily high costs of rearing children, working parents are simplifying the details by sharply limiting the number of children they bear, with primarily good results in the quality of family life.

Parents who make a positive decision to have only one or who, if they cannot have more children, can overcome the hurt and feelings of failure that often accompany the inability to have more children, raise happier only children.

What better environment for a child than one in which he sees himself and is appreciated for who he is? What easier environment in which to establish one's own identity? "In the end," says Emily Kramer, mother of a teenage only, "the important thing is a warm, loving, and supportive environment that respects the individuality of the child."

4

The Inner Workings of the Twosome

Tiffany Lydecker, thirteen, says, "I guess you would think it's more difficult for me because my parents were divorced when my mom was pregnant with me. It's not. Being the only child has made Mom and me as close as possible."

"I have a single mom. We're like roommates," Helena Nitashian brags. "We talk all the time and do special things together."

In the past, single parenthood, like the only child, has been labeled negatively by researchers and in the media, but with the increase in single parenting, outcomes are being re-evaluated and a new legitimacy for single parents is firmly established. An entirely new population of single mothers and fathers consistently proves that only children raised by one parent thrive largely because of the dedication, love, and determination of that parent.

The single-parent, single-child family is a familiar unit today and, most important, a widely accepted one. At any given time, single parents head one out of every five households[1] and that number is increasing. Conversations about broken homes and broken families, once prevalent, are rarely heard these days and have little import as marriage rates decline and more men and women choose to have children before they marry, if ever. Because living arrangements and marital status change, "over time, it is estimated that more than half of all children will spend some time in a single-parent home."[2] In fact, by 1998 "the norm of the stable, two-parent family was close to becoming the exception for American children rather than the rule."[3]

You may have opted to be a single parent from the start or you may have become one through death or divorce. Whatever the route, the number of single parents is on the rise. By 2000 there were roughly 13 million single mothers and more than 2 million single fathers.[4] Judges are awarding an increasing number of fathers custody because they are competent and effective single parents; fathers' care and the outcome of their parenting are indistinguishable from those of single mothers in important areas such as the child's self-esteem, school performance, and well being later in life.[5]

Extreme positions have been taken, from ones that hold that family structure makes no difference to that it makes all the difference in a child's long-term outcome. After decades of study, the conclusions are that "parental divorce or being born to unmarried parents does not lead to problems. Many (perhaps most) children who grow up in single-parent families or in stepfamilies will not be harmed seriously in the long term."[6] Other long-term research reveals that "children adopted by single parents are as well adjusted as children adopted into two-parent homes";[7] this is in spite of the fact that in the United States, older, more difficult children are often the ones most available to singles who want to adopt.

There are equally encouraging findings on the educational front. Cornell University researcher Dr. Henry Ricciuti looked at a large number of white, black, and Hispanic six- and seven-year-olds and discovered no relationship between results in reading, vocabulary, and math related to having one or two parents, even if the single-parent family has a lower income.[8]

Given the new family landscape, single parents, male or female, are just as able to provide the elements of a healthy family, including the ability to communicate and listen and to affirm and support family members; a sense of play and humor; continue with rituals and traditions; and the ability to model the value of service to others, and the value of seeking help with problems.[9] To achieve these desirable traits, the single parent needs a positive attitude and the willingness to assume all the responsibilities entailed in raising a family alone.

The majority of children born during this century will live with only one of their parents. During the next decade and a half alone, two-parent homes with parents between the ages of thirty and forty-four will drop by four million.[10] The elements of choice and financial stability are certainly factors. Although half of the pregnancies in this country are unintended, the half that are planned are done so with strong feelings. The overriding drive for so many single mothers and fathers is the desire to nurture.[11]

"I decided when I was a teenager that I wanted to be a mom," says Megan Martin, who became a single mother at thirty-four after electing not to marry the baby's father. "I was trying to get pregnant, but when it happened, I realized Jessy's dad was not the man I wanted to spend the rest of my life with."

In her essay "Mother of One," Lisa Shea had a similar take: "It wasn't until my son's father and I separated that I understood my notion of family didn't necessarily include being a wife, and that I may have wanted a child more than a marriage . . . often in our conversations (with other mothers) I detect a subtext of delight in motherhood, disappointment in marriage."[12]

Being able to fulfill that dream of having a child to love, however you achieve it, remains a complex task, but not nearly as difficult as it once was. In these cases, one child is a very determined choice, usually for very positive reasons. Owing to greater financial stability and life experience, single parents, especially those who have actively made that choice, enter parenting with a profound commitment. Assisted reproductive technology (ART) and more international adoption possibilities allow single men and women to become parents, frequently toward the end of their childbearing years.

Becky Reed, a thirty-eight-year-old California attorney, is typical of many women in their thirties and forties who have long wanted to be parents, who assumed they would get married or stay married, and who believe they can successfully parent alone, as Megan Martin does. Reed was a woman on a mission three years ago. In June of that year, she turned thirty-five, then the minimum age for single-parent adoption in China, and by July had filled out the paperwork. Reed had her daughter in her arms the following summer. "I adopted Tori because I wasn't going to wait to be in a committed relationship. I already had waited.

"I feel strongly, particularly because I'm single, that I don't need to create a child to be a parent," she explains. "For me, conceiving my own baby was just not an option. I didn't want to bring a baby into the world who would have no father because of my choice when so many babies exist who need homes and will never know their fathers anyway. If Mr. Right came along and he was right for me *and* for my daughter, then I could see co-parenting."

More and more middle- and upper-class women who find it impossible or impractical to adopt in this country, and can't afford foreign adoption, intentionally become pregnant with sperm donated by a friend, obtained from a sperm bank, or by another ART method. Thirty-two-year-old Jennifer Blomstrom spent considerable time planning for motherhood and elected artificial insemination. Like Reed, Jennifer felt no need to wait for the "perfect" relationship to have the child she wanted. "I have been able to find love, companionship, and sex without entering into the church and state-sanctioned institution of marriage."[13]

As the many permutations of family become better understood and accepted, there is a realization that two parents are not always better than one. In an inharmonious, combative home, a child can suffer irreparable emotional damage. Given an unloving, cold environment, your child will probably be happier and better adjusted in a single-parent living arrangement.

If you're new to "solo parenting," explain the changes clearly to any child old enough to understand. Go over the reorganization that will take place in the household, such as new living arrangements, altered schedules, new caretakers, and new chores, make as few shifts as possible early on, and be aware that your child may not adjust as quickly as you would like. Give yourself some time to adjust, too. Don't be hard on yourself when things don't fall into place or run smoothly immediately. It may help to let your child know if you're tired from work, need his help, or want some time to yourself. If not overdone, this type of directness makes a child feel important.

Single parents, male or female, have incredible stress from juggling the responsibilities of a child, a home, and a job. When you think you're doing poorly, one third of single parents in your situation or a similar one thinks so too.[14] Take on each challenge knowing you can survive it.

Nonetheless, when simply getting through the day seems impossible, consider your child's feelings, too. Explain that you love him, but don't offer the ugly details of support checks that haven't arrived or of your ex's latest love interest.

Your child needs to be reassured that he is loved by as many people as possible, and that includes your ex, if you have one. Preserve the other parent's image as best you can by keeping negative feelings to yourself. Be quick to move a conversation headed in that direction toward something that happened to you at work or to upcoming plans or events that involve your child.

For women who choose to be single mothers, the demands and frustrations can be as great as they are for those who became single parents through divorce. This is especially true during a child's early life, when it may feel as if you can't possibly meet the demands.

The only child who lives with one parent does not have to be shortchanged. A single parent can offer advantages not possible in a two-parent household, provided he or she can triumph over the stress and exhaustion that often accompany single parenthood. If there's a former spouse or former partner, keep your relationship amicable so you can have his or her help, even if only occasionally. Every bit of assistance eases your burden. One woman who succeeded without help from a former spouse is Terze Gluck. "At first, right after my divorce, I was in a panic," she admits. "I was desperate for another adult to be around. I found myself a single parent and turning to my daughter. Now she's my main companion. Our relationship is very close; very involved."

Lisa Black has also successfully negotiated being a single parent. After raising her seventeen-year-old daughter alone from the time she was three, she says, "My daughter and I know one another better than parents and children in larger families. I also have time to know her friends."

To diffuse the weightiness of the twosome or when the day or hour feels out of control, try humor to lighten things up. Tell a joke or do something utterly outrageous such as chasing your child around the house or painting clown faces on each other. When life seems overwhelming, you might try turning the music up loud and dancing, inviting your youngster to join you or going outside for some fresh air to revitalize both yourself and your child.

Beware of the Intensity

A family of two provides unique companionship and with it the danger that your life and your child's life can become too intertwined. "I sometimes feel we're too close and too dependent on each other," sighs Harriet Kean, whose son is in college. "For so many years, because his father was not involved in his rearing, it was the two of us against the world."

The single parent is or feels totally responsible, often overwhelmed. He or she wears a number of hats—a parent hat, a professional hat, a personal hat. It's especially difficult to define and separate the roles because of the intensity of a two-person relationship.

"A triangle," as Dr. Sandra Leiblum describes the threesome, "is inherently unstable. In it, you have different relationships—mother/father; father/child; child/mother—for interaction. In the twosome there is nothing to dissipate the intensity." Her advice: "Make sure there are other significant adults in your life. Don't look to your child for praise and confirmation."

When you do not have a special man or woman in your life, you tend to elicit your needs from your child and, as they get older, you expect them to be your emotional center. Single mothers plead "guilty." "A lot of my emotional stability comes from my daughter. She's all I've got," says Rita Graham. "A good part of my happiness revolves around her and wanting to be there and do for her. I've used our closeness more for my happiness than hers."

"I complain about men incessantly to Abigail," confesses Ms. Gluck, "and she tells me she doesn't want to hear about it. I say so many things to her that are inappropriate, but with her strength and good sense I don't think I've harmed her, but I think I could have."

As your child ages, it is also easy to lose sight of who's the parent and who's the child. The lines can become blurred without your being aware. Be sure you don't view your child as a substitute for an adult. "My mother leaned on me," explains a displeased William Royale, now married with an only of his own. "I became the man of the family at ten when my father died."

Ms. Royale was undoubtedly unaware of the pressure she exerted on her son. In a three-party system you have an objective ear to help clear away the childrearing "garbage" that you might not realize you're carrying around and projecting onto your child. As a parent alone you don't have the benefit of another adult's perspective.

One thirteen-year-old tells of his enormous relief when his mother finally found a boyfriend. "I was let off the hook" is the way he expresses it. Russell Courti's mother burdened her young son with decision making and turned him into her all-around escort. Russell had no social life because he felt going out with his friends was betraying his mother.

Very often children see things more clearly than their parent. Russell analyzes life since the boyfriend arrived: "I think it's good for her to be away from me and good for me to have a life of my own."

Set Time Aside for Yourself

Single mothers of one stress the need to fulfill themselves beyond their role as parents. Jan Callahan raised her only alone from his first years of life. "I had to learn that there was time and space for me as a person. I felt guilty because I wanted time for myself. It does seem to be becoming less difficult for women to take time away from being a mother."

Those who have chosen to be single parents may find it more difficult to set time aside for themselves. Many of these parents have waited until their thirties or later and are so thrilled to have the child they always wanted that they want to be with that child as much as possible.

"It's important to stay alive and vital as a person as well as a parent," stresses Lisa Black. Find a creative outlet for yourself such as an exercise class, photography or potting, painting or playing a musical instrument. Start or join a book or investment club, be involved in something other than work and parenting, and in the process you may make new friends. A new or expanded involvement in an interest gives you something more to talk about when conversation focuses too much on your child or your problems. If you don't have anyone to leave your child with or are pressed for time, get on the computer, go to favorite web sites, chat with friends, write some therapeutic e-mails, or investigate a place you would like to visit or a topic that interests you. You need time to recharge either by yourself or with friends and family members—without your offspring.

Daisy Grisori is straightforward about having a life of her own. "I go out a lot. I'm very social because I believe in meeting my own needs and that makes me a better mother."

Sandra Steadham argues vehemently, "A stressed mother [or father] is not much of a parent either. I make certain that there's some time for me." When a single parent becomes entrenched in job and child, life gets exceedingly dull. Steadham details how this can happen: "In the beginning, I was not adding anything to my life on an adult level to keep me fresh or give me relief. By Monday morning I had seen only the inside of my office and 'playland' for an entire week. Eventually, I made arrangements to have a sitter on Saturday nights that I pay for whether or not I go out. If she is unavailable, she must find a replacement, someone I approve, by Wednesday. It's a great incentive."

"A lot of single mothers are in the same situation," says Helen Amonte, who was a single parent of a single child for ten of her daughter's twelve years. She found that single mothers band together to help each other out. "Since Jessica was four, I have had a friend of hers come with us when we go away for the weekend. The mother reciprocates, giving me some time for myself."

Enlarge Your Circle of Support

"Being alone in the house puts different strains on the child," remarks child analyst Ava Bry Penman. "There is no relief, no one his size, no one his age for comic or other relief. Parent and child have only each other to talk things through or to yell at. In essence, there is no other person with his standing or nonstanding; no one on his team. To ease the stress, widen your world."

You can't raise your child without some outside assistance. You need others to turn to for ideas and, at times, moral support. A third party or parties who can influence your child, be involved in child management now and then, and share recreational activities provides extra support. When parent and child are the same sex, an adult of the opposite sex provides another point of view. If parent and child are of opposite sexes, an adult of the same sex may well serve as a role model or in the least be a figure with whom the child can identify. But, warns Professor Leiblum, "It is not an easy negotiation for the outsider. The best advice for a third party of either sex is to woo the child so that he feels special and valued for his own sake."

In a society that's still pretty much psychologically, if not actually, based on couples, the single parent and child are not always the most welcomed guests. Build a larger close grouping of family and "new" friends who have no connection to your previous married life, if you had one. Friends and family provide a cushion, the feeling of a safety net—someone to call in the middle of the night if you are frightened or sick or need help with your child. "It's a good idea," says Jane Mattes, a social worker and founder and executive director of the national organization Single Mothers by Choice, "to prearrange the telephone contacts, even if you never use them."

Find people who have been or are going through single parenting themselves to guide you. Sheila Ellison, author of *The Courage to Be a Single Mother,* recommends a single-parent support group that meets regularly with the children, who after dinner can go off to play games while the parents talk. "It's important for the kids to develop friendships with other kids in the community who are experiencing divorce and its aftermath. This group of mothers and children became extended family for us."[15]

If there's no local single-parent support group, connect with a group online. Arden Holmes, a single mother who adopted her child at fifty, believes, "The best support comes from other people who are in a similar position. I had to have surgery, but had no relatives or help to care for my son, who was two at the time. Two women I had 'met' in a singles support group online offered [to help]. I believe that singles help singles more. While I was recovering, the people who brought me lunch or took my son for the afternoon were single-parent friends. The busiest, most pressured people seem to be able to handle and give the most.

"I feel I have much more in common with other single moms. We go out with the children at least once every two weeks and talk much more frequently. If one of us has a problem or concern, we call the other. You can't do it alone," stresses Holmes. "You need other people."

Making new friends is not always easy when you have the limited time most single parents have. When deciding on groups to join, consider your preferences so the people you meet will at least have like interests—a good basis for forming friendships. Take a course at a local high school or college to be sure you get out on your own and meet people. Exercise clubs and church groups are good places to break new ground. Try reconnecting with a favorite high school or college friend whose circumstances may have changed, too. Friends from the past know your history and share your interests—and possibly your perspective.

There are many organizations and activities that can open new territory. Parents Without Partners, a national group with local chapters, has a range of events—from fishing trips to dances and parties—that include parent and child. Says Penman, "People who are more social tend to have a better perspective."

The family of two has built-in freedom to plan or pick up and go on a whim. Capitalize on it. You and your child have an open market on interests to explore, sports to try or perfect. Each may very well lead to new, exciting, and compatible people.

When the weather's right, check into camping. The American Camping Association provides a wide array of sites. This may be the year to learn how to ski, sail, or play chess. Depending on your child's age, the choice of adventure that will lead you to new people is broad—from modeling with clay to mountain climbing—and your choices need not be costly.

The voids that are endemic to single parenthood do not have to be filled by you. "One should not think that raising a child is the task of one adult," advises Dr. Michael Lewis. He recommends forming families of multiple adults—two women and their children, for instance. "You have to give the single child a larger social network for his well-being as much as for your own," he adds.

Stevanne Auerbach, known on the Internet as Dr. Toy and the

author of *Dr. Toy's Smart Play*, is an expert on child development, play, and toys, and is also a mother who raised her daughter as a single parent. "I shared a home with another single mother when our children were toddlers. We took turns looking after each other's child; we shared suppers and knew we had someone to call on in an emergency. It was good for the two children and gave each of us a respite." You deserve an escape from the grind, but you'll have to make a conscious decision to find or arrange for it.

"When grouping families works, it's a great alternative," agrees Leiblum, but she adds a caveat: "If the only thing that brings the two families together is their single status, it might not be so wonderful. Plus you run the risk of sibling rivalry developing."

Stephen Baylor, the custodial parent of seven-year-old Jerry, is forming another kind of network primarily made up of relatives. "I'm trying to build him a support group so that he is not totally dependent on my opinion of the moment. He has a surrogate grandmother next door and his mother picks him up every day after school. He is very close to my brother; they play soccer at least one day on the weekend."

Building a support network also plays a vital role in praising the child and providing acknowledgment to the child of who he is, especially when the noncustodial parent is inaccessible or there isn't one.

Make an effort to stay in touch with relatives and take the time to travel, if necessary, to visit with them. Take advantage of ties beyond family, too. "I keep in touch and involved with the other families who adopted when I did so that when Tori is older she will know people who came from the same situation she did and realize our life together is not totally unusual," explains adoptive parent Becky Reed. "I worry about what will happen when she realizes Mommy and Tori don't look the same, when she asks, 'Why don't I have a Daddy?' But that question would come up with any child I adopted. It had nothing to do with her and everything to do with China's attitude toward baby girls. With the help of the families who adopted when I did, we'll figure out an explanation so we don't damage our children's self-esteem."

Single mothers who have been artificially inseminated by a known donor who elected to remain anonymous, or by an unknown donor, will face similar questions about paternity. Above all, remember that you did not fail because you did not provide a father or because the child's father lives elsewhere. Single Mothers by Choice has its own online support site to help mothers struggling with this and other issues.

Stacy Coleman, who has been divorced since her son was fifteen months old, relies on the Internet: "Where I come from, I only know one other person who is divorced. Online I can vent, and there are people who understand. The fathers who write in about not being able to see their children help me to understand how my ex-husband feels. There are good financial discussions and important information about drawing up wills.

"If you feel like crying, you can type in whatever is bothering you and someone will write back, 'I know how you feel.' You realize you are not alone and that others have been wherever you are and the situation has gotten better."

Josh Grant, the single father of a two-year-old and an advocate of online support, talks about a single fathers' online list. "At one point my daughter had a rash. I knew it wasn't diaper rash; it was strange bumps, something I had no experience with. Immediately, I had three people telling me what it might be, how to treat it, and suggesting I also have a doctor take a look. You 'talk' to other parents who have experience in areas you may know nothing about. You can trust them to give you an unbiased opinion. I think the biggest reason I relied on the online support group was I didn't want anyone I knew seeing my mistakes."

Check the single-parent web sites and bulletin boards or join a single parent list.serv to give you online support (see Resource section). You'll receive advice from other people who have been in similar situations or have had similar experiences. You can also find or form your own local support group by posting a message on your child's PTA bulletin board or in its newsletter, at the community center, local gym, or with your house of worship.

A backup system relieves some of the tension and guilt many single parents feel. And when you're "strung out," you will have a place to ship your child so he can have some fun and psychic feeding and you can have some peace and quiet.

Once There Was Enough Time

Single children, as we have seen, benefit from the added stimulation of parental attention. In the single-parent household, this advantage is a double-edged sword. In an effort to compensate for the absent spouse, single parents go overboard and as a result fatigue becomes a major factor.

"After the office, I was faced with the grocery store, errands, a house that needed dusting, and a child that looked at me pleadingly," admits Ruth Hague. "It was me or no one when Jeffrey wanted to play a game or hear a story. I felt pulled in too many directions."

The best thing a single parent can do is to find a way to unwind before picking up his or her child. Listen to music during the commute or read the paper or a book. If using public transportation, shut your eyes for a few minutes to clear your head. Be gentle with yourself, if only for five minutes, before tackling your parental responsibilities so you'll be able to listen and really connect with your child. All this is impossible to do if you bring your work home with you when a few short evening hours may be all the time you have together during the week.

Single parents do everything two parents would do. Without the division of labor between spouses, the demand on a single parent's time is far greater. You must determine what can be put aside temporarily or dispensed with completely. The more exhausted you are, the more miserable both you and your child will be. Keep your social schedule manageable and assign your child chores without overloading him. Work together—you on cooking, him on setting the table; you on laundry, him on sweeping out the garage—always working toward a goal of doing something pleasant together when you are finished: a television program, a computer game, a walk, or sharing a book.

If you're a full-time, at-home single parent, be sure to take breaks from your child during the day. Relax when he naps, or go for a walk or run when he's playing at a friend's home; figure out what relaxes you and try very hard to fit it in. As a calmer parent, you are more likely to be able to short-circuit confrontations that will only add additional stress to your single parenting. You don't want to take your frustrations out on your child because he has or probably will have upsets of his own. Every child does.

Take the pressure off yourself to be everywhere and everything to your child. If your child has a father or mother who is available, ask him or her to bail you out. Seek assistance from grandparents. And lean on your friends for practical help and emotional support, which you will certainly get from other single parents. Or find paid help as Sandra Steadman did, if you can afford it. Hire a sitter occasionally to play with your child, even if you are home preparing dinner or want to read the mail in a warm bubble bath. Find a student who lives nearby—a few grades ahead of your son or daughter—to walk with or supervise your child's getting on and off the school bus. Sitter dollars preserve your precious time and are well-spent investments in your sanity as are dollars spent on someone to do the jobs you dislike.

Jane Mattes suggests changing your priorities, especially during the early, highly demanding years. Let the housekeeping slip. Forgo four-course gourmet dinners. Move things with low priorities for you down to the bottom of your list or remove them entirely. When your child is older, you can reinstate them.

To ensure the most pleasant relationship and time together, be consistent, which is possibly the most difficult assignment for single parents because it's so easy to waiver with one child. Think ahead by planning for food and prepare your child for what's to come—"we're leaving after two Ferris wheel rides," or "in ten minutes." Always, follow through so your child knows you mean what you say. Most of the single-parenting issues that overstress you are manageable if you are kind to yourself and get sufficient sleep. And swallow your pride; ask for, and accept, help.

Only children in single-parent homes need to feel that they are part of a family. Routine, knowing what you will be doing and when you'll be doing it, provides that sense of family and security, especially for the school-age child. In families with several children, absent one parent, routines and schedules happen, but in the one-parent, one-child home it is often advantageous to dispense with schedules. Why not eat dinner at 9 P.M. if there are just the two of you? Will it make much difference if we don't bother to set the table? We could skip making beds today—who will notice? In this way, life for parent and child can quickly lose any semblance of order.

It's well established that children need routines. If you alter eating and sleeping patterns, you are flirting with potential problems. Turn mealtime into a special time for your family of two, serve "real" meals, stick to homework schedules and bedtime rituals. The child in the one-parent family needs as much structure as the child with two parents or five siblings. That child needs to know what to expect and to have things to look forward to.

Single parenting is almost never easy. Although more "older" women choose to be single parents, many still in their twenties take that course. At age twenty-five, Carolyn Edy gave birth to a child she decided to keep. Her assessment is clear and valid for most single parents today: "Whenever I complain that single motherhood is hard, I've got my mom and grandmother to tell me I have it easy—I don't have a husband to take care of as well. I'm hopelessly in love with my child."[16]

Reed agrees. "Parenting is wonderful even on the really hard days." But even when good support is available, few single parents wish to add to their families. "My parents were very supportive," says Reed. "They gave me some of the money to go to China, but I would have done it without that help. They buy juice and clothes, like other grandparents. I could not afford to go back for another child. If I could, I don't think I would. I have this philosophy of one child per person. I don't think I could be fair to two children time-wise. For me, it's simply not feasible since I have to work full-time."

Some single parents re-examine their jobs and decide to cut back on the number of hours or days they work. At the very least, they leave work on time. Others, more and more in our virtual, connected computer age, figure out ways to work from home one or more days a week. Whichever route you take, you will be trading one benefit for another. All parenting is a sacrifice to some degree, but if you can make your sacrifices without feeling deprived (a learned approach), you will enjoy your child even more.

As committed as you may be, there will be times—many times—when you don't want to be, can't be, or shouldn't be with your child. There is a very fine line between too much time and involvement and too little. While dual parents of onlies need to step back, the greater concentration between onlies and single parents demands some separation.

PART TWO

Parenting an Only Child

5

Working Attitudes

Most mothers and fathers as they embark on parenthood have an ideal, often a hard-and-fast plan, about how to raise their child. Some believe in strictness, others in leniency. Some parents are very open with their children, others choose to be closed, keeping their thoughts and feelings to themselves. Still others choose to be formal and proper while their counterparts may elect to be more casual and less restricted by social graces. New parents are guided by a basic childrearing style similar to one of these, one they may well be perpetuating from their own childhood.

Because of the only child's centrality in the family, she is especially vulnerable to the full force of that style. In *Family Situations,* published in 1941, authors James Bossard and Eleanor Boll spelled out the childrearing arena as it remains today: "Whatever the family is like, the only child within it receives the concentrated force of all its influences."[1]

Thus, a rearing belief that worked for your parents doesn't necessarily work with the only child. Although a chosen parenting style may be sound, adjustments and concessions must be made. Without them, parents can hamper their child's healthy development and make his or her life needlessly trying.

Forty-one-year-old only Iris Kitter reflects: "It took a long time to realize I was unhappy as a child, not because I was an only child, but because I don't think my parents had the coping skills to make me feel protected. I wish they had been able to be better parents for their sake. They weren't able to say, 'You're the kid, we're the grownups,' and then follow through. I know so many people who had siblings and it wasn't a happy thing either. Whatever was wrong or right in my childhood was not because I was only a child. I never felt if I had brothers and sisters everything would be all right."

The parents' approach to rearing has far more to do with the child's behavior and eventual outcome than does the number of siblings. It is during the child's first two years that nurturing habits—good and bad—become established and ingrained. For this reason, it is prudent to establish good practices, ones that work for the only child as soon as possible.

Most parenting pitfalls are universal; however, they are more intense and require keener vigilance with an only. Stumbling blocks can be turned to your child's advantage when parents assume a constructive and positive attitude.

Perhaps one of the most workable attitudes for raising an only is that of Anne Marie Soto, who at age forty has a thirteen-month-old. Like many mothers of young children today, she is more mature and sure of herself than mothers of earlier generations. "I don't think of her as an only child; I think of her as a child of older, settled parents. Since I work, she doesn't get all of my time and I don't spend a lot of time worrying about whether or not she will end up with any of the traits normally assigned to only children. I tend to be a Pollyanna about life and don't worry about things that I can't do too much about."

Think Big

A healthy balance of involving yourself with your child and disengaging yourself from your child's life, of spending time with a child and having time alone, of protecting your child and fostering independence, of allowing freedom of expression and adhering to the rules is particularly vital for the successful rearing of only children. In large families balances are frequently reached by default.

There are, for example, only so many evening hours parents can devote to helping with homework or reading stories. These hours must be divided by whatever the "child load." On the other hand, it's relatively simple with one child to supervise homework and to spend the entire time after dinner reading fairy tales or dinosaur adventures. A child quickly becomes dependent on your support, even if it's only your physical presence. Hovering at homework time does little to encourage initiative or independent learning.

In order to achieve a livable balance, parents of onlies must think big; they must operate as if they had a clan. There's no question that with one child it's much simpler just to "do it." Take dressing. It's certainly faster to dress your five-year-old than to spend an hour arguing with or prodding her. In the multisibling home, so much goes on in the morning that children dressing themselves is a given, not open to arbitration as it is in many single-child families.

"I can't get her to dress," says Arlene Unger, voicing a common complaint. "It's not a question of disliking school. She loves school. She simply wants to procrastinate, to play in her room. It drives me crazy and she knows it."

To motivate children to perform requested tasks, parents often resort to bribes. In general, bribes have little long-lasting effect and can be damaging. Repeated use of food bribes, notably candy and cookies, can lead to obesity and eating disorders later in life. The best recourse is a precise explanation of what you expect from your child and when you expect it done. Your outline should specify that the request is fair and cannot be argued. If it has a benefit to the child, tell her—brushing your teeth prevents cavities; drinking milk helps your bones grow; going to bed on time gives you extra energy to play. When reasoning fails (not too often with an only child), take action. For the dressing dilemma, psychologist Frank

Main recommends bagging your child's clothes and putting them and your child in the car. To his knowledge, no child has arrived at school nude with brown bag in hand.

Thinking big means delegating reasonable responsibilities early on. A four-year-old can carry her cup to the sink; at five she can make her bed (hospital corners are not required). Setting the table, clearing the unbreakable dishes and containers, turning out lights when leaving a room, and putting away toys are tasks young children can handle. School-age onlies should be encouraged to fill their own backpacks and select their clothes for the following day. Adopt and promote the notion that this is everyone's home; everyone helps.

Don't demand or expect 100 percent cooperation or 100 percent perfection. Facilitate cleaning up after play by arranging labeled, open containers in accessible places. If it's disconcerting to watch your only doing the work by herself and pitching in makes you feel better, get her started then leave her to her chores. Tidying up is but one of many challenges your only must learn to deal with on her own.

Expect resistance for years to come, but be persistent in requesting help. You are developing your child's sense of responsibility and sense of pride in jobs successfully completed. Pretend you have four children whenever you ask your only to help. Think: toys for four scattered about the house! It takes fifteen minutes to make four beds; a half hour to pack four lunches, especially if the requests are for four different kinds of sandwiches.

"This is not a restaurant" is a handy response to the only who says she doesn't like dinner. Helen Amonte, an only child, remembers her father's position with warmth and a grateful sparkle. "He came from a family of fourteen so he was very strict. He ran our small household as if it were the real world. I had to eat what was put on the table and abide by rules that had governed his childhood home."

One of the reasons many couples have only one child is so that they can have more time to pursue their own interests. Spoiling your child with constant assistance and accommodating each whim simply defeats that goal.

Wynne Maynard details her life since she stopped teaching: "I'm almost too involved in my son's life. My activities center around Brandon: school, the neighborhood civic association that plans activities for the children, team sports. I don't think it's particularly healthy. I worry that I'm overdirecting his life, but it's hard to break away."

If you are not watchful, you can devote more hours to one child than you would to two or five. Thinking big can help you keep a suitable balance.

Am I Doing It Right?

You may not know. Many women who are having their first baby have never changed a diaper or seen a neighbor's child progress from two months to two years. This gap in life experiences is comparable to reaching the age of thirty without having had to face the death of someone close. With the breakup of the nuclear family, the distance between relatives, the decrease in family size, and repeated location changes, more people are by themselves more of the time and see less of the growth process.

"I didn't know a thing about babies," says Dawn Childs. "When Trent was an infant, the three of us took a short trip. The baby didn't urinate and I panicked. Fortunately, my husband has another child from his first marriage. He said, 'There's never been a baby that didn't pee.' I said, in my naivete, 'There's always a first time.' Of course, my husband was right." Dawn's gap in experience with babies is not unusual today.

Errors in judgment come with the territory. Parents enter parenting with the idea of being perfect. They set their standards too high and worry about every little thing or get bogged down by the unimportant aspects of child rearing. Almost every parent makes mistakes or decisions they believe are harmful or perhaps irrevocable, and generally they aren't.

"None of us knows how to do this," says Maureen Springer, mother of a nine-year-old only. "There's no road map or blueprint. I put up with things with my child that I would not put up with from a partner or a friend."

Parents of onlies tend to think a child's problem stems from his or her singularity. When in doubt, investigate. Find out if other children the same age are having difficulties akin to your child's. They probably are. Ask teachers and other parents, and if the problem truly is upsetting you, consult a professional.

"The more parents are with other parents and children, the more they can learn what they are dealing with," advises child analyst Ava Bry Penman. "Park benches are one of the greatest teachers. Talking with other parents in the playground or at school is an enormously helpful and informing experience."

Susan Davidman was too embarrassed to admit to her friends that her seven-year-old followed her around the house. "I was positive he stuck to me because he was an only child. Quite by accident, while watching a soccer game a mother was describing the difference in independence among her three children. Her oldest, a teammate and seven like mine, she said, had to know where she was every minute. 'I go down to do the laundry, he insists on coming with me.' I was relieved."

"At two-and-a-half, Hillary was timid and fearful," laughs Diana Warren, who was not laughing four years ago when Hillary "held my leg and refused to enter her nursery school classroom. I decided she was so attached to me because she had my constant attention. Hillary is an only, not yet three and ruined by her mother. That's what I told myself."

"I could not get my six-year-old to bed at night," Penny Dauber, the twenty-eight-year-old mother of Max, explains. "That task finally accomplished, he would wake at three or four in the morning and beg to come into our bed. He cried, he stormed. Max was pathetic in the middle of the night. I spent hours feeling as if I were a failure. I knew I had done something that was bound to ruin his adult life, but I could not figure out what I had said or done or what had happened to ruin his sleep patterns. I tried talking to him about what might be causing his irrational behavior; I tried bribing him; I even threatened him, knowing that was wrong. I was desperate."

None of the above trials is unusual nor can they be linked to being an only child. Do not berate yourself and become convinced that a disturbing situation has in any way been caused by your child's single status. Most times these are normal developmental stages and difficulties that any child may experience.

When you have only one, you can spend more time fretting over the inconsequential. It's snowing and he's playing with a friend who refuses to go out of doors. You chastise yourself for not inviting the friend you know is big on making snowmen and who would willingly go outside for healthy, invigorating fresh air.

Missing one day out in the snow is not going to change a child's life. If you had three children, you would not have the time to think about which one was doing what; you'd be pleased that they were all safely occupied and happy. In short, try to think and act as if you had many. Much easier said than done.

Moderation Is the Goal

In the opening scene of the film *Terms of Endearment,* actress Shirley MacLaine portrays a mother who almost falls into the crib nervously attempting to confirm that her baby is breathing. We are meant to believe that she does this with great regularity. Her concern is real; her action a bit out of proportion.

Many parents develop similar rituals and patterns, such as those who, fearing germs, permit no one near their young child, who record each of the baby's bowel movements, or who have not gone to a movie or dinner without the baby in eighteen months or longer—year after year they stay home, terrified to leave the child for a few hours with a baby-sitter.

First-time parents are often too consumed by parenting chores to think about how they are relating to their new charge. Are they being domineering, easygoing, too rigid, too lenient, too protective? Consider your approach; the goal is moderation.

Attempting to shield your only child is perhaps the easiest trap into which you can fall. When the child begins to walk, smothering parents are right behind her to scoop her up before she topples. When she cries, they drop whatever they are doing and rush to her to eliminate her discomfort. When she plays with other toddlers, they are appalled by normal arguing and intercede on their child's behalf at every turn of a pull toy or collapse of a block building.

Stand back. Let your child work it out herself. As soon as you start interfering, tears will flow and dependence will begin to blossom. "I'm guilty," nods Iona Gills, who regrets having acted on her every anxiety. "Leo is afraid of his own shadow. He's eight and he won't go into an empty room without company. He doesn't go on the slide or jungle gym with the other children. He watches. I did it. I spent his first five years telling him to be careful. He's afraid he'll fall off a bicycle, afraid he'll drown in a pool, afraid he'll choke on his food. He cuts his meal into the tiniest pieces before he'll put it into his mouth. That's exactly what I did for him for years. How can I blame him? There were times when friends told me I was going overboard. They were right, but I couldn't see. It was Leo, my only child, and I was terrified something awful would happen to him."

Fear that harm will come to your child is a powerful motivator for being overly protective. Once recognized, the fear can be managed, if only by avoidance, as Sherry Anderson explains. "I was so terrified of playground accidents that I stayed away from the playground and similar situations. I felt I would transfer my anxiety to my daughter. I knew I would hover dreadfully, so I arranged for others to watch her and I took their children for different sorts of activities that I was more comfortable with. As it turns out, my daughter is physically pretty bold."

Not all parents worry irrationally about their onlies. Being overly concerned has to do with a parent's personality and pathology more than the singleness of the child. Any parent can fall prey to his or her own insecurities. The fears and resulting overprotectiveness that *seem* more pronounced and more prevalent among parents of onlies are by no means limited to them. Parents of onlies may be anxious, but so are other parents.

One woman, the mother of six-year-old Kim, sets the record straight when asked if she feels she is overprotective. "We don't do that, not to the extreme we're accused of." She tells about a friend of Kim's who sometimes comes to play. Alice has two siblings. "By the time her mother finishes giving me instructions and asking questions about where they are going to play and will I be sure Alice's hat and gloves are on and what am I giving the girls for lunch and reminding me that Alice can go to the bathroom by herself, I feel as if I'm some kind of incompetent.

"Last time the father dropped Alice off to play, it wasn't good enough that I yelled hello from upstairs, he had to see the whites of my eyes. After explaining exactly where Alice was permitted to ride her bike at home, he asked me to walk outside and show him how far I let Kim go on our property. No one can tell me that because I'm the parent of an only child I'm overprotective. Alice's parents have cornered the market."

Even a "crawler" can be allowed to take risks (obviously within safe limits). Letting go creates a parental pattern that encourages independence as the child grows older. Overprotection can go far beyond preventing risk-taking. Many parents are so fascinated by their one that they hold on too tightly for too long, continuing the pattern begun in early childhood.

Betty Plumlee is careful not to criticize her parents when she tells of spending her college years at home. "My parents liked to participate in what I was doing. When my friends were going away to college, they asked me if I would stay home and attend the local college. They said, 'You're our only one.' So I stayed."

Andrea Balfour was not as accepting of her parents' protectiveness. "When I graduated from college and announced that I was moving into an apartment with friends, my parents became hysterical and made me feel guilty. It was almost as if I had said I was moving into a bordello. I wasn't surprised. My parents' way of approaching me was not new. In high school my mother was very jealous of my friends. If I was out every night of a week with friends, I would hear, 'This is not a place where you hang your hat, this is a place where you're supposed to be. This is home.' I don't make those kinds of demands on my children. I don't want to be in and on top of their lives."

When parents of onlies don't let go, a mutual dependency develops. "When she was twenty-five, we moved," Ruth Palmer's mother relates. "She said she would be fine without us; she was living in her own apartment. Fortunately, we returned after only a few months. The entire time we were gone, Ruth had stomach problems and was unhappy, but she told us only after we had relocated near her. She's thirty-five and I keep a room for her. I've vowed never to leave her again."

"When I was young, my mother was very apprehensive and overreacted all the time," recalls adult only Niki Sanger. "She was that way about herself, too. I'm sure her nervousness is the reason why I threw up on the kindergarten teacher the first day of school."

Nervous attitudes are hard to conceal and sooner or later are absorbed by children—witness Ruth's stomach problems and Niki's apprehension about starting school. Control your concern and worry. Hysteria over every minor fever and rejected morsel of food creates tension. Find a middle ground and try to stay in it. Remind yourself that children are very resilient—take a few deep breaths before you overreact.

Certain Concerns Are Realistic

National awareness of children's deaths by senseless shootings and bombings has heightened all parents' fears. But, there are other legitimate reasons for parents of onlies to worry. Lynn Murphy has cause for being obsessive about her son's health. "He was premature and on a heart monitor for six months. I'm crazed by the fact that something might happen to him and he's my only chance. If at fifty, all of a sudden, I had no child, it would be totally devastating. You can never replace a child, but at least if you had another one, the devastation might be bearable."

"We love Joey so much, I don't know what we would do if anything happened to him." Tears form in Helen Umberto's eyes as she speaks. "We considered—although it's out of the question—having another child, just in case."

"I had one child die before Justin. I know kids die. I feel terrified of that," acknowledges Marney Yoto. "You have one child. In a way you have no safety. These things happen. I know firsthand. They don't always happen to other people."

Some parents become irrational in their fear of losing their child. One mother admits to worrying constantly and visiting Internet bulletin boards that deal with grieving the death of a child. Many parents of only children report that the fear lessens as their singleton gets older.

Fearing the death of a child, especially an only child, makes good biological sense. Your genetic future is tied to that single child as well as to your future plans and your hopes for her future. Your total "investment" in one child is enormous. You have made an entire commitment to one person; hence your loss will be somewhat greater than if you had several children. "If you have the fear," advises Dr. Zeeman, "be conscious of it so that you verbalize less of it to your child and control your panic in situations that worry you."

"I have a tendency to catastrophize," admits Dawn Childs.

"There's so much to worry about, but I wonder if I worry because he's an only child or because the world is so damn scary?" It's natural to worry about the death of a child; the fear arises at different times with different intensity for different people.

Although perhaps unfathomable, parents whose only children have died find ways to live with their agony and loss. Dr. Kay Talbot, who studies and works with these parents as a grief counselor, says, "Our grief does not necessarily get better; it gets different." From her perspective as a parent whose only child died at age nine, Talbot believes parents who lose their only child "must consciously decide to survive our child's death and find our own personally meaningful ways to 'live life alive' again."

In her study, "Mothers Now Childless: Survival After the Death of an Only Child," she notes that having another baby is not always a viable choice. Women find other ways, often through volunteer efforts either directly with children or in one of the helping professions, to retain their definition as mothers "as a part of a new, more integrated identity which acknowledges the child's death but also preserves the child's memory and honors the woman's past life as a mother."[2] Dr. Talbot is quick to point out that "losing a child and the role as that child's parent is not a 'typical thing,' but all parents know that this can and sometimes does happen."

The death of a child is always devastating, but having other children will not necessarily ease the pain of such a loss because each child is special, unique, and irreplaceable. If you can accept and acknowledge your terror, you'll have an easier time reveling in the wonders of your only-born.

Don't Focus on Oneness

The consequences of zeroing in on a child's singleness can be serious, as forty-eight-year-old David Cornell well knows. "It became a family issue to have another child. Although my parents had decided against it, they often talked about wanting one. Since they were not satisfied, I was not happy being alone."

Feelings of oneness are often created by parents. Having an only is an easy thing to hang your hat on when something goes wrong. You don't have to look at yourself. You don't have to look at your marriage. You can say, "If there were another child, this would not have happened. We would be happier; we would do more."

Tina Nukkom, like many who have had family size decided for them, adjusted her thinking to avoid focusing on oneness. "My husband and I never sat down and had an official plan about how many children we would have. In the back of my mind I assumed we would have more children," explains Tina, whose son is eight years old. "At thirty-seven I was diagnosed with breast cancer, and for me and my husband another was no longer an option. I was very angry when the decision was taken away from me. Now I feel good about having one. We feel fortunate and blessed. I realize this is the way it is so we're taking advantage of the opportunities of having one child."

Meg Reese's mother was not only dissatisfied, but also extremely needy. "My mother always made me aware that I was an only child and that she wanted more children. I was reminded that I was the only thing that she had and that it was important for us to be close. A lot of my mother's emotional needs were being met by me."

If you feel strongly that it would have been nice to have a larger family, say so, but say it matter-of-factly—don't lace it with emotion and guilt. Follow up immediately by adding the advantages of your small family. Most people wonder how things would have been "if," yet it's far healthier for your child to understand that his parents are happy and feel complete as a family. When your child is old enough to understand, you might want to explain why you decided to have one child or why you could not have more children. Here's another way to think about your child: It might not make any difference whether or not she had a brother or sister because each child in the family perceives parenting differently, each sibling is in essence an only child. Keep focused on the positives and highlight the gains for your child, who may not see them as clearly as you do. Then, drop the issue permanently if you can. Only children are children first.

Whose Life Is It Anyway?

You're so connected to your single being that you feel every hurt, every slight. Neighborhood teenagers knocked over her snowman and broke her sled; she wasn't invited to a classmate's birthday party; the children in her class laughed at her because she forgot to do a homework paper. Every embarrassment she faces affects you. Each mistake or mishap you take as your own.

Gracie Downing retells tales of first-grade adjustment. "He was utterly miserable, I could not ignore it. This was my only child. The boy who could not wait to get to kindergarten was refusing to get dressed and working himself into a state until he threw up. He trembled in line and burst into tears on entering the classroom. I was beside myself. I envisioned twelve years of struggling to get him to school. I didn't sleep and lost five pounds in the weeks before he adjusted to his new school. Watching him suffer was heartwrenching."

Speak to mothers and fathers with more than one child. You will find they don't sleep either when one of their children is unhappy about a team's losing streak, or a daughter is crying her eyes out over a boyfriend who dumped her. Ask parents how they feel when their children don't get into the college of their choice, are bullied on the playground, or don't get invited to the seventh-grade dance. Their tales will be as sad and unsettling to them as Gracie Downing's was to her. If you have children, you identify with their pain. You worry. But if you have a singleton, you can immerse yourself totally in her distress.

You can stew until you find yourself interfering in your child's life. You'll find time to argue with her softball coach about the length of time she played in the last game, to call and "speak to" the mother of a child who calls your son names, to get in the middle of everything as Felice Robert's mother did.

Looking back, Felice Roberts, an only with two sons in their twenties, has misgivings about being an only child because of her mother's attitude toward her. "Sometimes I felt smothered because I received too much attention. Anything that happened to me happened to my mother. She was so attached. I remember screaming at her as a teenager that she wanted to live my life and would probably want to have my labor pains for me. I wanted the right to make my own mistakes."

"I wanted recognition for my accomplishments, but my mother was too busy worrying about what I was doing," explains adult only child, Andrew Witter. "If I scored three touchdowns, instead of saying 'Great job, son,' she said, 'You could have broken your leg.' She tried to control my life through overprotection and fear."

"My parents were too concerned about what I was wearing, who my friends were, what I was doing," notes Barbara Lumpkin, age thirty. "I felt my likes, dislikes, and opinions were second-rate. You begin to think that you don't have good taste, valid opinions, and aren't capable of making sound decisions when someone else is making them for you."

Parents of one go to great lengths to help their child negotiate obstacles or avoid them entirely. There is no concrete formula that lets any child skip over the pains of growing up. Alone, without a brother or sister, fighting her own battles is her lot. She will cope much better if parents accept her situation and she fends for herself early on, especially among her peers. Help out only when necessary or when asked. The rest of the time, back off.

Born in the mid-forties, an era of large families and limited parenting knowledge, Edie Mulligan feels "I was the object of all my mother's neuroses. She was so focused on me that it was intrusive; she was overly possessive. It was clear to me that if I had a sibling, some of this tension would be deflected onto another victim. As it was, I was the only victim and I was desperate for company—someone to share the burden. I was a kid with a very difficult mother."

The closeness and scrutiny that may befall the only child can be troublesome. It can backfire and cause a child to rebel. "I say I will raise my child differently than my parents did," declares high school honor student Jennifer Walsh. "I say to my mom, 'I'm not going to do what you've done to me all my life.' My mother is the queen of nosiness. She always has to get involved. She has to know how I'm doing in each class. She still chases me around the house and tells me to go do my schoolwork. She looks in on me every ten minutes because she has nothing else to do; she doesn't give me telephone privacy either. When I'm on it, she sits in my room. She interferes and I don't like it."

"As far back as first grade," remembers Victor Smythe, a college freshman, "I had an antipathy for my family's presence at school. I simply wanted a private and independent section to my life."

Noted pediatrician and author Dr. Sanford J. Matthews cautions women in *The Motherhood Maze:* "When you slip into a secondary spot in your own life, subordinate to the life of your baby, you can never receive enough emotional feedback to keep you adult and vital . . . And when you live your life for your child, the child is robbed of so much. His triumphs . . . are so much a part of your triumphs that they are lessened by your intrusion . . . You just have to keep in mind that these are their own lives, not yours, that they are living. The women I know who do the best job of mothering are those who are involved in themselves first."[3]

Ariel Divers, age twenty-two, complains bitterly of her first thirteen years, those preceding her mother's return to work. "Because I was my mother's career, there was always a sense that I was an extension of her. That's where a lot of the pressure came in. It happens to all daughters to a degree, but it is more intense when you're the only child. I was her major definition of being a good mother and a good person."

Hospital fund-raiser Andrea Balfour offers sound advice garnered from her experience as an only child. "Don't depend on your child to fulfill what you may have wanted in your own life. Parents should busy their lives so that the single child is a member of the family and not its focus."

One factor working for current and future only children is the desire of most mothers to be autonomous and productive in their own right. Women who are starting their families now have a different attitude. Sandra Steadham explains hers. "My own self-esteem was not balanced on the fine edge of whether or not I was a mother or how my child turned out. I wasn't going to try to prove my life through my daughter. I can easily allow her to be her own person."

Jody Cohen maintains that she has "enough in my life and my life with my husband to diffuse the concentration on my son."

Self-direction takes part of, but not enough of, the concentration away from the only child. You can function so that your child thinks she is a precious gift to humanity and create an ego problem or you can think and act in terms of what might be the best for your child—the best school for her to go to, the best activities for her to engage in, the best experiences for her to have, the best values for her to develop.

Parents of onlies have the time and energy to nurture their single offspring in warm and constructive ways. Yet the factors that allow parents to focus on their only children and that make it easy to raise great kids are the very ones that can snag them. If you can maintain a relaxed attitude about rearing your only child, always bearing in mind your goal to be moderate about your concerns and fears, the specifics will work out quite easily.

6

The Specifics

Assume you have adopted a calm attitude about raising your
child—you plan to raise him as if he were one of three, and you
know you can control your instinct to be overprotective. Still, you
must be cautious not to become so fascinated with this one young
person that parental guidance and discipline go by the boards. You
can instill good values, enforce rules, and work out differences
without sacrificing your child's childhood or enthusiasm.

There are harmonious, simple solutions to the possible trouble
spots—too much attention, too much parental assistance, too
much power within the family—in raising a child without siblings.
Given a genuine understanding of the only child's position, rearing
one is far less taxing than raising two or more.

Center Stage: Pros and Cons

By definition, an only child has the leading role. He's the star, the
center of attention, the recipient of applause, praise, and the material items you, and those close to you, can afford and wish to give.
For some only children, center stage is not what it's cracked up to

be. Being the recipient of the full impact of parents' attention and affection has enormous drawbacks as well as benefits.

"I was my parents' entire life outside of work. On the one hand, I received a tremendous amount of personal attention; I liked that. On the other hand, one can't readily hide things from parents. Being the central figure is the same thing I didn't like," adult only Kenneth Briggs states frankly.

Antique dealer Bill Sheehan was less fond of his single status than Briggs. "Being the center of attention sounds like it would be a good thing, but much of the attention is negative. I did not like being front and center all the time. If there were more kids in the family, the attention would be spread out. If parents are not taking particular notice of you on a specific day, as an only child you are still their main concern."

An obvious lesson to take away from Briggs and Sheehan's comments: Don't constantly scrutinize your child; overlook something he does that you may not like but which may not be important in the scheme of development. If he's been on the phone too long with a friend or stayed up reading too late, pretend you don't notice every now and again. Give your only a sense of privacy and his own identity, something he would automatically get if you were caring for more than one.

The personal attention that Briggs and Sheehan found disturbing is usually a strong positive if not overdone. In a two- or three-person family, the child listens closely to adult conversation. There are opportunities to impart useful information and solid values when parents discuss their jobs, a family tragedy and how they plan to help, a surprise they are plotting for a friend, a social crisis or charity they support, possible destinations for a pending trip . . . whatever. The potential to learn is ever-present.

Mary Kelly Selover's parents capitalized on this advantage. "At the dinner table we talked about books and world events. When I talk to friends from large families, they say they talked among themselves and the parents talked to each other. The children didn't have the chance for adult conversation or to be treated as mature people."

"I've been talking to Dan since he was an infant," remarks Lois Angel, whose son is a senior in high school. "We have read to him, given him books to read, answered his questions, and spent a lot of time discussing life with him. The combination has made him confident and put him way ahead in school."

Rachael Cronbeck, like so many parents of onlies, sees the same advantages. Speaking of her accelerated five-year-old, Rachael remarks, "She's just starting kindergarten in an advanced group, but is able to do first-grade work. She loves to learn and I have the time to teach her. Even at her age, I can see the benefits of not having to divide my time between two children."

Referring to her only, Donna Stultey thinks a child who "starts life with the self-confidence that comes from people always telling her that she's the best, she's terrific, she's the brightest, is armed for being knocked down as opposed to the child who thinks there's always another child who may be better. Let her start out at the pinnacle."

Stultey is right in one sense, yet for the only child, too much emphasis on being the brightest, the prettiest, or the most talented can create undue pressure and a sense of failure if she can't measure up. What children, onlies in particular, need are not vacant or empty comments, but actual successes in whatever they are doing—riding a bike, making a new friend, solving a puzzle—to build their confidence. Individual accomplishments provide the strongest armor in the world beyond home.

The only child is in the enviable position of not being compared to or pitted against a sibling at home. Don't slip into the habit of measuring him against his cousins or classmates. And don't brag to others about your child's special qualities or achievements. Here, one mother boasts of her four-year-old's progress: "She's into the phases of the moon; she reads the advertisements . . . anything in the newspaper that catches her eye and is of interest to her. She's easily reading at a third-grade level. She goes into the bookstore and picks out the books that she wants and reads them." To many people, such vauntings are obnoxious, providing more fuel for the stereotypical fires that emanate from the only child's being her parents' star.

Similarly, depending on a parent's interest, it is not unusual to find an only child who shares and excels in that interest. By the age of seven, an only child with a mother or father who is a baseball fanatic might easily recite batting averages of players in the National League over the past twenty years. Friends will tell the parents the child is brilliant. Once out of the child's and parent's earshot, they will call the performance pretentious and believe that the parents force-fed the statistics into their child.

It's the rare friend who wants to listen while your advanced reader reads from *Hamlet* or proudly solves complex math equations without paper and pencil. It's all well and good, but keep it in the family. Save showing off for grandparents who relish their grandchild's every accomplishment. Within limits, boasting has its place on Internet web sites created for discussions of only children. These parents are open to only child successes and tend to be highly supportive of accomplishments even when they are presented as blatant bragging.

Delighted to discover an area in which the only child does well, many parents go way beyond encouraging or nourishing. They drive their child to fine-tune the skill or talent to the exclusion of other developmental areas. "She was playing that way at ten," a mother whispers smugly to her neighbor in the second row of a large concert hall. The mother of the sixteen-year-old on stage devoted her life to sitting in the living room making sure her daughter practiced the violin. Summers were fully occupied with lessons; the daughter remained ashen and imprisoned when other children were tanned and free. She is indeed musically precocious—her playing is of concert quality—but she is unhappy and not well connected to her peers. Her parents, however, are pleased with her success.

Balance Receiving with Giving

In his position of priority, an only expects as much from you as you are willing to give. He will take for as long as it comes his way. In this respect he is no different from his "sibling-ed" friends. The difference is that parents of onlies who have the wherewithal are prone to give to excess. If an only receives too much for too long, he will eventually demand his anticipated rewards and you will have fed the stereotype of the impatient, spoiled only child.

Jack Crummley, an only himself and the parent of an only, consciously tried to avoid raising a spoiled child. "We were always doing something with or for Candy, but she didn't get everything she wanted."

In many families an only child is on the receiving end for years and years, possibly a lifetime. For Susan Longrahm, who was thirty-nine at the birth of her daughter, the problem was exacerbated by the fact that her friends' children were grown. "Shelly was born to a group. Like ourselves, our friends were older; most of their children were in high school. She thought that she had ten sets of fawning grandparents.

"Our friends rarely visited without bringing a gift for her. By the time she was walking and talking, she was at the front door searching handbags and packages and asking, 'What did you bring me?' After she had been talking for a while, her behavior stopped being cute. We were mortified. We explained to her that people didn't have to bring her a present, especially if it wasn't her birthday or Christmas, but she was conditioned like Pavlov's dog. She salivated at the sound of a crinkling shopping bag. As a last resort, I told friends to stop. It was over a year before we 'broke' her; she was eight years old before her eyes went to people's faces before she surveyed the content of their hands."

As parents you have a responsibility to prevent gestures—even well-meaning ones—that may be detrimental to your child. You would stop your child from consuming another brownie or dish of ice cream if you felt it would make him ill. Tell relatives and friends to stop indulging your only when you feel their graciousness is not constructive.

You can successfully short-circuit an unpleasant chain like Shelly's by demonstrating the importance of giving. Your child's ego will not be permanently scarred if you state firmly, "You can't always receive; you must give, too." Follow through. Establish a pattern of having your child give away toys he's outgrown to a local women's shelter or children's hospital. Suggest your child give away a toy each time he receives a new one or have your child assist in collecting her old toys for a garage or yard sale every year (you'll want to save a few representative or favored ones that have special meaning to your child or to you). Your child can also be involved in going through his clothing, too, to pack up for giving to your friends who have younger children or to a clothing drive at school. As your only ages, be supportive of school community service projects. Ask questions about his involvement and how he enjoyed it.

For birthdays of family members or for Christmas and Hanukkah celebrations, have your only shop with you and pass out presents. Instead of signing your child's name to gift cards, take the time to get his signature (a scribbled line or bunch of illegible letters will do). When your child is invited to a friend's or classmate's birthday party, ask what he would like to give as a gift. If his suggestion is too costly, offer alternatives, then try to comply with his gift-giving preference. He may have a toy that he thinks the other child might also enjoy. Giving a gift that he likes himself heightens the joy, and handing it over is much easier if he already owns the item.

Suggest your child give a small gift to a friend of yours or a grandmother because she did you a favor or just because you love her. The gift can be a few cut flowers from the garden, a clay "art piece" molded in school, or a drawing sketched in your child's free time. Stop with your child on the way home from school or practice to pick up Dad's favorite dessert or a book Mom's been wanting to read. Volunteer to cook dinner, rake leaves, help clean a friend's, neighbor's, or relative's garage, if it's not something you regularly do. Enlist your son's or daughter's aid and talk about how pleased everyone will be with the gesture or completed job.

Teach Sharing and Respect for Others

The notion of sharing attention and time is the most difficult for young children. Nonetheless, during the pre- and post-adolescent years, it is necessary both by discussion and example to cultivate the tools of sharing and feeling for others. Parents must realize that an only child has a focus different than children who have siblings. There are hundreds of children's books that discuss sibling relationships—the arrival of a new sibling, fighting, loving, helping your sibling. A scant few tell a child about the problems and prerogatives of being an only-born. If your child does not bring up the subject, you should.

By first or second grade, make him aware of his circumstance in a direct conversation. Explain that sharing is not something he is forced to do when he is at home. Use examples that are on his level: He does not have to fight over who sits in the front seat of the car, who names the new puppy, or who eats the red jelly beans. Tell him straight out that although he is privileged in regard to sharing, he is not exempt from caring and making contributions to the family.

Involve your child as much as possible in activities that do not center around him, such as team sports, dance classes, summer trips, or camp programs. Volunteer your time and services—and your child's—to people outside your core family: Take an elderly aunt for a ride; help build a booth for the hospital fair; pack old clothing for the homeless; gather and deliver unused toys to needy children.

When a classmate is absent from school for an extended period of time, have your only call to find out how he is feeling and send a get-well card. Have your child offer to bring his assignments home to him or to call him each day after school to keep the home-bound student up-to-date on class events and news.

If the only child is surrounded by equals outside the home and has some "basic training" at home, it is more than likely that he will adapt and adopt the amenities former generations feared were lacking in only children. Early on there has to be a sense that everyone in the family has rights, that people in it share and cooperate with each other.

In the Duncan household, calculated measures were taken to introduce this concept to three-year-old Phoebe. "We've made sure Phoebe realizes that she is not the center of the universe," explains John Duncan. "We purposefully put only one television in the house. If she wants to watch something and we're watching something else, she has to wait. She has to sit with us when the family is having dinner. Certainly we could let her go off and do what she would like, but we don't. It's better for her to figure out now that we have interests and priorities just as she does. Only children must learn that they may be the only child in a household, but they are not the only person."

These are subtle lessons the only child must receive simply because he is the central figure. His position grants him the last chicken leg, the lone steak bone, or the remaining cookie. Train him to ask if anyone would like the last scoop of mashed potatoes. Occasionally one parent should take it. Cut the last piece of cake in half; forced sharing gets the message across.

The only can quickly learn to expect all things to go his way. "You're always the winner when you're an only," says Evelyn Wolff, an investment banker. A basic home introduction to competition prepares a child for later challenges. When starting a game with his parents, the only child goes first. He will not always have that advantage when playing with his friends. Get him used to going second or last and to losing.

"When parents always give in, an only child's social negotiating skills might be constrained," warns author Dr. Sharon Ramey, developmental psychologist at the University of Alabama in Birmingham. "The fear is that only children become unduly self-centered and demanding because of the context that they've been in. I rarely see that," Ramey notes, "because the parents who chose to have one child are especially thoughtful and actively do things to prevent that from happening."

Set Boundaries; Define Acceptable Behavior

Because no one else vies for a parent's time, it's no real inconvenience—in fact it's often pleasurable and rewarding—to keep your only child company while he practices piano, writes his autobiography, or rehearses his part in the class play endlessly. It is also normally not a problem to allow one young child to speak or to interrupt you whenever he wishes.

When you allow constant interruptions, regardless of how clever or endearing, others will rightfully find this rudeness inconsiderate. As your child gets older—and louder—and has lots to say, he will provide more fodder for the singleton's unwanted and unwarranted stigma of self-centeredness.

Necessity brings behavior boundaries to the multichild household. Without them, as any mother of several children will attest, chaos prevails. Onlies, too, need firm guidelines. Assume your three-year-old has good verbal skills (which many onlies do) and a three-year-old's foggy concept of politeness. An only will not learn restraint from competing for "talk time" among siblings; parents have to begin curbing interruptions. Stop him when he interrupts you; tell him he must wait his turn to speak within the family as well as outside of it. Make him wait for his turn. If you are diligent about enforcing this rule, by the age of five, your only will be saying "excuse me" when what he has to say cannot wait.

Hand signals are more effective and less upsetting to both parent and child than forceful verbal requests to be quiet. When you're on the telephone, a stop sign with your hand warns a child that he may not speak until you have hung up; one finger held up tells him that you'll be off in a minute. Present hand signals as a game to the toddler, as "law" to the older child; make sure he comprehends each cue.

Reinforce your youngster's adherence to your rules. When another child is rude, point it out. If your child says "excuse me" at a gathering, tell him on the way home that he did exactly the right thing. When he waits for you to end a telephone conversation, thank him. Praise goes a long way in achieving the goal and conveying the message that he has company on this planet.

If you're prone to tolerating repeated interruptions, you'll probably be inclined to overlook your only's breach of other behavioral contracts: to sit still in a restaurant, to clean his room, to put away his bicycle, or to limit his telephone conversations to ten minutes. Parents of one must exercise extreme firmness. Little things left unchecked become big things as a child matures. A young child who talks back to his parents may not be taken seriously, his words excused by "he didn't mean it" or "he doesn't know what he's saying." He means it and he knows. Do not let him off the hook.

Many parents of onlies prefer to sit down and "talk it over." They say, "Now, Lisa, you must understand," instead of saying, "You may not speak to me that way," or "Daddy is busy, you will have to wait." Having one child is often equated with having plenty of time for deep analysis of the rights and wrongs of hitting one's friend or talking back to one's grandmother. If you're tempted to adopt the "let's talk it over" approach, remember, parents with more than one are enforcing rules and laying down the law. Long-term, doing the same can only benefit your singleton.

Children act and react better when boundaries are established. Minus sibling friction, fewer rules and regulations are necessary. But without them, you end up reluctant to punish or not knowing what form to give the punishment. When you finally must punish your child, you run the risk of overreacting and enforcing a penalty too severe for the infraction. Limitations also provide an important frame of reference for your child when he visits the homes of his friends. If for no other reason than children do not like to be different, give your only solid guidelines at home.

A case in point: Four-year-old Casey Cowine was hitting his playmate. His mother told him to stop immediately or he would be sorry. "Casey became irrational. He screamed at me, 'You always say you are going to punish me and you never do. You just say you are and you don't.' He carried on like this for a full ten minutes," according to his mother, Olivia Cowine. "He was begging to be penalized. It dawned on me that Casey's friends were sent to their rooms or had privileges taken away if they disobeyed. Casey had been such a good kid that we had little reason to punish him. I could see that he felt strange because we weren't treating him as other parents were treating their children."

It's okay to make reasonable demands on your only child and to revoke liberties for deviations from the rules. "We had very strong rules about eating out," Brenda Tyson says. "From the time Billy was two years old, he was told that if he didn't behave, if he walked around or disturbed other diners, he would remain at home with a baby-sitter. We were lenient at first, but repeated our threat regularly. By age four, he was a pleasure in restaurants."

For "wait time" in restaurants or other public places, pack a few small toys, coloring books, cars, or your child's current favorite amusement. Since the only child has no one with whom to play, he can busy himself with his toys until the food arrives, the airplane is boarding, or the event begins. Playthings make it much simpler for the only child to adhere to your restrictions.

Marsha Shutz proudly tells of her success in setting boundaries and making demands on her fourteen-year-old. "Nina is given many chores and she knows I expect them to be done . . . When she tests me, not very often now that she is older, she is punished. When she was younger, I took away her favorite television program or sent her to her room; lately it's her telephone privileges for the day or a week, depending on the importance of the task she neglected to do."

Some families use contracts as a method of control with teenage only children. One mother outlined her program with her son: "At thirteen when he got his own telephone line, he signed a contract to keep his grades at a certain level or we would remove the telephone. When he reached driving age, the same applied—if his grades were not up to par, his driving privileges would be revoked."

Discipline shows you care. By overlooking your singleton's minor indiscretions you may actually contribute to the very problems you are trying to avoid. Early on, bedtime should be honored without endless stalling and requests for water, more light, fewer covers, another stuffed animal, or the window opened (or closed). Granted, with one it is easy to alter a routine or give in to a single demand. Be firm and be consistent.

Because you have only one, you may let small transgressions such as forgetting to feed the cat ("But, Mom, Joey is waiting outside for me") or tossing underwear on the floor slip by. Of course, you don't mind feeding the cat or picking up one pair of tiny boy briefs or one set of blocks. When this child turns teenager, it will be clear that the easy way out was a grave error. One size-five pair of briefs will have become two- or three-week's dirty laundry barricading his bedroom door. The two-handled training cup you carried to the sink will have mounted to snack dishes from what seems like the entire tenth grade.

Too Much of a Good Thing

Very simply, don't do for your child what he can do for himself. Otherwise you'll find yourself in the position of Sherry Maculsky, the mother of nine-year-old Bobby, who compares her son to her brother's three children. "They have been forced to learn to do more things for themselves. Bobby can still con me into running his bath water. A nine-year-old is perfectly capable of doing that on his own. He still hasn't learned to tie his shoelaces. When I try to withdraw my assistance or attention, he rebels."

Like Bobby, Carla Vozios's son's "frustration tolerance is zip. You tend to do everything for one because you have no other responsibilities. He's very dependent. If you do too much for them, it comes back to haunt you. At the age of nine, he still asks me to get him a drink," Carla sighs.

Refuse. Suggest he do it himself. Start early and realistically or you will find yourself slipping into the pattern of doing it for your child because it's faster and easier than arguing. Don't expect your two-year-old to tie his own shoelaces, but you can insist that a five-year-old get undressed, put his clothes in the hamper, and find his sneakers in the morning.

The expectation that things will be done for you can carry over into adulthood and marriage. The indulged only-child-turned-spouse may experience rocky going early on in a marriage while the marital partner adjusts to picking up caretaking where the only's mother and father left off.

At the age of seven, Justin Yoto assumes a lot will be done for him and he expects more than his share of attention. His mother thinks, "That's definitely because he's an only child. If a child calls you and you have three children, he may have to wait, but my son has been responded to immediately and it's difficult for him not to be. Unless you're actually doing something, you can't make up something else to do. You are there to get the jacket, hold the jacket, and zip the jacket. I see it as absolutely damaging to do those jobs for him."

"There were things I should have been doing for myself, like breathing," jokes Larry Brand. "My mother did not let me be on my own early enough. She made all my arrangements; she got so involved in my projects that she took them over; she made sure I ate enough by outlining what was on each shelf of the refrigerator. She tried to insulate me from the world and it would have been better for me if she hadn't. When I went to boarding school as a teenager, I had a hard time adapting—away from home, nothing was done for me."

The only child receives a healthy dose of individual care, especially if his mother and father belong to the current older, more affluent generation of parents. Many only children always have someone interacting with them. If a parent is not home, the child is at school or involved in some form of recreation. If the child is home and parents are at work, arrangements are made for a caretaker to amuse him.

Henry Wallman, himself an only, questions the merits of occupying a child full-time. "There was a period of time when my son did not have much to do and I felt constrained to play with him. It was my memories of being alone, because I had been ill as a young child, that interfered with my judgment. Leaving him to fend for himself might have been better."

When you're not sure if you're doing too much for your child, compare what you do with parents who have more than one child. Many parents of onlies complain that they cannot get their preschool or young elementary-school-age child to play alone. Some of this has to do with age, some with training. If you've allowed your child to rely on you for all forms of entertainment, it's time to break the pattern. Fill a basket with your child's toys and explain it's time to play alone for a few minutes. Initially, limit the time to two or three minutes. Send her back to her toys each time she seeks you out. Set a timer if you need to, so the pattern-breaking becomes a game of sorts. Depending on your child's age you may want to stay in the same room with her. Eventually, you will find she can amuse herself for half an hour or more and you will be able to move around the house.

Always being available or having someone available to entertain your child will not help him explore and learn on his own. If only children have carefully selected toys and activities, they will learn to amuse themselves. Toy manufacturers consider the problem of independent play when designing their products. According to an executive from one of our country's major toy companies, "Most toys, 90 percent, are designed for individual play and to stimulate the imagination." Three- and four-year-olds, for example, can play computer picture games and learn math from special computer programs without adult assistance.

As soon as your child can dial the telephone, post his friends' numbers, instruct him in telephone etiquette, and have him make his own play dates. Take over to confirm pick-up and drop-off arrangements.

No matter how much planning you or your child does, "only" parents are called on more than other parents to fill in for missing companions. It's difficult to throw a football or play Monopoly by yourself. Here, two-parent households have an advantage: Generally one or the other parent enjoys, or can tolerate, an hour of board games or twenty minutes of wrestling on the living room floor. Young children are so delighted to be with a parent that the parent's choice is acceptable. Be selective. When parents submit to activities they loathe and stay at them too long, the enjoyment is lost to both parent and child.

There's no way around doing time in the entertainment department, but indulging an only child—toddler or teen—has the potential for your participation to become standard fare in the child's mind. He will then expect you to play a game every night or, worse, watch him play a computer game. Yet saying "no" hurts parents more than it hurts the child. "I couldn't stand watching Elena founder. She would be lost with nothing to do," Alice Rand comments. "It pained me to refuse a quick game of dominoes."

It's easy to lapse into a pattern that you come to dread, as Ben Grisori's mother well knows. "I had the hardest time telling Ben that I would not read him his favorite book. The book was a nightmare for me, an endless nonsensical series of cartoons about cars and trucks. His 'please, Mom's' uttered in an experienced pathetic tone far beyond his four years weakened me almost daily for months. I grudgingly read the book cover to cover."

Inadvertently, the problem was solved. "One day Ben caught

me in a bad mood and I blurted out, 'I hate that book and I'm not reading it.' Instead of becoming annoyed with me, he looked me in the eye and said, 'I'll get a different one.' It was that easy." All onlies do not respond as agreeably as Ben did when a parent deviates from an established program, but a flat refusal is always worth a try.

Money Matters

"We are able to offer him anything and everything he wants. That's very pleasurable to me. My parents were not very well-to-do and could not give me the things I wanted." Chemical engineer Roger Clemens, like many parents, derives satisfaction from being able to provide well for his child.

The only child is likely to live in a financially secure environment. He is apt to receive most of what he asks for—a teen tour through Europe, the same style shirt in several colors, and a back-up pair of sneakers. He will be the first to tell you: "I get almost anything I want"; "My mom buys me more expensive clothes because there is one of me"; "My grandparents give me money whenever I need it"; "You get lots more stuff and you don't have to share it."

There will be no lessons from siblings who are stuffing their piggy banks or saving up to buy their next toy or video game. Unlike his peers with brothers and sisters, the only child may be indulged without regard to cost or to the financial realities he will encounter when he sets out on his own. Therefore, the only-born needs a careful indoctrination in money matters.

"There is a difference," explains Maxine Sobel, mother of a twenty-one-year-old, "between indulging and spoiling one child." The difference rests in a parent's underlying motivation. Parental guilt can be a strong factor in only-child families. Some parents feel they must compensate for the absence of siblings, using the excuse that a child needs more things because there is no at-home playmate; others employ material indulgence to make up for extra time spent at the office. Splurging to temper guilt has no reward beyond a child's ten minutes or few days of instant gratification.

How you offer a possession is far more important than what that object may be. If you attach strings to your gift—"you must start performing better in school, keep your room neater, help your mother, share it with your friends"—you might as well not bother. "Gift persuasion" is rarely effective and never constructive.

Setting limits on what you are willing to buy serves as strong evidence that you are not attempting to buy your child's love and affection. You can teach good money sense and instill a respect for its value by drawing parameters. For example, starting in kindergarten, children receive monthly book order sheets at most schools. Permit your only a given number of books each month—two to four books or a set dollar amount—rather than allowing him to choose as many as he would like. When you buy clothing, give him either/or options. "You can have the red shirt or the blue shirt, not both." In restaurants, discuss the prices of different selections on the menu.

"We made a conscious decision when Philip was two to restrain *our* spending and his," explains Bonnie Fales, who used school fairs, carnivals, and outdoor markets as means of educating her son in money matters. "When we went to flea markets, for instance, we told Phil he could buy one thing. If he selected something too expensive—over a dollar-fifty was our limit until he was eight—we told him that he could not have it. At five, he was pointing to objects and asking, 'Does this cost too much?' We patted ourselves on the back, sure we had succeeded in our efforts to train Phil to be conservative about money. Watch," she adds humorously, "he'll turn out to be the Donald Trump of Louisville."

Let's say you can afford to give your child pretty much what he wants, except maybe the outrageously expensive cars advertised in the F. A. O. Schwartz toy catalog. Don't do it. Pare down his Christmas and birthday lists by taking into account what he will receive from relatives and friends. Your child may be the only one on both sides of the family or the lone young person among your group of friends. The number of gifts can—and often does—become excessive in the one-child household if parents don't act sensibly and attempt to short-circuit a deluge.

Although they have the means to buy the extras their sixteen-year-old only child would like, the Wegners encourage self-motivation. "Our son has a very small allowance. When he wanted a bike or wants to go to a concert, he has to earn the money by mowing lawns, doing yard work for other families, or doing chores around our house. He understands that we are not going to meet his desires or needs for the rest of his life. He knows, if he wants luxuries, he will have to get them himself."

You may choose to have your child do small jobs around the house to earn his allowance or decide to pay him a bonus for those jobs. He may receive large monetary gifts from family and friends or just a few dollars on each birthday. Whatever the case, it's a good idea to open a savings account for your only child between the ages of six and eight. Take him with you to make each deposit; show him how the interest has been added. Watching his own savings account grow is a rewarding learning experience for a youngster.

You can indulge your only child if you balance your giving with a strong sense of values, as the Wegners are doing. Restricting spending as the Fales did with Philip directs the young child and gives him a sense of proportion. Your own spending patterns are just as influential. If you are extravagant, don't be surprised if your only also spends lavishly when the resources are available to him. It is wise to remind the only child that he is fortunate to have as much as he does, that others are not as lucky. Encourage a spirit of charity by your own actions.

Who's Running the Show?

"I've failed utterly. He's in charge," confesses Bonnie Markham, the mother of five-year-old David. "If we had more children, we would have to be more structured. Our style is not to have routines and that leaves more room for him to take over."

The likelihood of a child ruling the roost is far greater when there are no siblings. If permitted, the only child can direct the course of his parents' lives—be it insisting on an expensive addition to his toy holdings or demanding a sleep-over guest the same night you have an important dinner engagement.

Rebellion against your going out is one of the most obvious indications that your child is seeking control. There will be others: The only child may demand his dinner now or insist he'll take his bath later, when "this minute" is far more convenient for you. He'll explain that he needs you to come home immediately from a shopping expedition or to "hurry downstairs, it's important." You drop what you are doing to discover he wants you to see his drawing or comb his hair.

This little being can have you racing around the house on command. Many a parent of the only child feels as if he or she has become a personal servant. Every time you accommodate him unnecessarily, he moves one step closer to controlling you. Try this: Stop dashing when your child calls; start insisting that if he wants you, he must come and find you.

Only children know their power. By age six or seven, they will tell you that you have no excuse for dropping the indulgences they have come to expect. After all, yours may remind you, "You only have me." You can avoid such unpleasantness by stating the special nature of whatever treat you provide and by making it clear that the treat or occasion has limits. If you take your child into a toy store, for example, specify what he may purchase, if anything, or how much he may spend before you enter.

Special time should be just that and announced up front. For instance, ask your child if she would like to go for a bike ride or work on a model airplane after dinner as a "special treat." Use those words. Stipulate time limits and conditions. You might say, "We can go to the zoo, but we must leave by two o'clock." Or "You can stay in the park for one hour, then we must go to buy you shoes for Uncle Robert's wedding."

Don't weaken once you've taken a stand. Parents of onlies are known to succumb regularly and readily to requests to stay a little longer, to read one more story, to stay up a few extra minutes. Whether you're refusing a nightly game of cards, an afternoon cookie from the bakery, or five minutes longer at a friend's house, saying "no" takes practice, but may be one of your more liberating responses.

Stop control before it starts by going out regularly during your child's early years. When your going out is a given, adjustment will be easier. Don't allow long periods to lapse between dates. If you do, you and your child will reface the trauma of separation each time. And if you exhibit the slightest hesitation or concern, you reinforce unpleasant and upsetting behavior. Be prepared for tears and tantrums, possibly verbal assaults such as "you don't love me" or "how can you leave me?"—sure signs that an attempt to take over your social life is imminent. Once made, don't back down or change your plans.

Bev Rogers details her experience (extreme, but not unusual) with her four-year-old: "We hadn't been out in months for a series of reasons, then we arranged a dinner date with new neighbors. They picked us up, and while we were putting on our coats, I could see Becky was getting anxious. Then it started, the 'pleases' which became shrieks of 'don't leave me.' She worked herself into such a state that she threw up on my husband's shoes. It was very embarrassing. The neighbors had the decency to wait outside while we dealt with Becky and Len's shoes. I calmed Becky down and gave the sitter instructions, then forced myself out the door, prying Becky's hands from my coat sleeves. I did not enjoy dinner."

Advance reminders of bedtime rules or a pending date help a child prepare mentally for your leaving. Take reminders a step farther by illustrating the idea of grown-up activities. Tell the truth: "When you are a daddy [mommy], you will have same privileges."

"What we are doing would bore you." "You would have to be quiet for two hours." "The play we are seeing is very scary." Acknowledge his feelings: "You don't like having Mom and Dad go out." Reinforce the fact that you will return that evening by saying, "We will kiss you when we get home" or "Do you want me to wake you when we get back?"

When a child is old enough, give him a say in sitter selection, assuming you are fortunate enough to have reliable options. Choices give the young child a feeling of control over his life. Have him help plan something special to eat or do with the sitter: Make a pizza or popcorn; play a game you don't enjoy, but your child does; rent a children's video; permit him to stay up a few minutes later than normal. If you have thought ahead and made good arrangements, there's a better chance that he will be occupied and happy when you walk out the door.

Expect some sulking or pleas, but there is no reason to assume he would be any happier left home with a sitter and a couple of siblings. Demands for parents to stay at home are not restricted to the one-child family. The difficulties in leaving two young children have more ferocity—one child simply eggs the other one on.

Steps to dethrone the young dictator and extricate yourself from his clutches are imperative. Suppose your child has, through a series of procrastinations, maneuvered his bedtime up a full hour. He's gained an hour of your time and lost an hour of sleep. Proceed slowly. Give a warning notice: Explain that he needs his sleep and that you plan to slide his bedtime back, fifteen minutes a night or a few minutes each night over the course of a week. He'll give you a hard time. Be assertive and leave no room for negotiation.

The older the child, the more difficult the demands. "Chicken? I'm not eating it. Get me a pizza." If, for years, you have been at his beck and call to pick him up from school, or drive him here and there when he can transport himself perfectly safely by walking or riding his bicycle, he will not out of the goodness of his heart accept your refusals.

The child who becomes used to having things his way may

continue to expect the same outside the home, in school, and with friends. Roger Clemens acknowledges that his son was "very intolerant and very demanding. He believes he can demand from his friends the kind of attention he got from us. It was more of a problem at age twelve than it is at seventeen."

Stephanie Kirby, eighteen, admits that having control over her family caused her problems with friends until very recently. "I was autocratic and inflexible. I wanted to do what I wanted to do when I wanted to do it. I didn't have the bend that's needed for smooth friendships."

To prevent a pattern of domination with friends from emerging, periodically ask your child's teacher, coach, or other leader of activities about his ability to get along. Find out if your child is cooperating with the authority figure and the other children, asserting himself, and compromising when necessary. Encourage day-to-day contact with other children. Have your child visit friends in their homes and have friends into your home. In effect, create sibling relationships so he gets noncontrolling behavior modeling from other sources.

The only child should have a say in family decision making, but that say should be limited to age-appropriate areas. At no age should your child determine whether or not you go out in the evening or where you go, but he can be involved in deciding where the family will take its vacation or what movie the three of you will see. There's no harm in letting a child select the paint color for his room or rearrange his furniture the way he would like it. And you might ask him to plan the seating arrangement for Thanksgiving dinner if you have no strong feelings. But the prerogative ends when he says, "Aunt Sarah can't come" because he doesn't like her. If you concede on Aunt Sarah, then there's no doubt about who's running your show.

A regular family meeting is a highly effective tool for settling disputes as well as planned time for the family to be together if all of you have schedules that make being together on a regular basis difficult. Elect officers (the child as president, of course), follow modified meeting procedures—call the meeting to order, make motions, call for the vote. Meetings are not the time to lecture, but rather to settle arguments over privileges or unacceptable behavior, to plan vacations, to name a pet, or to talk about fun projects. A democratic atmosphere goes a long way toward easing tension.

The Wedge, the Pawn, and Other Manipulations

The only child can "divide and conquer" by adhering so tightly to one parent that the marriage is threatened, a problem not uncommon in one-child families. "Once I had my son, I couldn't think about anything else," admits Angela Sapio, a thirty-three-year-old computer programmer from Illinois. "If Terrence was sick, I was a basket case. He drained me, my time, and almost my marriage. He clung to me and developed a pronounced stutter. With urging from friends, I returned to work when he was five. Terrence's speech improved and the distance let me see that I was destroying not only his life, but my own."

The dynamic works this way: When a child is made to feel too important, he can come to believe that he can replace your spouse or has a more powerful status than your partner. This situation worsens if you involve your child in negative conversation or offer negative comments about your partner. Make a great effort to keep your adult life a separate, strong unit by going out as a twosome and spending whatever is left of the evening together after your child is in bed.

Although the only child normally does not have to compete for love, there is the risk that parents will vie with one another for the only child's affection. In this small family, such a rivalry seriously jeopardizes the child. Because an only lacks intimate relationships with siblings, it is important that the two relationships he has be substantial and pleasurable.

Balance can be encouraged by assigning special care time for each parent, especially if both parents work. Regular intervals with a young child ensure an all-important bond with both parents and lay the groundwork for good communication when the child is older. "Regular intervals," not constant ones, is the operative phrase here.

Given the opportunity, there is a danger that the only child will play one parent against the other. Take the case of Aunt Sarah. She's actually a loathsome human being; all three of you know it. The wife sides with the child in banning Aunt Sarah from a family gathering and a list of her faults is bandied back and forth. The husband is forced to defend his aging aunt. A stormy atmosphere is brewing. The child, knowing little of the family history, is intrigued. Having indirectly instigated an argument, he can sit back and watch the show.

"Our son is a master at using himself as a wedge," reveals Edward Morris. "If he does something wrong, he disappears and leaves my wife and me arguing about how to discipline him. He has a tremendous talent for getting us provoked at each other for something he did or said."

Dr. Henry Wallman advises, "Whatever the specific problem, parents should discuss it quietly themselves, not debate the point in front of a child. Such an approach should be standard in any family."

Pitting one parent against another is a ploy that only children learn very early. "But Mommy said" is a classic example. If used successfully, it can undermine your relationship not only with your spouse, but also with your child. When allowed to operate for long periods, it renders both parents powerless. A unified front is essential. If you are caught off guard by this ploy, not sure how your spouse would respond, tell your child he must wait until you have discussed the issue with his mother (father).

Children have not cornered the market on manipulation. Parents of onlies must be mindful not to use their single child to their advantage. It's easy to cast an only in the role of go-between during parental disputes. Don't enlist your only child to carry needling messages or apologies that parents should deliver themselves.

Nor should the only child be placed in the position of marital arbitrator or parental confidant. He may have no one in his support system to use as a buffer for his feelings about your arguments and misunderstandings.

"Family problems are too personal to tell a friend," says Monica Heath, age thirteen, "You don't want to spread it around when your parents aren't getting along."

Parents can become overly dependent on the only child, pulling him away from friends and peer events to attend adult functions or to go away for the weekend. Parents of one rationalize these decisions by telling themselves that where they are taking their child and what they are doing is more educational or interesting. This may well be true when your child is young, but as he becomes a preteen or teenager, contact with peers and fulfilling his own commitments are equally important. When it comes to a choice between going with parents or playing for the team, appearing in a theatrical production over the course of two weekends or attending a going-away party for his best friend, the only child should cast the deciding vote.

7

Great Expectations

"I think about what my son will be and he's only three years old," says Rosemarie Simmons. "We can give him the advantages of our profession [husband and wife are commercial artists] and that would give him a bit of a head start, but he's very different from either of us."

Parents have fantasies about babies before they are born. While the fetus grows and moves about in the womb, parents make predictions: "This will be a very active baby; this one's going to be a crier, an athlete, a fighter." As years pass, the fantasies change form.

But with an only child, there is almost always a level of expectation that is too high. No matter how much you restrain it, it's there. If you're honest with yourself, you'll recognize it, as will your child at a very young age.

Chances are your only will do well in one or more areas because of the special opportunities and attention her onliness affords her. For example, in a study of families with three children, the addition of each child was linked to a reduction in the child's verbal test scores.[1] Only children show up with more frequency among leaders; they are intellectually advantaged and socially well adjusted. But do you want to put your one child under extreme pressure to succeed?

Raising a child is supposed to be fun. Enjoy it; don't turn child rearing into a competition in which your child must be the best—best academically, best athletically, best dressed, best all-around camper. You will gain endless rewards from your child in respect, love, and consideration if you delight in her accomplishments and minimize her shortcomings as they surface. Forget the presidency. It's one of countless options open to the only child.

When parents impose their visions on a child, the child readily picks them up. Aspirations don't have to be verbalized for a child to understand that they are present—as well they should be. Sociologist Sandra Hofferth at the University of Michigan Institute for Social Research found that "expecting a child to finish college is associated with an increase of six full points on a child's reading test score."[2] If parents have no hopes for a child, the latter may believe that anything or nothing is acceptable. Everyone, including children, needs something to strive for. When goals are attained, self-esteem is enhanced. But if expectations are too high, the child's self-confidence may be undermined when she cannot reach parental goals, and her desire to succeed may vanish.

In the classic book *Between Parent & Teenager* by Dr. Haim Ginott, one of the most respected authorities on childrearing, a seventeen-year-old commented on expectations gone awry, " 'In my father's mind there is a picture of an ideal son. When he compares him to me, he is deeply disappointed. I don't live up to my father's dream. Since early childhood, I sensed his disappointment. He tried to hide it, but it came out in a hundred little ways—in his tone, in his words, in his silence. He tried hard to make me a carbon copy of his dream. When he failed, he gave me up. But he left a deep scar, a permanent feeling of failure.' "[3]

Judith Miller, an office designer, elucidates the goals her parents established for her. "They began when I was young and never changed. The day my father died, he still thought I should have been the Jane Pauley or Barbara Walters of television news. My father regularly referred to me as 'my daughter, the Northwestern College student,' or 'my daughter, the summer intern in Washington,' 'my daughter who works for Xerox,' or 'my daughter who works for the ballet.' It was never just 'my daughter.' I always felt I fell short no matter what I did. If I could have been my own parent, I would have accepted me for me."

Miller, like many onlies, extended herself to meet her parents' every dream. "They were told I would be a boy so I felt a need to do things a son would have done. I learned to fish and play golf. I even went to the fights with my father. An only must work harder to please her parents."

Andrea Balfour endured the pressure for years before she got out from under it. In grade school, she recalls, "Once I asked my father to listen to a poem that I had to memorize for a class. The first time I went to him, I really didn't know it and he told me not to come back until I had it perfect. Only perfection was allowed. I performed perfectly until I left Tennessee to go to college. I almost flunked out after my first semester. Away from the constant observation of my parents, I felt free. I wanted to have fun and I did."

Parental expectations were absorbed into sixteen-year-old Jennifer Walsh's personality. "Ever since I was very young, I have always been in the top classes and involved in so many activities that I can't stop now. Even if I were under a lot of pressure, I couldn't stop because that is the kind of person most people know me to be. Half of what I do is for myself, half is for my parents. I don't want to let them down and I don't really think I want to break out of that mold." When asked if she thought they would love her any less, she hesitates before responding. "I suppose they wouldn't, but they would be disappointed, very disappointed."

Doing one's best does not seem to be good enough for many parents of onlies. Martin Bronson's parents were perpetually disappointed. According to the forty-year-old only, he never lived up to their ideal. "If I got a ninety-eight, they said, 'Why didn't you get a hundred?' When the basketball team didn't win, my father said, 'Why didn't you get the extra point?' They demanded an improved performance for everything. I was not permitted any mistakes in any area."

Warning Signs: Too Much Pressure

A "pressure cooker" mentality has seeped into academics and sports, and parents are turning up the heat at younger and younger ages. Parents who are driven and, "hoping to raise the next Tiger Woods, are enrolling kids in elite leagues or travel teams before they show even a glimmer of potential stardom."[4] Parental violence and unacceptable behavior in different forms erupts on children's sports fields while distressed children, some not far beyond toddler age, try to fulfill their parents' dreams. According to Sean McCann, director of sports psychology at the United States Olympic Training Center, in their enthusiasm parents often don't realize how much pressure they exert on their children.[5]

Watch for danger signals that indicate the pressure is too great, that the extra push you think is helping your child is counterproductive. In the younger child, stress shows early. You can tell you are being too demanding when your child begins to turn to your spouse or partner on a regular basis for entertainment, consolation, or affection. A young child will walk away from the parent who insists that a dive be executed precisely or book read aloud without errors. She will march to the parent who accepts her skills at her level.

Overemphasis on excellence is also easy to spot in the school-age child. A drop in the quality of schoolwork, extreme sensitivity to mild or constructive criticism, or a lowering of her own standards are indicative of an overstressed child. If she feels—or says—she's lazy or dumb, if she appears to have stopped trying or asks to drop a sport or extracurricular lessons, you may be driving her too hard, expecting too much.

Because only children expend great amounts of effort to satisfy their parents, it may be wise to rethink your only's involvement and to listen to what he may be "telling" you. Onlies can be very hard on themselves, so when the pressure seems too much, consider allowing your child to drop an activity, or in the least, pull back and ease up. Block out time so that the three of you can be together or play together. If something needs to be cleaned, all of you set yourselves to the task. Work in the garden together, go apple picking together, clean a closet together, paint a room or piece of furniture. Share the task at hand to remove the focus from whether or not your only child is doing the task well.

Look at Your Child Realistically

Make an honest evaluation of your child's talents and abilities, then offer opportunities to expand her strengths. If she's only a mediocre gymnast and she says she doesn't like it, let her stop training. Take your child's age and developmental level into account. Your three-year-old probably doesn't have the muscular development and co-ordination to swim a perfect crawl—wait until she is five or six before you critique her strokes. She still has plenty of time to make the Olympic team.

There are various reasons why parents impose unrealistic expectations on their children. Ava Bry Penman explains one root of parental expectation. "We all have to face our childhoods when we face our children. That's the biggest challenge." Parents tend to want their children to have the successes that eluded them in childhood.

Evelyn Hanna spent long periods of time agonizing before she learned this lesson. "The first blow came when my son entered second grade. The teacher put him in the slowest reading group. I was sure she had made a mistake and insisted that Neil be retested. I had convinced myself that he was going to outshine anything I had ever accomplished in school. In my head he was going to be the academic fireball I had dreamed of being. It took months of me telling him he could do better and torturing him by making him redo papers the teacher didn't want to see again. Finally I accepted the fact that he didn't have what it took. With the help of the school principal I learned to focus on his positive attributes—his popularity, his athletic abilities, and warm personality. Those should have been enough for me from the beginning."

There is also a tendency on the part of the parents to take responsibility for how a child turns out instead of accepting that that's how the child is. "She's not reading because I didn't spend time with her each evening teaching her the sight words." "He's not slamming the ball out of the park because I didn't have batting practice in the backyard twice a week." "If I had taken him to visit the Stock Exchange or down to the bank with me more often, he would have been a financier."

From a child's point of view, following in a parent's footsteps seems like a tough road. When a child doesn't have a brother or sister to compare herself with, to say I'm doing better in this subject, worse in that subject, she starts relating to the parent as she might otherwise relate to a sibling. In discussing his seventeen-year-old daughter, Joe Michalcewicz details a hazard that can befall only children. "Parents become the only child's performance model. I have a successful business career and that puts pressure on my daughter. She looks at me and wonders if she will have the same success."

Pressure intensifies when both parents have excelled. You can reduce some of the distress by offering bits and pieces of the struggles you've had to reach your position; you might want to include some of your failures along the way. Measuring up is magnified further when each parent wants something different for the child. A mother who wants her son to be a lawyer and a father who wants that same son to be a conductor with the Philharmonic can make it nearly impossible for the son to meet either dream.

To ease the burden, make it clear that your child should make her own path by choosing something that particularly interests her. Tell her you understand that her choice may be quite different from yours. When you don't explicitly give a child room to be herself, the situation can appear hopeless and impossible.

For parents of one who are consumed with dreams of greatness for their single child, popular humorist and author Fran Lebowitz offers sage advice in *Social Studies*. "Your responsibility as a parent is not as great as you might imagine. You need not supply the world with the next conqueror of disease or major motion-picture star. If your child simply grows up to be someone who does not use the word 'collectible' as a noun, you can consider yourself an unqualified success."[6]

Every child is unique and reaches goals or doesn't reach them because of how she internalizes a wide range of influences: her parents plus her relatives, her teachers, her friends, her neighborhood, television programs she watches, favorite web sites, books she reads, the clown she loves or the stuffed dog she is afraid of, the store clerk who is abrupt, the slide that is too high, the spelling words that are too boring.

You can't help having high hopes for your only child, but they can be tempered. The new crop of onlies are more likely to have parents who are much more prudent. "I would like my child to go to the most prestigious and finest schools and be recognized as excellent in a career such as law, writing, medicine, or architecture, but I don't tell her that," explains Sharon Stein-Cardonsky, mother of thirteen-year-old Lauren. "She understands that she must take her schoolwork seriously. We are trying to be very low key and quiet about our goals for her for fear of a negative reaction."

High school senior Scott Scranton talks about his academic record. "My parents expect me to get good grades, but they realize that I'm not an Albert Einstein. As long as I maintain B's, they're pretty happy."

Whether or not your child excels academically, she probably has strengths you can encourage and in which you can take pride. Being proud is very different from living vicariously through your child. Being a role model by expressing contentment with your own pursuits is more effective than expressing your dreams for your child or being a tough taskmaster.

Dr. Deborah Matro, a psychiatrist in private practice and an assistant professor of psychiatry, highlights another reason why parents should rein in their dreams. "Parents must recognize that a child has his or her own dreams to fulfill. Whether it's an only child or a child with siblings, if parents exert too much pressure, they are not allowing the child to develop his own sense of self-worth. The danger is in the parent not being interested in and not supporting the child's dreams. In devaluing or dismissing your child's own goals, he will get a sense that nothing matters. You must convey to the child that what he wants and what he does matter."

"I wanted to be a ballet dancer," teenage romance writer Felice Roberts angrily reports. "My mother wanted me to be a pianist. There was a constant conflict between her love of music and my desire to dance. I wound up being neither."

Demanding performance from a child who may not be capable of meeting the expectation or interested in it is frustrating for everyone and could create a backlash the effect of which might not be seen for years. To reduce the amount of pressure on an only child, Dr. Sylvia Saltzstein highly recommends that parents have other activities and interests so that there is less time to focus on every inch of a singleton's progress. It's a step in the right direction just to be aware that putting all your energy into your child may not be the best thing for her.

The Super-child Syndrome

A "stage mother" mentality can consume parents regardless of how many offspring they have. Everyone today seems to be pushing for "star" children. Learning tools for the in-utero set, infant swimming lessons, and computer programs for toddlers supposedly give youngsters a head start. Books promise to have a child reading by three and toilet trained in one day. These high-pressure tactics, once thought to be the exclusive territory of parents of one, have become pervasive.

Nevertheless parents of onlies who feel they have "one shot" at creating an outstanding child remain the ones most easily swayed by the desire to give their youngsters a jump on the group. Parents of singletons have more time to push a stroller from museum to museum and to follow the directions on each gimmick that claims to create a superior child. "Only" parents—like all parents—can jeopardize their child's natural progress.

"My mother overdoes the lessons: piano lessons, gymnastics lessons, ballet lessons. Every day after school I go somewhere for a lesson. I have no time to myself," complains Mitzy Finn, age nine. Like Mitzy, many children, only and otherwise, are overprogrammed, overprodded, and given little choice in how they spend their free time.

Parental efforts to create super-children are being condemned by child-care experts. David Elkind, former president of the National Association for the Education of Young Children, was so alarmed by the trend to hurry children along that he has devoted a book to the topic, *Miseducation: Preschoolers at Risk.*

"Formal training," points out Dr. Elkind in his book, "has no lasting benefits for preschoolers." A good many only children advance amazingly well without any prodding. They are motivated and stimulated by their parents' interests and activities and by their routine input, which is generally greater than in the family with two or three children. "Gold-Medal parents who enter youngsters in athletic or other competitions before they are five are miseducating their children, putting them at risk for no purpose," warns Elkind.[7]

It's hard not to worry that your child will be at the back of the pack if she is absent from the regime of karate, tennis, soccer, and ski instruction. Of course you want your child to be accomplished, but a sense of reasonableness is in order.

Some children have strong preferences, and parents should honor them. Don't force your seven-year-old to show ponies if she would rather paint pictures or brush her dog. The same liberties should be given the older child. Permit her to train in areas of interest to her or to compete in activities she enjoys, not the ones you feel will make her a stand-out success.

Informal training when force-fed to children can be just as damaging as premature attempts to advance your child. Cheryl Lincoln, a Midwest mother, reports proudly, "We read Tim *Beowulf;* he's very mature." Five-year-old Tim, however, cannot dress himself. Like many parents of onlies, this mother has no point of reference. She has so much invested emotionally in Tim that it's difficult for her to see that he's headed off track, and that she's the one derailing him by her own efforts.

Look at the big picture: Isn't your child's health, eagerness to engage in activities, learn, be with friends, and relate well to people more crucial than having a shelf full of Little League trophies or having been exposed to *Beowulf* before first grade?

The Race to Educate

It's almost impossible to ignore the emphasis and pressure on children to do well in school. "Higher education has become a preoccupation for children even before they reach puberty."[8] Stakes are high and most parents know it early on. Peter Relic, former U.S. deputy assistant secretary for education, remarked, "Parents lecture you [kindergarten teachers] on the realities of a competitive economic world and high test scores of Japanese five-year-olds. Parents' overzealous and ill-timed concerns are not lost on the children, no matter how young. That kind of anxiety is contagious."[9]

Elizabeth Harrison was unduly influenced by the head of her daughter's nursery school. "This woman was positive Jacqueline would get into the city's gifted program and advised me to have her tested. Of course, the mere hearing that my child could get into the gifted program went right to my head. We did eventually have her tested and she did well, but not well enough to get into the program. That set me back. It was an ego thing at first; it bothered me.

Now I don't feel that competitive for her. I don't necessarily want her to be a lawyer or doctor. I don't want her to be someone who is so driven that her whole life is her career."

The race to educate can be very distressing to parents of only children. The first point at which they may be "brought up short" is when kindergarten readiness is measured. It is particularly difficult for parents of an only to accept that their child is not ready for school or to be told that she was initially overplaced and should repeat a given year. In spite of parents' extra efforts, a child may need more time.

Let's assume for the moment that you have a son about to enter kindergarten. Your son's birthday is one month before the cut-off date for your school district or the private school that you hope will accept him. Your son, solely because he is a boy (boys tend to develop physically and mature emotionally at a slower pace than girls) or maybe because he is small or because he cannot sit still for extended periods of time, is not truly ready to start school. Do you hold your only child back until next year? You wouldn't dream of it. Correct?

Like many, you would probably feel that starting him the following year would be a reflection on you. Theoretically, you have had ample time to work with him. He has had more attention, more learning experiences, more exposure to the outside world than many other children. And what's more, people might accuse you of not being able to "let go."

School readiness tests are very reliable indicators of a child's developmental age. This is the age at which a child's mind and body work together to perform tasks and function with a certain ease. It is developmental age, not chronological age, that determines school readiness. Prekindergarten and transitional classes have been initiated for children who need some catch-up time. A "late" kindergarten start can only have positive effects on a child who is not yet ready.

Parents of one can become myopic. If you banked on raising

an exceptional child and she's average, you must adjust your expectations accordingly. Don't lose sight of the fact that an affectionate, kindhearted kid will give you more joy than one studious, self-directed child who has no time for fun.

"I wanted my son to be a fulfilled, happy person, satisfied with his life and career," says Harriet Kean of her college-age only who is studying to be a photojournalist. "He was directed to have good, honest values, which he has." Harriet Kean set an attainable goal for her son, a goal that was reached without painful brooding and disappointment for parent or child. Realistic expectations—be they educational or social—bring gratification to all parties.

Blinders On

"My mother thought everything I did was perfect, but I knew everything I did was not perfect. From her point of view, I could never do anything wrong, yet I knew my grades weren't always terrific and I knew I wasn't always getting along with my friends. Therefore, I could never rely on her for a straight answer about anything," states William Sheehan.

If a child cannot get a reliable reading from her own parents, where can she get it? The only has no sister to tell her that her makeup is silly, no brother to tell her she's out of line with a friend or that her behavior is bothersome.

The kid can do no wrong, you think. Not my child! She's perfect. She's innocent. You balk at the mere suggestion that your toddler provoked a fight or your innocent-looking adolescent was smoking dope or snorting cocaine at the junior prom. Couldn't be. You are adamant about that.

It could be. The only in your house has a personality that may be very different outside the house. Reconsider before you staunchly defend her. The proverbial wool may be pulled tightly over your eyes. Parents of onlies, because they have so much invested, have a hard time accepting that their child may have done something unacceptable or potentially harmful to herself.

Joy Smarak is unable to look up as she tells of learning that her only child was using drugs. "We were so close that I refused to believe what the principal of her high school was telling me. As the principal related the events, I replied, 'Impossible,' although the pieces of his story were fitting together and pointing directly at my daughter. By the time our meeting was over, I bravely told him that I would look into it. By the time I got to my car, I was drenched in tears. I knew his accusations were on-target. My child was smoking pot, and God knows what else she was using. I had been denying it and unable to challenge her because I didn't want to see or know."

Parents of one must try to be objective and attempt to see what is really going on in their child's world, whether that child is a preschooler or a teenager. They must be open to criticism about their child and search for the truth in what they are observing or hearing.

"'Parent wishing,'" as Dr. Matro calls it, "[is] being blind to a child's faults stems from a parent's desire to see the child as special because in doing so it enhances the parent's self-esteem. To accomplish this, a parent minimizes any difficulties that arise."

When disagreements, disparities, or frictions develop, listen to both sides. There's a fifty-fifty chance your child is wrong. If she's wrong, be sure she understands why. If a child lies, call her on it. It doesn't matter what her age or how small the dishonesty. You can tell yourself, "one child, one lie, not a big thing." You can tell yourself that you know the truth, that she has time to learn. She might not. Recognize your child's faults and deal with them.

Perhaps you've noticed your only bends the rules a bit when playing games and the bend is regularly in her favor. Or she might blatantly cheat. Cheating is something most children try sooner or later. Pretending you don't notice her tactics is the same as affirming them. Talk to her in private, not in front of her friends and not in the middle of the game. Ask her, Why is it wrong to cheat? She probably knows the answers: It's dishonest and in time her friends will not want to play with her.

Your only child may have a less serious fault that you would rather not notice. Let's say she's a hoarder. It appears that she is hoarding not only her own possessions, but also barrettes and nail polish that belong to friends. Talk it out, don't wait for her to outgrow the tendency. Maybe she borrows, but forgets to return. Help her remember to bring things back to their owners. A fault may be as minor as forgetting to make her bed, clear the table, or call her grandparents. Don't ignore it because small things are often the ones that shape personality and help turn a young person into a considerate adult. For the forgetful only child, post a list of reminders.

Perhaps your only has feelings that are too easily hurt. Only children are used to kid-glove treatment at home. When a friend slights them, they are instantly crushed; the initial response is, "So-and-so doesn't like me." Some parents of only children are shocked that another child might not like their child. In the course of your child's life there will be many people who won't like her. Be prepared to face this reality. You can help your child deal with her feelings of hurt and rejection by asking her to tell you what happened and by offering suggestions for handling the situation should it be repeated.

Removing the blinders can also be overdone. Says Stacey Gibson, an adult only who works in the human resource department of a large corporation, "They saw my faults almost to a fault. For my mother, being like her was terrific, but being different was wrong. There was a strong emphasis on being physically perfect. My hair had to be right; my makeup had to be right. If my nails were too short, my mother told me to stop biting them. If I wasn't standing straight, I was reminded. I always felt my mother wanted me to be something I wasn't."

Harping on perceived faults can be corrosive; it eats away at a child's self-image. Remember, there is no peer living in the house for the child to turn to for corroboration that her parents are being overly critical.

If you want your child to have faith in your guidance and to follow your advice (most of the time), take off the blinders, but be constructive in your evaluations and offer useful advice.

State-of-the-Art Child

Exquisitely dressed, perfectly mannered, impeccable use of the language. You want your child to do everything right.

Parents of onlies pride themselves on their ability to raise model children who can be taken anywhere—to the theater, to a concert, or to a four-star restaurant for a six-course meal. This state-of-the-art child is fully trained by the age of four and behaves as if she were a well-bred forty-year-old. She can sit still through three acts of Shakespeare, two hours of Wagner, and an entire gourmet meal without so much as a whimper or squirm.

Psychologist E. W. Bohannon talked about such demands on the only child back in 1898: "It may be gratifying to some parents to have a child of theirs, while yet in knee breeches or short dresses, spoken of as a 'deep thinker,' or a 'perfect gentleman,' a 'perfect lady,' etc., but it is a pleasure of a cheap sort and paid for at the price of stunted and abnormal growth."[10]

Although he exaggerates the consequences, Bohannon makes the point: The perfect child stands to miss out on her childhood. There's no room for mud pies, tattered jeans, and swells of laughter. Forced structure often leads to frustration and/or behavior problems in other areas.

Parents with a number of children have difficulty keeping tabs on behavior. They easily overlook a napkin not placed on a lap; they are off in another part of the library when one of their children races through the stacks playing Indian. In the case of perfectionist parents, siblings may not divert the scrutiny, but typically, when there are three children in the house, none of them is perpetually under the microscope. Instead of hearing "Stop biting your nails" every day, a child with siblings may hear it every third day.

Parents of onlies must force themselves to look the other way occasionally: Let her out in the gaudy outfit she assembled, no matter how much it offends your sensibilities; let her think you don't notice the eyeliner that's blackening her ten-year-old lids; leave her bed messy if she made it, no matter what company you have coming. A dirty face or clay under the fingernails is a good indication that your child is having fun. Demands to stay clean, be neat, and act properly are horribly annoying to a child.

Don't ask your youngster to accomplish tasks normally mastered at a much later age. For the very young, holding a fork properly is downright hard work, a giant accomplishment that should be cheered. Not every two-year-old speaks in complete sentences; your five-year-old may want (and need) her training wheels for another year; and your eight-year-old may feel safer and go to sleep faster with a night light.

"Hold your fork correctly" and related demands are requests to keep low on your priority list during those early years. If she manages the fork, great. If not, focus on easier jobs until her manual dexterity improves. Not much is gained other than a modicum of parental ego satisfaction when the popular opinion is that your child is mature for her age. Dr. Steven Reiss, psychologist and professor at Ohio State University has another take: "Parents who brag about their children's looks, dress, or social graces are vicariously satisfying their own desire for status."[11] The child's elegant manners and eloquent speech may make her seem older, but her emotional level is probably much closer to her real age.

Select restaurants and intellectual outings that are suitable, that stimulate her interest and broaden her perspective. Frequent family restaurants where a child can feel comfortable if she wiggles in her chair or wants to investigate the rest rooms several times during the course—one course—of the meal. Attend puppet shows, children's theater, and musical presentations that talk to her on her terms.

Babying the Baby . . .
Or, All Grown Up at Four

Many parents push their children ahead with one hand and hold them back with the other. The extremes regularly snag parents of only children. Either end of the rearing spectrum leaves the only child vulnerable to being overly coddled or forced into maturity too quickly.

Pet phrases such as "you'll always be my baby" and "little guy" do not encourage separation. Not permitting her to sleep over at friends' homes, to go to the movies with friends (once safety is no longer an issue), or to attend overnight camp—these and similar restrictions—contribute to keeping the baby a baby.

"My mother babied me," says Henry Wallman. "She was very anxious because I had been ill as a young child. She was concerned about any physical activity that was risky. I'm not talking about being a trapeze artist, I'm talking about ice skating or biking."

"It's hard to let go of an only child," notes Marney Yoto. "Your child is getting older; you don't have another one coming up. To be able to let go is probably the key."

Physicist Frank Owens, an only child who is raising his own only child, believes that "you have to give a child more and more responsibility so that eventually he feels good about dealing with the world. During my younger years I had no confidence in myself because of my parents' excessive regulations and their unwillingness to let my sense of responsibility grow. It hit me during my teen years. At eighteen or twenty I was scared to death to ask a girl out on a date.

"My approach with my son is very different. I am less rigid and give him more responsibility so he can think positively and feel good about himself."

When the only child has a steady diet of being treated gingerly, she cannot learn how to do things for herself. If she doesn't learn to make her own decisions, she will ultimately be unable to make sound choices for herself. Babying the baby, while comforting and safe for some parents, is detrimental to your child's flourishing independence.

As dangerous as shielding your child is, too much exposure to and too much time spent in an adult world is equally unhealthy. These experiences do not replace hours engaged in fantasy play, rugged afternoons of snowball fights and sledding, or time spent on swing sets and jungle gyms. Do not slip into a pattern of treating your only child as a grown-up because everyone else in the household is adult.

According to only child Amy Sommer, "I benefited from going to the office and the opera with my father, but I grew up too fast. I did not feel part of my peer group until I went to college. Everyone told me my friends would catch up, but you are who you are at the time. As a child, I was much more comfortable with older people. I would not want my child to feel as much an outsider as I did by being an adult too young."

Within the close-knit unit of three, only children work to elevate themselves to their parents' level. Be cautious if you notice your child competing on your level. A daughter, for example, may be eager to prove that she is smarter or more clever than her mother; a son, braver or more rugged than his father.

Surrounded by adults, an only child may well seem, and in many cases be, more grown up than her peers. One mother, who grew up with a sibling, phrased it this way: "My daughter is never after me to do kidlike things. When I was her age, I was a monster, always demanding to be taken to the movies, swimming, or ice-skating."

"It's a different perspective when you are the only child," states Emily Bauer, an adult only and mother of two sons. "You grow up more quickly because you go visiting with your parents or are part of the company when adults visit your home. My children do not have as close a relationship with my friends as I have and had with my parents' friends because they have each other."

If your friends become her friends to the exclusion of peers, she will get along well with adults, probably wonderfully, but she won't have the foggiest notion of how to deal with children her own age.

Parents of onlies have a clear option. Bunny Eldridge, who raised her only child in New York City, accepted her son's not wanting to go to restaurants or be around adults. "We did not thrust him into the adult world when he didn't want to be there. We hired a sitter and, as he got older, let him stay home alone or with a friend."

Onlies Need Not Be Lonely

In the past, only children were automatically thought to be lonely children. Today if isolation or loneliness strikes the only child, it does so in spotty, temporary episodes. Although time alone is essential for developing creativity and the ability to function independently, only children must have companionship from both parents and peers.

Human beings are inherently social. A child who keeps to himself and is lonely as a result, has learned this behavior. With child care and group activities a way of life for very young children, it is easy for onlies to socialize. From the earliest years, parents should surround their only child with playmates and keep up this practice through elementary and high school.

But exercise moderation when scheduling a child's free time. There's a danger of overloading an only child, believing that because he is alone you must compensate by filling every waking hour. A balanced combination of free time and social time teaches onlies both to amuse themselves and to benefit from the stimulation of others.

Certainly by age two a child can relate to another child his age for brief periods. Set up play dates with friends' or neighbors' children. Understand that there may be conflicts about sharing and that the children are more apt to engage in parallel play most of the time they are together. Begin leaving your child for short intervals of half an hour. To make the arrangement equitable, switch homes regularly.

"I made a point of keeping up with play dates starting when Justin was barely eighteen months old," recalls Marney Yoto. "In fact, three of the children from back then are still his good friends. Not only is it important for the child, but it's also important for the mother of one to have someone to talk to about childrearing."

Parents who have several children are not nearly so desperate to make play dates as parents of onlies. You can be made to feel like an annoying salesman reciting his telephone pitch. "I've had to make as many as seven or eight phone calls to find someone for my daughter to play with. It's a good thing that I felt secure that she's a great kid or I would have started taking the rejection personally. Mothers with other kids don't have the same compulsion to make plans. They simply say, 'Play with your brother.' The worst is when parents say things like, 'It must be tough on you. Do you play with her when you can't find someone?' Of course I did, but I would never admit it then," confesses Caroline Russell.

Sandy MacDonald had a different approach. "I was not my daughter's constant playmate," she recalls. "When she was little she would come home from school and pretend things for hours; she became accustomed very early to being very social and to being very self-sufficient in terms of playing."

Seeking preschool playmates on a regular basis can be time-consuming and frustrating but worth the effort until your child is old enough to do it himself (the Russells' seven-year-old has been making her own arrangements for the past year). Kelly Paul, mother of a four-year-old girl, advises, "The best thing to do is plan in advance."

Don't wait until the morning of a day off from school to find out who is available. Make calls and firm plans a few days ahead. When possible, set up steady engagements: Every Tuesday after nursery school he plays with John; every Friday with Scott.

What happens when you don't socialize your only child early? Jan Callahan knows. "My son had a hard time with nursery school. When he was very young, I was his playmate, his only playmate. It took five weeks before I could leave the building without a scene."

Early socialization will not prevent anxiety about separation for every child, but it will reduce its intensity and duration. Lisa Danford, who had exposed her son to other children before he could walk, was mortified when he suddenly, at the age of three, refused to attend his two-hour, twice-a-week nursery school sessions. "I had a child who was a school dropout before his fourth birthday. I disliked the idea that his reluctance just fed the mouths of mothers who thought the problem was caused by Jimmy's singularity." For Jimmy Danford, early play proved beneficial; his hesitancy to attend nursery school was short-lived.

Susan Leites reaped the highest reward of early interaction when her son began nursery school. "On the first day when the mothers were supposed to stay, my child said, 'Why are you here? Go home.' "

During preschool years some children, onlies or otherwise, are just not ready—or not in the mood a particular month or week—to be on their own. If separation is a problem and you are able to keep your child home with you, take him out of nursery school for a week or two until he feels more comfortable about leaving you.

"These bouts of anxiety are not unusual in this age group," observes nursery school director Paula Cole. "However, separation anxiety is more acute when the first born is expecting a brother or sister than it is with only children.

"Many times when there is an only child, that child is used to being left," notes Cole. "With one, it's easy to drop him off with a friend, relative, or sitter. The only child is accustomed to being with other people and does not feel the same anxiety as the young child who is trying to make sense out of the changes in his family."

Friends Are Vital

"My daughter is very connected to me," states Lisa Turk, "and that strong connection is why I make sure she's involved with other people, especially children her own age. She calls my good friends 'Aunt' and is close friends with their children. I make sure she is comfortable in their homes, which is part of forming close relationships."

Parents of onlies who do not offer early interaction with other children and adults may pay a price. "I suppose it's my fault," remarked a distressed Maria Louise Endicott as she attempted to get out of the clutches of her hysterical five-year-old. It was September and the tenth day of kindergarten. "She's never been left with anyone other than her grandmother. I never let her play at anyone's house. I just never left her," she lamented, embarrassed and on the verge of tears.

On consideration, this woman's mistake is apparent. What may not be so obvious is the fact that grandparents, aunts, and close adult friends are not substitutes for playmates who are near in age and who live in what initially are unfamiliar surroundings. No matter how much a parent prepares a child for school, preparation is more effective when it is learned from someone his own size.

Nor are siblings a panacea for emotional adjustment to peers outside the family or the find-a-friend problem. "My kids," points out Shannon Woodriff, mother of three, "want friends to play with. There's no stature in playing with a sibling; no degree of acceptance into their peer group can be gained from playing with each other. Plain and simple, they want to be with a friend, not their sister or brother. When they are forced to play together because there is no alternative, they fight."

In short, parents with more than one child will also have some arranging to do. The process is much briefer and simpler if you can send your child out the front door and have friends right there.

The benefits of a neighborhood cannot be undervalued, especially for the only child. "I don't think my daughter feels lonely at all because we live in a development," says Gail Shore, the mother of a six-year-old only. "On any given day there are twenty children out there with their bicycles and I make sure she constantly has a lot of children around her."

"I had a happy childhood," notes thirty-year-old Harvey Swann, "because I had friends in my neighborhood. I could always walk to someone's house if I wanted company."

Anne Marie Soto talks about her situation. "I often jokingly say if my daughter had her way, she would be the youngest of five. We live in an old-fashioned neighborhood and the other children are crazy about her. They stop by to take her for walks. If we lived in a different environment, I could see having one as a problem. As it worked out, I have the benefit of neighbors' children, and when I can't stand it, I send them home."

A teenager at this point, Nancy Armour's son blossomed through neighborhood existence from the time he was two until he was twelve. She says, "It's important to try to live in an area which has friendships geographically built in. That's where John learned give-and-take, how to get along with older children as well as younger children. The ten years of a neighbor network were one of the most important factors in his life. The neighborhood was like a family; he was a person within it."

John Armour confirms his mother's analysis. "I never yearn for a sibling, even when I'm alone and no one is home. Sure, there are those odd times it would be nice to have a brother or sister to play a board game with, but as I get older, I wish for a brother or sister less. Friends are more important in my life."

There are a lot of misconceptions about the only child's supposed wish for a sibling. When they have friends nearby, most only children don't think about it and few dwell on the subject. In response to the question Does your child ask for a sibling? many parents of onlies answered as Gail Shore did: "Lia never asks for a sibling, but I make a conscious effort to have her in many afterschool activities and make sure she has play dates regularly. I don't rely solely on the neighborhood children always being available."

Even major cities have pocket neighborhoods with large family populations. New York City attorney Howard Vogel and his wife recommend moving to the parts of the city in which children are the rule rather than the exception. "We did not change apartments early on in our son's life and it was harder for him to see his friends."

Raised in rural Florida, Judy Lynn Prince's mother went to extra lengths to be sure her daughter's free time was filled by peers. "My mother imported children for me from a very young age. We lived twenty-five miles from civilization in a town with a population of two thousand and that's counting dogs and cats. She carted friends back and forth for me."

As technology increasingly "runs" our children's lives, the lack of immediate access to friends becomes less of an issue. "We live in the middle of nowhere," says Lorraine Brewer, whose daughter is entering the eleventh grade. "After school and on weekends, when my daughter was much younger she complained she was bored. Now, she comes home and gets on the computer and 'talks' to her friends online. There's so much less isolation for onlies now; groups of her friends are online together. It's better than the telephone for teenagers. She feels totally connected without being face to face."

Not all onlies see proximity to friends as a significant factor. "I grew up in the country in Vermont without neighborhoods," says Candice Crummley. "It was a car ride to get to a friend's house, but I never said to myself, 'I have no one to play with.' I was never lonely. My parents planned well in the sense that there was always something constructive for me to do. They filled in my slack time."

Once you've created a friend-filled environment, your child is on his own. "You can't make your child popular; you can only make popularity possible," notes Nancy Armour. "A child either has that knack or he doesn't." Onlies often do.

After decades of watching children in classrooms, teacher Deejay Schwartz believes only children have the qualities that ingratiate them to others. "I find that onlies are friendly and very interested in the other children. I don't notice that they seek friends as much as they attract friends because their inner direction makes them creative and interesting."

What parents of only children can do is encourage their child to be with friends, to participate in group activities or team sports, all of which expose a child to many different points of view. Sometimes a busy social life simply is not in that person's nature. Some children prefer to have fewer friends; whether this preference is dictated by their singleness or temperament is open to debate.

"Abigail is a loner," acknowledges her mother, Terze Gluck, "but she is not at all lonely. If I try to force more play dates on her, she quickly tells me that she is the best judge. Unless I see signs of stress or unhappiness, I leave her to her two or three friends. Her attachments, however they appear to me, mean something to her."

Evelyn Wolff remarks that she, too, always had one or two good friends. "I found it difficult to make casual friends, but had no trouble making intimate friends. I still don't have problems with close friends."

A pattern of a few close friends is apparent among only children. Lisa Denne Reilly is another example. "I don't have trouble forming a few good friendships, but I do have trouble going out in a crowd and making lots of shallow acquaintances."

Best friends of onlies at all ages can be and often are sibling replacements. Adult only Helen Amonte says of her twelve-year-old daughter, "Jessica always has had a best friend. Onlies look at friends as siblings. Her friendships are very strong."

Ninth grader Leslie Porter is serious when she discusses her friendships. "My best friend, Caroline, is like my sister. Being an only child makes me closer to my friends. I'm sure I relate better to my friends than most."

If your only seems to need someone beyond his day-to-day friends, the computer opens outlets for sharing secrets and problems that the only child might not want to or be able to discuss with a parent. Consider helping your child find a safe online group who can be on the receiving end of confidences and confessions that other children may share with a brother or sister. Whatever your child's age, you will want to monitor online access to protect him or her from dangers and inappropriate information.

Be it one dear friend or an assortment of buddies, friendships are the keys to successful, happy only childhoods . . . and lives. "My friendships were more important to me than to children from larger families," notes Richard Dewhurst, "because friendship was my contact to the outside world. I tended to make very good friends and kept them."

In the scheme of friendship among children, Dewhurst is in the minority. Because of the shuffling that goes on as children switch grades or parents relocate, it's the rare individual—with or without siblings—that holds onto his childhood friends throughout his life. Michael Thompson, a psychologist and school counselor in Cambridge, Massachusetts, stresses that "a long-term friendship isn't a developmental need . . . not every child needs a best friend every year," especially when they are young. "On average," he adds, "childhood friendships last for a year."[1]

Lessons Friends Teach

Children determine their self-worth in large part through relationships with and acceptance by their peer group. How only children interact in childhood influences their adult relationships. Friends teach onlies important lessons in standing up for themselves and for their rights.

Onlies must have the opportunity to work out normal conflicts and anger that they don't get in a small family unit. Absent the normal arguing (and making up) between brothers and sisters, the only child can have difficulty understanding fighting and may fear it or shy away from it. To the only who has little experience with peer quarreling, a fight can mean lost friendship or companionship.

Ellen Stern, the mother of two, feels a major deficit in this area. "The fact that I grew up without sibling competition made it very difficult for me to compete in other situations. I have a hard time telling my children how to argue or work out a problem they may be having in a social situation because I was not in that position very often. When I was, I backed off or withdrew. To this day, I can't deal with people in a tactful, diplomatic manner."

Although Stern blames her lack of siblings for her inability to approach conflict head on, most believe the "skills" to argue and handle conflict can be learned from friends. Ganie DeHart of the State University of New York found that "sibling relationships and friendships provide substantially different interaction contexts for your children and require them to use different social skills and strategies for managing conflict."[2] In short, a fight with a sibling is very different from a fight with a friend. Relationships with peers teach effective communication and discipline in handling aggression—vital coping skills that can't all be learned at home. These are lessons in power and consequences that children learn outside the family, as painful as they may sometimes be.[3]

An explanation from parents of what to expect in friendship will serve the only child well. Tell your child that he does not have to acquiesce during every disagreement and that friends will not necessarily desert him if they have an argument. If your child is particularly timid, role-playing will give him skills to deal with peers. However, the best instructor by far is experience.

In the course of growing up, every child faces some difficult issue. A boy who is small will learn to use his mouth instead of his body to equalize his chances in a disagreement. Similarly, the only child who feels deprived of shouting matches over a bicycle borrowed without permission and the continual abrasiveness created by sibling rivalry will find a friend with whom to do battle when he has the urge. And when he needs a confidant because it feels like both parents are against him or are unapproachable, he will pour his heart out to that same friend. Only children are resourceful; they find ways to meet their needs.

Professor Henry Wallman is a firm believer that a child doesn't have to live with siblings to learn how to deal with near- or same-age children. You can create situations that, while not exactly like sibling relationships, offer many of the same experiences. Clubs, teams, scouting, religious organizations, and instructional classes offer the only child plenty of opportunity to learn the art of encountering someone his own age successfully.

But, you may not be covering all the bases if your child regularly plays with one friend at a time. Adult only Marguerite Fitzsimmons offers a word of caution: "I saw Donald very much as I saw myself as a child. In grammar school I was jealous of best friends if they had other good friends; I could not share my friends well. I noticed a similar reaction in Donald as a youngster—he would get along well with one child, but when he couldn't have that child to himself, the situation became difficult for him."

The way around this potential problem is to involve your child periodically with small groups of children. As he gets older and makes his friendship preferences clear, there will be little else you can do in regard to jealousy other than helping him to deal with it by talking with you about his feelings.

Since socializing with other children is paramount to the only child, wise parents will ignore minor annoyances to protect key friendships. Refrain from belittling your child's friends and diminishing them in his eyes. Most friends your child selects have merits, but at times parents can't see them.

Keith Adams lists the faults of each of his ten-year-old's friends. "Daniel has the worst taste in companions. Tim is dull; Parker has no sense of adventure; Brandon is boring . . . What does he see in these kids? Can't you find him some interesting friends?" he complains to his wife.

"I go down a whole list of playmates"—Barbara Cross shakes her head in perplexity as she speaks—"and David says, 'No, I don't want to play with him . . . or her.' Months later I find out that one child I had suggested is the class troublemaker; another is into baseball, a sport in which David has no interest; one of the others

David finally tells me doesn't like to be touched. David is very affectionate and 'touchy.' David's instincts were right for him. My feelings that so-and-so appeared to be a bright, fun child were meaningless from David's point of view. I have learned to respect what he says rather than forcing a friendship he doesn't want and won't last anyway."

"In the best of all worlds," advises only child Bob Parlapiano, "you have to trust your child's judgment in choosing his friends. I grew up in a tough, sixties-seventies drug environment, but I never had to hide from my parents the fact that someone I knew died of an overdose. I knew my parents wouldn't say, 'I hope you're not hanging around with that group or doing drugs.' "

Parents of one should think of twelve-year-old Hallie Borg when they are tempted to criticize their child's buddies. "You have to rely on friends a lot to keep you company," she says. Choosing and making friends is essential to the only child's well-being and social functioning.

The More the Merrier

"My mother, because she was one of five and I was an only child, made an enormous attempt to keep an open house so I would have lots of friends around. Often ours was the place friends came to after school. It was a welcome place," Katie Crosby recalls happily.

"As a parent of an only child, you have a real responsibility to have children into your home and to have your child visit other friends' homes often," says family therapist Fredda Bruckner-Gordon. "They need exposure and give-and-take experiences in their early life."

Rita Graham discusses one choice open to older onlies. "When my granddaughter [age sixteen] came to visit this summer, I told her to bring a friend. They both stayed for six weeks. My granddaughter has other friends in my area, but this was closer to sisters living in the same house. They had their fights; they loved each other; they hated each other; they borrowed clothes and talked late into the night. If you make your home available to friends, your only can act out many of the sibling experiences."

Not all parents or grandparents can invite a child's friend to stay for a month or more—and most parents would not send their child to someone's home for such an extended period—but it is not a major inconvenience to cook one more hamburger for dinner or prepare an extra peanut butter and jelly sandwich for lunch. As frequently as you can, invite one of your child's friends to stay for a meal. When you can bear them, sleepovers create a great sense of comradeship among children. Your child will delight in sharing his room as often as you allow it. An extra person changes family dynamics, exposes your only to other people's quirks, and diffuses the focused attention the only child normally receives.

Some of the most trying times for only children are adult events they are forced to attend. It is the sole complaint seventeen-year-old Astrid Lance has about being an only child. "When I had to go somewhere I didn't want to go and I knew there would not be any other children around, it bothered me more than anything else. I would have liked a brother or sister for those occasions."

If your young only child has to accompany adults, arrange for one of his friends to go with you or try to have someone for your child to play with wherever you are going. When visiting in another state, ask your host or hostess to set up play time with one of the local children—a playmate can be slightly older or younger—or to hire a teenage baby-sitter who will take your child to a park or play games with him.

Special outings—the museum, the circus, a movie, a magic show, children's play—are more fun when a child shares them with someone his own age. Jennifer Walsh remembers, "I always hoped for a friend to come along when I was younger because my parents would not go on rides with me or do the more adventuresome activities." A companion brings excitement to the dullest event or the most boring excursion. And the guest's parents, especially if they have several children, will be grateful. Your expedition will win your only a warm welcome in their home, a place where he can see other rules and other family styles.

Whenever possible, invite one of your child's friends to join you for short vacations as well. For Nancy Armour as a child, more would have been merrier. "During summer vacations I wanted to go to the same place that I knew my friends went every year so we would get to know a lot of people and it wouldn't be just us. I felt isolated with my parents. Vacations and holiday meals were the two times I found being an only child depressing."

During the first six or seven years, when it is unlikely a parent will allow his child to travel with another family, plan vacations with other families who have children compatible with yours. "When we plan our summer vacation, we plan to be near friends who have a child the same age as Justin," explains Marney Yoto. "We've done that in the past and will do so until he is ready to bring a friend along."

"I keep a friend for the whole vacation when we go away during the school year," says Lorraine Brewer. "That limits our traveling to relatively close areas and fewer trips because we can't afford to pay for another person on an expensive trip that includes an airline flight. But without a friend, at age sixteen, she would be bored out of her mind." Another possibility is to ask the parents of a child you would like to include in your vacation if they could help with part of the expenses. Generally, if you are gracious enough to invite someone's child, the parents will offer.

To widen your base and enhance the festivities without friends, include family members in your plans. Schedule once- or twice-a-year vacations with relatives who are far away. Plan to meet your brother and his family or your cousin and her family at a convenient location for a week, weekend, or brief holiday celebration. In the only-child family, cousins become—and should be—elevated in importance. Send your child to visit his cousin Christopher during a school holiday or for a week in the summer.

"I have a girl cousin about my age," says Mary Kelly Selover. "She was a surrogate sister; she did everything with us—went on vacations with us and was at our house fifty percent of the time. We're still very close."

"A single child needs a support system, a safety net. We're building one by getting together with cousins as often as we can," explains Carla Vozios, who drives four hours one way on a weekend so that her son can be with his cousins and get to know his aunt and uncle well.

In addition to adding interest and warm feelings, reaching out to family and friends has long-term feedback. Those who surround your child during his growing years become his memory bank of experiences. He will have people as important in his life as the most superlative sisters or brothers, people who share his past and with whom he can laugh and recall the "good times."

Alone, but Not Lonely

The growing years will be less problematic if your child has learned to play well by himself as well as with others. During the often distressing adolescent years, when rejection by friends can be a factor and there is sometimes a shortage of appropriate activities, the only child should do well because he has learned to occupy himself with independent projects.

Suzi Rudd Cohen, whose daughter was an only child until she reached eight years of age, is "convinced that only children are more industrious and resourceful because they are alone and have to amuse themselves."

Marguerite Fitzsimmons, who originally thought being alone was a serious drawback, re-evaluates as her seventeen-year-old only approaches adulthood. "I see alone time as a strength. Donald is very self-reliant and very clear about what to do in an emergency. He's comfortable as a teenager entertaining himself—reading a book, doing a project. He is never bored and never says, 'I have nothing to do.' He has a great imagination and I think that's from having to entertain himself. He was forced to be creative."

As the parent of a young only you may hear, "I have nothing to do," or "I'm bored" more often than you would like. To encourage creativity and spark young imaginations, ask your child to practice being bored. Explain that there is nothing wrong with doing nothing and within a few minutes—probably after serious complaining—your youngster will have discovered or dreamed up something to do on his own.

Larry Brand was a high school and college track and basketball star—hardly a loner in the sense we commonly mean it, yet that is what he considers himself. "My first inclination is to be alone, yet I have no problem with people or being part of a group. I don't tend to seek out others; I'm very content by myself. If I have projects to do, I find it fulfilling to do them alone."

The capacity to entertain oneself serves a person well in later life. Everyone has periods of time in which they are without other people. It is more enjoyable when that time alone is productive. It's a positive feeling to know how to be by yourself without having to run, without having to be busy every minute. There is a strong tendency on the part of parents to fear that their child is lonesome and, hence, deprived. When your only is happily occupied with an endeavor, view his contentment as a plus. Don't feel compelled to be his playmate or to find him one.

Learn to read your offspring: Some require a lot more social interaction than others. If a child needs friends and doesn't have them, he will feel lonely. Bill Sheehan's parents paid no attention to his need for playmates. He says, "I felt like Robert Frost. The only thing to do after school was wander around, climb trees, and occasionally set fires in the then undeveloped woods. It was horrible for me." If, on the other hand, he's good at entertaining himself, being alone doesn't necessarily mean loneliness. Time alone is valuable, but don't overdo it.

Parents' nights out can be, but don't have to be, especially hard on the only child. Emily Bauer explains: "Having a sibling was not something I dwelled on, but I did think about it when my parents were out and I was home in the evening. I was alone a lot. As a result, I was very sensitive to my children's having companionship. I spent more time with them and shared my interests with them at a younger age than my parents did with me."

Parents of single children who make a concerted effort to be with their children in the evening rather than out every night will be doing their onlies a service. Parents who work and have frenetic business or social demands can diminish loneliness by making plans to fill up what would otherwise be empty time for the only child: sleepovers with friends, dinner with a favorite aunt or uncle, a videotape to view, preparations (package wrapping, card writing) for upcoming holidays or birthdays, photo album organizing, or room rearranging.

Twelve-year-old Lauren Benito lists her one dislike about being an only as "often being lonely until my parents come home from work at about seven-thirty." A few hours alone before dinner are not cause for concern, but if husband and wife can alter their schedules so that one of them arrives home earlier a few evenings a week, Lauren and only children in similar circumstances would be happier.

The ideal solution is to have one parent home whenever possible. A child accepts parental absence more readily when one parent is present. "Our professions call for each of us to be out one night a week, on average," explains attorney Richard Cooper. "Since Emily was an infant, we have alternated nights out. In her six years, she's probably been without one of us on a weekday evening maybe ten times when our commitments overlapped. She doesn't and didn't, even as a toddler, care which one of us was with her. Although we had full-time live-in help, I think covering for each other has made her content and secure."

Helen Amonte, a single working mother, found this viable solution to loneliness: a nonworking mother in her child's class who was interested in a companion for her children after school and in earning some extra money. "Jessica stayed with the same family after school for six years and whenever I was away on business or had an emergency. She learned what it is like to have siblings."

No matter how perfect your arrangements, a favorite baby-sitter cannot measure up to a parent who plays a game, takes his child out to dinner, or becomes involved in an activity that is important to the child, be it baking a cake or building a model spaceship. *Not* acting your age is important if you, like many of today's parents, are older and have only one child. Sociologist Monica Morris found that children of older parents (who are often only children) recalled their childhoods more fondly when their parents were "generous with themselves and their leisure time." One of Ms. Morris's only-child subjects states, " 'You know—being older, as they were, they didn't—we didn't—do a lot of kid stuff.' "[4]

Child development researchers Sharon and Craig Ramey, both older parents, suggest finding aunts and uncles and other people who are younger to be involved in the rough and tumble. "We see twenty-eight-year-old dads versus Sam's fifty-seven-year-old dad . . . and we just play differently with him. I don't think it's horrible, but finding substitutes to complement who you are will benefit your child."

Ross Yearwood, whose father was forty-seven when he was born, feels being available is the main factor. "I was fortunate in that my father retired when I was in the ninth grade. He had a great deal of time for me." Willing involvement by a parent (or parents) forms bonds that will endure, whatever the age of the child . . . or parent. Isn't this part of the reason for having only one?

PART THREE

Making the
Right Decision

9

Just One More

She's everything you've ever wanted. Adorable. Bright. Fun. And a bonus: She's affectionate. You ask yourselves, why not quit while we're ahead? Why not?

It's easy to understand why doubt and indecision arise. Not too long ago, being a parent, more pointedly being a mother, was the main reason for existence. Fallout from this attitude exists and puts considerable pressure on the current childbearing generation. Will you be swayed? The forces are many; their tug is strong. On good days, when your only is being a dream child, you may think, I can do this again.

Until recently, parenting two or more perfect children was the dream, the family status that was envied. "There may be more social pressure to have two children than to become a parent in the first place," reports Dr. Denise Polit-O'Hara, a social science researcher and authority on the family.[1]

Because more women choose to or need to work, the pressure to have second and third children is decreasing somewhat. However, many still think of parents of onlies as offenders against family tradition—the old one, that is. On online bulletin boards and in Internet chat rooms people voice their opinions boldly. The whispering that accused you of ignorance, craziness, or laziness, once confined to bedrooms and telephone conversations, is out in the open. People feel it's their job to tell *you* how many children to have or to let you know you are cheating your child by not providing a sibling. They take pleasure in proclaiming that their decision to have more than one is right; yours is not. Every time you turn on your computer, chances are you will see some sort of attack on having just one or on how you parent. There are just as many supportive boards that will confirm your decision and share tips on parenting an only.

In spite of all that we have seen that is positive about the only child, opponents can pull dated tidbits from the recesses of their minds and fire away on their keyboards for all to read. Those you see have no compunction about examining your parenting skills microscopically. Should your only have frequent colds, they will tell you your child stays up too late. Should she refuse to eat at a friend's home, you will be accused of being overprotective. Should she hit another child, you will be told you don't know how to discipline. Should she say thank you too often or not often enough, you will be labeled too demanding or too lenient. Even today, criticism can be the bane of life for the only child's parents.

"My husband and I decided to have one child when we were dating and long before we got married," Wendy Shields explains. "You can't imagine how many times we've had to defend that decision." Mrs. Shields represents so many one-child parents when she adds, "I can supply you with a very long list of the legitimate reasons we chose to have one, but the truth is simply, we don't want another child."

Those who had trouble conceiving, or experienced miscarriages and difficult pregnancies or deliveries are often emotionally thrown back into a time they would like to forget. People don't realize, unless they've been there, that the number of children you have is a very private issue for parents, that implying what should happen in someone else's home is not their business, and that they are in fact being judgmental.

For decades, parents of one have been viewed as defective or selfish, in much the same way that women who elected to live apart from their husbands and children were viewed as incompetent, unfit, or peculiar. It doesn't matter that these women voluntarily made their decision, believing the fathers to be better parents. Similarly, antiquated notions about how many children to have linger.

Remember, you are wiser than those who are judging you. The practice of raising an only child has gained wide acceptance. But the pressure to have a second baby, even when mild, can propel couples into months and years of anguish. If you're young, steel yourself. This pressure, when combined with the natural instinct to have children, can readily wear down your resistance.

If you have only one or are planning to have only one, be prepared for rude comments and criticism that may make you wonder about your decision. Sometimes the pressure is insidious, stemming from an unknown source and eating away at you when you least expect it. As pressure mounts (and it will), keep in mind what you have read about only children. It should be perfectly obvious at this point that a sibling is not required to help parents raise a happy, well-adjusted child.

In an extensive study of almost three thousand children, onlies and children from two-child families were compared in the same psychiatric clinic. There was no difference among the children older than five, and among those under five years old, "a higher portion of only children had problems that did not warrant a psychiatric diagnosis." The researchers concluded that this finding indicated that parents of onlies were not being "more overprotective, but . . . more willing or able to seek medical advice."[2]

Dr. Deborah Matro, a practicing adult and child psychiatrist, gives further proof of the only child's adjustment. "There is no noticeable correlation in my patient load resulting from being an only child versus having siblings. If anything, adding a child when you truly don't want one or are ambivalent is more damaging to both parents and child." No therapist would disagree.

Although you should never have to justify or defend your position, there are times when you may feel you must. To keep "attackers"—that's what they will begin to feel like—at bay, quote the study or Dr. Matro as often as necessary. You want the offense to believe that you are responding intelligently and that you are in perfect control of your emotions at all times.

The instant you show any sign of weakening, be it to your husband or wife, significant other, your neighbor, mother, father-in-law, or best friend, the vise will be set in place and the handle turned periodically to apply more pressure.

Grandparents Are Most Enthusiastic

"How can she do this to me?" exclaims Fern Nicks when referring to her twenty-nine-year-old daughter, who flatly refuses to consider having another child. "As a mother and grandmother, I want to have many grandchildren. It's a legitimate feeling. There's nothing like being a grandparent."

Grandparents tend to produce the greatest tension with periods of enormous guilt—yours. Sure, parents and in-laws are all for "it." If the one child you have already created is wonderful, grandparents will want the success duplicated. And if your only isn't their ideal, they will exude hopeful confidence that the next one will be better behaved, more loving, a great quarterback. The new baby will compensate for whatever is the perceived flaw or failing in the child you already have. If your parents don't express their desires to you, there's a good chance they are bemoaning their plight to their friends.

As far as grandparents are concerned, the more the better (unless, of course, they are called on for financial support). While the children will be wearing you out, they'll be making their grandparents feel younger. Grandparents have long forgotten the school plays, the tears, the colds, the scrapes, and the disappointments that mother and father must tend to or work out. Most grandparents won't be walking the floors with your colicky baby or sitting long into the night in a steamy bathroom battling croup. More likely, they'll be a few states away or across the country, showing off the baby's pictures.

When the pressure sets in, hold firm. Andrea Spencer, Fern Nicks's daughter, stands up to her conviction. "I don't believe you can divide your attention fairly between very young children. My mother can mope all she wants, we're finished having babies."

Witness this common scenario between a daughter (the mother of one toddler) and her mother (the toddler's grandmother):

"We're talking about it, but we just started. Having another baby is a big decision," the daughter remarked in passing.

A delighted mother jumped on an innocent comment and turned it into a foregone conclusion. "Oh, I knew you and Chad would come to your senses. You've made me so happy."

"But, Mother, hold on," replied the daughter, beginning to feel panicky. "I didn't say we were having a baby. I said we were considering it."

"I know you and Chad will make the right decision. You'll give that grandson of mine a baby sister. Wait until I tell your father."

In cases like this, attempts at clarification are virtually useless. Arguing semantics ("I said we were *considering* it") or becoming incensed will not alter the exchange. The other party, whether or not she has listened, walks away remembering only what she wanted to hear. The old adage, "Give an inch and they take a mile," is in full swing. This mother has the news she's been waiting for and she's headed for the home stretch with the speed of an Olympic sprinter. Before the coffee cups are empty, her mind has raced beyond maternity clothes shopping; she's choosing layette accessories and starting a doll collection.

In many families, however, a straightforward, honest explanation of feelings, goals, and limitations can ease the stress between couples and their parents. Instead of feeling guilty because you are not producing grandchildren, present an accurate appraisal of what having a second child would mean to you, your partner, and your only. Highlight the plans you have for your one child, the advantages she will have because she is alone, and the strain you would be under at home and/or at work if you were to increase your family.

As baby boomers move into the grandparent role, they appear to have more understanding than their parents did of your generation's pressures and goals. If not, remind your mother and father of the stresses they were under with both of them working or scrambling to get you and your siblings to your collective activities. They may recall some of the financial strains of paying for your education, but, like excruciating childbirth or the painful first days following an operation, grueling times evaporate from memory. They may also be approaching retirement and looking forward to helping you out with your children.

When confronted with the facts, a parent can go off with concrete reasons and solid information to consider. Couples who have tried this approach say that their parents slowly reduced the pressure and soon dropped the subject entirely. Parents are not the only ones who will try to coerce you into providing a sibling. Knowing potential irritants in advance builds your inner resources and gives you strength to hold your ground.

Keeping Up with the Joneses

"I get pressure from other mothers, not from my family," Gin Choa laughs as she tells her "joke." "I couldn't find my diaphragm and said to my husband, 'I think Nancy took it.' She's suffering with her second pregnancy and she wants me to suffer, too.' Although I was joking, my friend really is trying to convince me I want another child."

Close friends are generally adept at lengthy and substantive workovers. Imagine a friend of yours: She knows you so well that she can cut very deeply into your emotional reserves. The process can cover a period of months or she can go for the jugular in a swift fifteen-minute telephone call. Without ever saying it, she'll imply that you're a lousy friend if you don't join her and have another child when she is planning hers. She may tell you that you'll be sorry later or she may try to convince you that you have nothing better to do.

A good friend can woo you with the fun parts of parenthood and with promises to cover for you whenever you call in distress. She may go so far as to propose car pool arrangements for nursery school and rides to junior high dances. "If you have another child now, the kids will be able to play together, grow up together. They'll be best friends like us." Don't bank on any of it.

Initially, the proposal may sound plausible and pleasurable, but on close scrutiny, it weakens. Planning so far into the future is simply unrealistic. Your friend could be transferred to another state before the children talk. You and she could have a fight that severs your relationship or strains its intimacy. And there is the real possibility that the children will dislike each other intensely. It happens. Often.

Jody Cohen reports repeated pressure from her contemporaries. "They say, 'How can you have just one? That's terrible.'" Jody tells them, "It's my decision and there is nothing terrible about it. I feel I can give Jordan everything that I want to materially and emotionally. It's very taxing to work all day, which I choose to do, and come home and give this child real quality time and attention and teach him. I don't think I should be torn in any more directions."

Sometimes it's not friends or family who exert the strongest influence. The times you, like Jody Cohen, are adamantly against adding another are the times pregnant women seem to multiply. They are everywhere, blocking supermarket aisles, crowding elevators, and being given hard-to-get seats on sardine-packed rush-hour buses. Conversations center on decorating nurseries and delivery dates. If you're on the fence, witnessing any combination of these occurrences or a single one is sufficient to start you reconsidering.

Isolated incidents can affect you powerfully: A mother cooing at her newborn in a checkout line; the pang you feel when a neighbor tells you about a camping adventure with her four children or how her oldest reads her youngest a bedtime story each night. It may be the loneliness, perhaps envy, you experience when you drop your only at a birthday party and watch mothers rushing to the dentist or a tap dance lesson with one of their other children. It may be a big brother teaching his little sister to ride a two-wheeler or a sister helping her baby brother master the art of walking. You wonder if your child feels left out.

Your child's social environment by itself can play havoc with your emotions and stir up enough unrest to send you back to the drawing board. Parents often feel inadequate when they overhear or engage in conversations with other parents. "Is this your first experience with soccer?" "Do you have another child in this school?" About the time you confirm the fact that one child is what you both want, signs appear on nursery school classroom doors with increasing regularity: STEVEN BROWN HAS A BABY SISTER—LORELEI. KATE ROFEE HAS TWIN BROTHERS—DAVID AND DANIEL.

In the park a well-meaning grandmotherly type who is out for her afternoon airing watches your daughter playing by herself in the sandbox and badgering you to join her. The woman sidles up to the bench and tells you with unquestionable authority in her voice, "She needs a playmate. Doesn't she have a brother or sister? That would sure keep her busy." It would, you nod in agreement, not saying a word because this woman has you thinking. Maybe another one is not a bad idea.

The sandbox/swing stage passes swiftly. If you're at this point, you're almost beyond zipping zippers and scrubbing crayon murals off walls. School and playmates, if not already in the picture, are in the foreseeable future. If you're not craving another child, don't allow passing comments to lure you back to the changing table. Conformity is a powerful force, but so are the forces that make you desperately want to keep the status quo: the special and extra time you have with your only, your job if you have one, your relationship with your spouse, and the freedom you have to move about with one. Or possibly, like Iris Kitter, you come to your own realization. "My neighbor said she would never have another one and we were both very up on having onlies and then she decided to get pregnant. I felt as if someone had kicked a chair out from under me. I talked to friends of mine who said, 'But that's not where you are, that's not what you want.' "

Hitting Home

Here are some lines you'll hear with some advice on how to handle them:

Line 1: "You'd better have another one soon."

Perfect and not-so-perfect strangers in idle conversation can arouse the guilt and second thoughts you were sure you had buried. Your doctor, for instance, might jokingly say, "If you're going to have another baby, you better do it soon." In his office you laughed, but at the dinner table neither you nor your husband can shrug off his inference. The doctor tapped one of your most sensitive emotional nerves—your age.

For those who still have biological time, the conflict between career and adding to the family is most disturbing. As noted pediatrician T. Berry Brazelton has pointed out, "Women who interrupt their careers to have their families feel they should have the second child soon so they can 'get on back to work.' "[3]

If you're seeking advancement at a "fast track" pace, a new addition will slow you down. A second child automatically means a cutback on the number of hours that can be devoted to a career. When you are trying to hold down a job, one child is a full-time project. Two children will give you two projects that compete with your career and its course. And don't expect much help from the government. In spite of the enormous increase in the number of women working, the United States lags way behind other countries in providing assistance to working parents.[4]

Line 2: "He needs a brother or sister."

This is the form of disapproval you will hear most often and the one that weakens parents to the point of succumbing. Dr. Brazelton sums up the problem: "With the increasing pressure on parents to limit their families, there is a parallel feeling that an only child may be 'spoiled' or may 'suffer.' These days parents feel that one child will be too lonely if both of them are working. They feel they should have a second child in order to give the first a friend and close relative."[5]

In an era of step-families, second families, blended families, and friends substituting as family, there are alternate ways to give your child support now and in the future. Vanessa Woodmere puts the issue in perspective: "You can't have everything in life; you can't have perfect conditions all the time. Zack's adopted and we won't be adopting another, but in his case I'm reassured because he'll have his grandnephews, my husband's grandchildren, to lean on. Because they are close in age, these four boys will be very connected and I want to do everything I can to promote that so Zack will have family when we die."

Katy Koontz, a second-generation only and mother of a third-generation only, prepares for the time when her daughter Samantha's grandparents, she, and her husband are gone. "My first cousin has a daughter about the same age as Samantha. I make a special effort to be sure the girls see each other at least once, but ideally, twice a year. It's a three-hour drive one way to their house after I've flown up to see my parents. But this cousin relation may well be her only living, family-of-origin, relative in a few decades."

If someone is brave enough to pursue the "you need another"

conversation, ask why your only needs a sibling when she has many friends and cousins. On this issue your ammunition is powerful and plentiful.

Why assume that a sibling will benefit your child? Library shelves are overcrowded with books on how to introduce a child to a "new arrival." Volume after volume—for both adults and siblings-to-be—is devoted to the anxiety-ridden task of ending a firstborn's reign. Rarely does a parent pull off the transition without a hitch. Usually there's a trauma that can linger for years. Some children never get used to being dethroned. They resent the arrival of a sibling intensely and cannot adjust. Many spend a good part of their childhood, if not their lifetime, trying to figure out what happened.

Consider the popularity of the book *Siblings Without Rivalry*, which rose to the bestseller list almost immediately after publication. In their first chapter the authors capsulize daily life with siblings and in doing so reveal what parents of an only child will miss: "It was pure happiness to discover that my misery had lots of company. Mine was not the only day punctuated by name-calling, tattling, punches, pinches, shrieks, and bitter tears. I wasn't the only one walking around with a heavy heart, jangled nerves, and feelings of inadequacy."[6]

"Conflicts with siblings seem to be an almost inevitable part of family living as children share space and resources."[7] The ritual bickering and friction in multichild homes are virtually nonexistent for only children. Only children get the first bath, the first and last good night kiss. They get bedtime stories tailored to their daily routines or current whim. Most significant, only children receive the time that siblings might not get simply because there isn't enough of it to go around.

Penny Lopez, twenty-nine, looks at sibling rivalry from the vantage point of her own childhood: "I'm badgered regularly about giving George a sibling, but I can't be moved . . . I won't be moved. I spent my early years until I went off to college in armed combat with my brother. We fought constantly. Can that tension and bellicose atmosphere truly be good for a child? I won't subject George to it. I don't think it's a healthy way to raise a child."

Most children need parents far more than they need siblings. According to Dr. Toni Fablo, "The absence of siblings can be compensated for by others, particularly their [only children's] parents, who not only interact more with only children than do parents of multiple children, but also may be more likely to act as brokers in arranging peer interactions for their only children."[8]

Line 3: "Give him a playmate."

"None of the brothers and sisters I knew," comments Frank Berlinger, an only who raised two children, "talked to each other. The older brother didn't like the younger sister; the older sister thought the younger brother was a pain. As long as there is an age difference, siblings never mix anyway."

Unless your children turn out to be of the same sex and less than three years apart, the goal of having them play together is unrealistic. In any case, children want and need friendships that are separate from family. Preschool "children who develop the greatest social understanding in the context of their sibling relationships may actually show the *least* direct transfer of specific behaviors or interaction strategies from sibling relationships to peer relationships."[9] Children with friends have been shown to be altruistic, cooperative, able to see from another's perspective, and friendly.[10] In other words, friends can influence your child's social and emotional development in many positive ways, including academic development. Children who have positive friendships have higher self-esteem and are more involved in classroom activities, meaning they valued school more.[11]

Even with several children, you will not be left off the scheduling hook. When one child is off playing with a friend, the other will be home complaining, feeling sorry for herself, and begging you to do something with her. When they are together, whatever the sex mix and ages, they will probably be squabbling.

For limited amounts of time, if they get along, the fact that one child is there to play with the other can give parents an occasional break. The peace and quiet will most assuredly be short-lived and sporadic and will never balance the time and energy sapped in settling disputes.

Line 4: "You're such good parents."

If you are raising something that approaches a "model" child, you'll be patronized. You may hear, "You're such a good mother. Tom's such a good father. You really should not let that talent go to waste."

What the speaker doesn't know is how much energy and time you put in and how fragile the "model" is. Today's five-year-old piece of perfection may suddenly refuse to get dressed in the morning, to eat her lunch, or to go to bed. She can sustain the turnabout for months on end.

The extent to which you really are good parents to your only child comes from the significant amount of time and energy you are able to devote to her. That's no easy feat given that most jobs are more demanding, require more hours, and are not yet entirely supportive of parents who have both work and family vying for their attention. Because you have only one you can be more relaxed, more rational, and better able to help her deal with her problems, encourage her pursuits, and build her self-esteem just by being there for her when she needs you.

Line 5: "Two are as easy and almost as cheap as one."

Don't believe that line for one second. "I see so many parents after they have had their second child," reports Lori Karmazin, director of the Counsel Oaks Learning Campus, a child-care center that services some three hundred families in Oklahoma. "They say, 'You might as well have four once you have two. It is so very different.' "

Just figure in the added man-hours. They're staggering. A 1947 French study reported that a firstborn added eighteen hours of housework each week, and when a second child entered the household, the hours jumped to twenty-eight. Studies in this country in the 1960s were a bit more conservative in their estimates, calculating the extra hours of child care only between five and twenty for each offspring. On an annual basis, housework hours estimated at a thousand hours with no children doubled to two thousand in a home with children under the age of six.[12] Granted we have conveniences that make swifter work of cooking and cleaning than in the sixties, but no gadget is going to replace or cut short the hours that must be devoted to caring and loving.

The familiar cliché "Two can live as cheaply as one" enters the picture here, in a slightly altered form: "There won't be much additional expense." Someone will argue that you already have the essential baby items: carriage, crib, high chair, and so forth. But what about baby food? Formula? Diapers? It's the rare mother who will dress her boy in his sister's pink snowsuit and lavender all-weather boots. Shoes don't generally make it to a second child, nor do serviceable play clothes and sleepwear, the bulk of a young child's wardrobe. Your oldest may still require a car seat, so you'd need another for the baby. The list goes on and expenses mount before you pay for nursery school, child care, or a family vacation. And, if you are financially secure and can easily handle the expenses of more children, advocates of a second child will be telling you to have another child simply because you can afford one.

Line 6: "If anyone can cope with another, it's you."

Perhaps money is not an issue. Pro-baby fans will try the angle that you can easily handle another child and your other obligations because "you're so organized and efficient." This comment is usually uttered by a nearly out-of-control mother with three children under five or your own mother who, after several years of pleading, will resort to any strategy.

Gin Choa, whose mother doesn't pressure her, speaks of acquaintances and friends. "I think they are jealous of my freedom. I don't have to keep George in day care all day. I can spend the afternoon with my son if I decide to pick him up early. Of course, I have the option because I work for myself, but I wouldn't be able to pick up two as often as I get George."

One more could burst your orderly bubble. Parents with households and children who function smoothly have been known to fall apart with the added, constant demands of an infant. Rather than being a snap, one more could cause *you* to snap. If you like a neat house, a workable schedule, no hitches, and no surprises, a second child may be out for you. There will be twice as many unexpected things happening, twice as many toys to clean up, twice as many cuts to bandage and training wheels to tighten and/or remove. There will be two bodies to feed and dress. If you work, those two little beings must be squeezed into snowsuits and carted off to the baby-sitter or prodded along to meet the school bus. When one is an infant and one is in kindergarten, for example, two early-morning stops may be necessary before you begin your own commute.

Line 7: "It's going to be a boy; I know it."

People who want you to have another baby don't give up easily. When they run out of the standard arguments, they manufacture new ones. "Give John the boy he's always wanted. I can just feel it. Your next baby will be a male."

The chances of that happening are a lot better than your chances of winning the lottery; however, you're still running odds of only fifty-fifty. And, you could wind up with twins or triplets, especially if you are over the age of thirty. Although the highest birthrate for multiples is among forty-five- to forty-nine-year olds, "the twin rate rose 63 percent for women aged forty to forty-four years" between 1980 and 1997.[13] And the likelihood of having twins is higher if either parent is a twin or there are twins in either family.

Jeb Ortstadt, father of three, laughs wryly as he says, "If I had any idea, if it had even crossed my mind that we could have twins, I would never have risked having what I thought would be one more. Our lives have been an utter shambles since the boys arrived."

"I'd have another," says Aurelia Barnes, "if someone could guarantee it would be a girl, provide full-time care paid in full, promise I'd never have to work again, and do all the chauffeuring."

Line 8: "What kind of parents are you to deprive your child of a sibling?"

That's what your harshest critics will ask. And since you want to do what's best for your child, when you hear, "You're not being fair to your child," you can't help doubting your decision.

If you're content with your choice, it's more than fair. The damage done by siblings is little discussed. "An idealistic conception of siblings is that they are always close, loving, and ready to care for one another. Unfortunately, this is only part of the portrait. Sibling conflict exists, and sometimes continues throughout life. In the absence of better means, aggression, violence, or abuse may be used to deal with it."[14] A shocking 65 percent of college students reported they were on the receiving end of severe sibling abuse such as kicking, biting, being hit with a fist, or being choked.[15] The residual effects of childhood sibling actions spill over into adulthood and negatively impact adults' feelings of well-being,[16] often in the form of lower self-image.[17]

In fact, adding a sibling may be extremely unfair to all three of you. Resentment builds when schedules get overcrowded and workloads seem interminable. When a husband has time for his wife, a wife has time for her husband, and both have time for their child and that time disappears, the pleasures of family life can begin to erode.

Line 9: "You're being selfish."

You may be told that you're thinking only of yourself, not your child. Self-interest is rarely the sole reason people decide against adding to their families. The decision not to have another child is complex and emotional. Analyzing it with someone other than a spouse (therapists excluded) will probably prove futile. When you are accused of being selfish, the best response is "maybe so." Very often agreeing, whatever the charge, is an effective way to end a childbearing discussion.

Once the discussion is closed to outsiders, you must still reach a decision based on your own energy levels, dispositions, dreams, and circumstances. Whether you would be bearing or adopting a second, your final choice must be a realistic one that recognizes and accepts your physical, emotional, and financial limitations. Maureen Springer assesses her decision: "My life is not my own. I absolutely love this child who drives me crazy. We were presented with another adoption opportunity, but my son was under two then, and he consumed us and continues to. We wouldn't know what to do with another child. It was a difficult decision because when you're an adoptive parent you don't know if you are ever going to get that chance again. You have the sense that if you say no, you are going to be punished; it feels as if people are saying, 'What kind of ungrateful people are you?'

"I think very active, all-consuming children are inherent contraception for their parents. I couldn't fathom having two children. I know that doesn't sound like a big family to some people, but to us, two sounds like an enormous family."

Most of us have grown up believing that a big family is a happy one. Women have been programmed to want to bear and men to want to "sire" those smiling faces that will appear in great numbers around the Thanksgiving table. If you come from a large family, deep down you may still feel that way in spite of the fact that you have demands and goals for yourself that are incompatible with a houseful of kids . . . or one more.

In final analysis, you, the parent or parents, have the right to decide the size of your family. You may want to be a single-child family, the fastest-growing family unit. Perhaps you don't know yet.

10

Pressuring Yourselves

Once you have made the decision to have only one child, it's very easy to be led astray by what others say is the right thing to do. It's equally easy to become your own worst enemies by fooling yourselves into thinking that you want one more. You may feel you've made mistakes with your child—didn't have natural childbirth, didn't breast-feed or breast-feed long enough, didn't read to your child every night, or take a long enough maternity leave—and want a second chance, not really a second child, to nurture in different ways.

You may have had a delightful infant, missed the terrible twos completely, and just know you'll be lucky again. Or vice versa, your child is or was a major challenge and you're looking for the perfect baby; after all, you've earned it. Once you think the matter is closed, from time to time you'll wonder and be unsure. If you think others can work you over, wait until you fully understand the job you can do on yourself and your partner.

A second baby should arrive in this world for only one reason: You want him. He should not satisfy anyone's notions of what is right or meet someone else's expectations. He should not be your latest hope for self-actualization or a cover for personal fears or feelings of inadequacy.

Ask Yourselves

Take your time in reviewing these questions and the issues they raise. Consider your reactions carefully.

Question: Are you, like so many couples today, getting too old to have a second child?

Age puts ample pressure on the mother who is approaching her biological deadline to give her child a brother or sister. As one couple stated, "Neither of us is a kid in terms of having kids."

"We're in the middle of the age issue," Lynn Murphy explains. "I'm forty, my husband's forty-three. I can still squeeze in another baby. Daily I say to myself, here's the good, here's the bad about having another child. But I like having one and I don't want to spoil that."

It requires a certain amount of energy to take care of an additional child, an infant at that. Be realistic—you may not have it. Radio talk show host Barbara DeMarco-Barrett, who had her son at the age of forty, believes that having another child now would be unfair. Her feelings stem from having a father who was sixty-three when she was born. "He didn't play with me like fathers do. He was loving, but his lack of involvement may have had to do with his age. If I had another child, I'd be fifty-one when he entered kindergarten. Not good."

As you may recall, parental exhaustion is a fact of infancy. Sleepless nights are the norm. Remember those early stages, first crawling, then walking? There's nonstop supervision closely followed by waiting on your offspring until he can open the refrigerator himself.

There's a sure-fire way to get a good idea whether or not you're up to another child. Borrow one from your sister or a friend, preferably an infant or toddler. Offer to baby-sit for the weekend or, better yet, a week. If such an arrangement is not feasible, spend a strenuous day with someone's child. Be sure to take your only along because you are investigating what it would be like to care for two children. Include a shopping expedition to the grocery store, lunch at a restaurant, and a movie, a trip to the park, or a local fair. Test your endurance and patience to the limits as they will be tested for years to come if your only has permanent company.

Question: Do you want to or can you safely be pregnant again?

Here, the decision weighs heavily with the female partner. You have a right to your feelings and, perhaps, fears. Some women report being loath to the idea of being exposed to doctors' probing and feeling as if their privacy has been stripped from them. Others say one labor and delivery was hard enough, and still others don't want the struggle of losing extra after-birth pounds a second time.

Those who experienced a high-risk pregnancy or postpartum depression with their first child are fearful of the same thing happening. Barbara O'Connor lost her first pregnancy. Her daughter Jenny was born a month early and spent two weeks in the neonatal intensive care unit, but most worrisome, she wonders, "Could I carry another baby to term?" Before the miscarriage and intensive care days Barbara was sure she would have two children. Even women who "sailed" through pregnancy and delivery are hesitant to add to their families believing they got it right the first time.

Question: Are you ready for the rigors of another adoption?

For Theresa Galinsky, the process took ten months with criminal background checks, involved home study, and endless paperwork and forms. She says, "You have to make a true commitment to do an adoption and we had grave hesitation about a second adoption. The rules change all the time about age limitations for parents. If you want an infant or baby under a year old, you had to be under forty-five, then it changed to under forty. We felt we hit it out of the park with this perfect child and we have no way of knowing what we would get next time.

"I told one of the mothers at the playground, 'It's easy for you, you can just go home and get pregnant.' It's more of a crapshoot for us than for other people. It was such a big, frightening step, an incredibly intense experience in a way-out part of the world that few people ever go to. Even the news correspondents don't go to this area we were in to get our son."

"It's possible to have so much heartbreak in adoption," recalls Tess Berkley. "You think you are going to adopt a baby and then the adoption falls through. I didn't want to go through that again. There can be problems for a variety of reasons; you get your heart and your hopes set and it doesn't work out. I didn't want to take that risk—I got one, the adoption worked out. I didn't want another child badly enough to put myself through all that twice."

And just as soon as you've reached a decision something will happen to shatter your confidence. For most of us, deciding the size of our family is an emotional roller-coaster ride that leads to more questions and unclear answers.

Question: Can you endure a repeat of the downside of early childrearing?

Many are blessed with an ideal infant who coos and smiles, eats and sleeps without incident. "After we brought Jenny home, she developed pneumonia, colic, and projectile vomiting," sighs Barbara O'Connor. "I'm still young, thirty-four, and my husband thinks I'll change my mind, but I won't. He's at the same point I was before I started educating myself about only children. Jenny was just too difficult as a baby for me to have another."

And after the first few months are you ready once more for seemingly never-ending bottles and diapers? The endless trips with your child to public rest rooms? Can you stand crushed beets on your curtains? Strained peaches on the edges of your chairs? Can you endure two more years of climbing over gates that guard the stairs? Or worrying about the baby choking on morsels of food that are too large and toys that are too small? Can you stand not knowing what's wrong with your infant when his skin is burning with fever? Are you resigned to spending hours in the pediatrician's waiting room for the essential checkups from birth to age three?

"We enjoyed taking care of our son when he was an infant," says Gin Choa who is thirty-six, "but George is four and as time goes on, we say, 'Well that's over.' We don't have to worry about him poisoning himself; we're done with diapers; he has great conversations with us. I don't think I want to give up another five-year block of my life for the moment-to-moment attentiveness it takes to get to the point we're at now."

Question: Are you up to the embarrassment and trials of early childhood?

No parent wants a repeat of the time the store manager stopped you on the way out to request payment for the pack of gum your child stashed in his jacket pocket; the time your child threw a tantrum in a restaurant and you were forced to leave before the main course; or reports from school that your child is being rude to his teacher or fighting with classmates. They're part of growing up before sound reasoning powers are developed. Some parents laugh these things off; for others, the memories haunt.

Husband Pressures Wife; Wife Pressures Husband

As with most marital issues, one spouse often feels more strongly than the other about adding a new member to the family. If you listen carefully today, you know that the scenario works two ways. It's just as likely that the man wants another child.

Male pressure tactics take many forms. They can be subtle or straightforward. Ask women you know—especially the ones who have jobs they enjoy—about pressure from their husbands to have "just one more."

One husband expressed his despair to his wife and to anyone who would listen: "I love pregnant women. They drive me crazy. I've tried everything to convince my wife to have another. She knows I can't resist a pregnant woman and that I want another baby."

In the afterglow of the birth of their son, Ron Childs said, "'Okay let's have that daughter,'" recalls his wife, Dawn. "I said, 'Let's wait awhile, let's settle into this.' The first few months turned out to be so difficult—the painful aftermath of the C-section, dealing with the baby's colic, and having no money to hire help. Ron recognized pretty fast that I was an unlikely candidate for a second baby."

Not all husbands readily accept or understand their wives' feelings on this matter. Melany Brooke, a single parent, remembers her ex-husband's rebuke with bitterness. "At times he would scream at me, 'My mother had six kids and you won't have two.' Then he'd shake his head and walk into another room as if there were some kind of flaw in my very being."

"It is not unusual for a husband to expect his wife to assume many of his mother's roles and that includes having babies," notes psychiatrist Deborah Matro. "Husbands often think if their mothers could do it, anyone can do it, or that the way their mothers did it is the correct way to do it. They tend not to recognize the options, including the reasonableness of having one child. They believe what happened in their families is the right way."

Historically women have been taught to be peacemakers, "good girls," and to acquiesce to a husband's demands. In the baby department, this is not such a splendid idea. The female's vote for or against probably should be counted twice since she is the person who most often ends up doing the lion's share of the work. Says Carla Vozios, "I don't care who you are, you can't be sane and work full-time because the majority of the child care and the housework falls on the woman. It's a condition perpetuated generation after generation."

Our idealized notions of division of child care and household duties have not been fully put into practice. Slowly, gender differences are surfacing, but as Scott Coltrane, a sociologist at the University of California Riverside, points out, while men and women agree that both partners' jobs are equally important, and that both should "share all aspects of parenting . . . studies of time use show that wives who are employed still do at least twice as much child care and three times as much housework as their husbands."[1]

Even when the woman's earning power and professional prestige are greater than her husband's, he does not necessarily share family responsibility. That is, not yet. Women's education and elevated status in the workforce are creating an environment in which change is possible. In families with dual incomes, especially when the wife's is substantial, child care and household chores are more likely to be equitable.[2]

Even so, as he persuades, the husband minimizes the burden by saying, "You'll only be tied down for a few years." He includes promises of enormous scope which, when put to the test, often turn out to be empty or near-empty ones. "You won't have that much to do with him. I'm the one who will play catch. We'll go to ball games. I'll change him and dress him. Didn't I do that with . . ." The offer is almost irresistible.

While doing research for her book *Halving It All,* Dr. Francine Deutsch, professor of psychology and education at Mount Holyoke College, discovered that men know better than to argue or openly claim that they shouldn't have to do housework or child care. But they continue to use age-old strategies for avoiding those responsibilities, such as ignoring requests for help, claiming incompetence, or declaring that the wife is better at performing the task since he has lower standards about the cleanliness of the house or how their child is engaged during his free time, and comparing themselves to their fathers who as a generation did much less. Like Coltrane, Deutsch concludes that while people talk about equal sharing—and some actually do it—many wives still handle 60 to 75 percent of household responsibilities.[3]

Fathers forget that the mother is the parent a child usually requests when he is sick or hurt or had a bad day at school or just wants a lap to sit in. The fact is "women often feel they can't compromise" when it comes to their children's needs. "They think it's important to be there for their kids as much as possible, even if it's at a sacrifice to them. Some go to extraordinary lengths to reduce the amount of child care they need so that they can be with their kids, or to create a child care situation that satisfies their conscience," explains Deutsch.[4] The mother is the one who will probably have to stay home from work when illness invades. And she's the one who will be in daily demand for homework and asked at the last possible moment to bake cupcakes or supply heart-decorated napkins for the class Valentine's Day party.

In some enlightened and liberated families, a bit of progress has been made in the last twenty years but as Deutsch notes, it's not uncommon for men to shy away from situations in which they have little or no experience.[5]

"Men don't think domestically," observes one overextended attorney/mother. "Maybe it's genetic. The female role is so ingrained."

Most men do precisely what this father of a two-year-old did. Here's his wife's version: "Bill heard the baby crying about two-thirty one morning and went to his room. Brent was bathed in vomit, as was his crib. Bill picked him up and carried him in to me. Wide-eyed and apologizing profusely, he nudged me awake. 'I'm sorry. I don't know what to do. How do I clean up this mess?' "

In many respects, not terribly much has changed since Dr. Benjamin Spock wrote in his 1945 edition of *The Common Sense Book of Baby and Child Care:* "Of course, I don't mean that the father has to give just as many bottles or change just as many diapers as the mother. But it's fine for him to do these things occasionally. He might make the formula on Sunday."[6]

Fatherhood brings longer working hours for fathers, a discovery that translates to more income with the birth of each child.[7] But that can only mean less time to help—possibly leaving only

Sundays (as Dr. Spock advised). Given these facts, the father of one is going to carry a far greater percentage of the "child load" than is the father of two or more. The pressure on parents with larger families to earn a living can be stressful. One football game *or* one ballet recital on the weekend may be a full load after a hectic workweek. In short, there is likely to be more sharing between husband and wife and a better division of duties in a one-child home.

The crux of the matter is that mothers are ultimately responsible for the endless details involved in raising children. Although both working mothers and full-time homemaking mothers do the same types of household chores and child-care activities, employed mothers spend hours equivalent to almost two full-time jobs to meet the demands of motherhood and work.[8] When there's an illness or a problem, the school calls the mother first. When a child needs a Halloween costume or wants someone to listen to him read, Mom's usually the first one asked. When he fights with a friend or feels sorry for himself, he looks to his mother for sympathy.

So when a husband or partner lays it on thick with a proposal for another child, a woman must ask herself: Do I really want to arrange for, watch over, provide for, feed, and feel for one more? Those involved in a twenty-three-year study of women who gave birth to children who were initially unwanted discovered that "a mother's attitude in the first year of a child's life seems to be particularly important to the child's later self-esteem." The finding has nothing to do with loving the child, but rather results from how much she gives in emotional support when weighed against other demands and desires in her life.[9]

One smart husband who finally agreed with his wife to keep their only an only summed up the strategic issue: "What Sally does or doesn't do, how she feels about taking care of Jamie and me, affects us every single day. If she's not happy, it's going to be difficult for us to be happy."

One would think that, because expectations for girls are as high as they are for boys in our current society, people would be indifferent to the gender of their children. Yet, as in the past, couples are more likely to go for a second if the first is female. If you have a daughter or when your first turns out to be female, get ready for more pressure.

Men and some women, although not as ardently as in the past, want a boy to carry on the family name, to inherit their anticipated fortune, or to run the family business. If you are the proud parents of one daughter, store away the knowledge that she can retain her maiden name and attend Harvard Law School or Wharton Business School when the time comes.

In terms of gender preference, Ann Luther, a vice president of a major corporation, sees a great advantage to being a female only. "Both of my parents treated me like a son; I was very much *their* child. Had there been a boy, I would have been my mother's daughter; my brother would have been my father's son. I would not have had the considerable exposure to the business world that I received. I'm sure it's my father's influence that led to my career successes."

Wives can turn on the pressure with as much ferocity as men. If a woman has a daughter, she may have heard that "boys adore their mothers." She may want to give her husband the son he always wanted or, conversely, she may want the daughter she dreamed about as a child while playing dolls. "Shocked by the birth of a son," Tracy Fields, who expected a girl and is approaching her fortieth birthday, says, "I'd still like to have a daughter."

Just as a husband "promises" to take over child care, the woman who wants another baby—boy or girl—vows that the husband will be exempt from all duties. In theory this works. He may not be asked to play checkers or to take his child to the park. What he will be asked to do, in large part, if not in full, is to support that child—no easy feat these days. He may not be willing or able to do it.

"Sure, I wanted another child," admits Douglas Angus, a successful civil engineer, "but there was no way we could do it without giving up every single pleasure in our lives. If I had to give up skiing and my boat, I would have resented that child—and my wife—enormously."

Paula Ferris, an advertising agency vice president, didn't care what costs were involved. "I just wanted another baby; I was willing to sacrifice some of my power and status at work. I had my second child and returned to the office, but some of my responsibilities had been delegated to others. That was hard to swallow at first, but I told myself that I still have my salary and a good job. It's rough. Really rough. There's no question our lives were easier with one."

Mothers of two like Paula Ferris can be extremely helpful to parents of one in the throes of indecision. Watch them in action; ask questions about how they manage and how they feel raising two children. Do they interact equally with each child? Are they closer to one child? Explain your concerns; seek their advice. Then take your investigation a step further. Make a list of the positives and negatives as they are told to you. Compare it with a similar list you prepare about your only. When presented in black and white, the picture becomes clearer.

The Wrong Reasons

Couples can want another child without being aware of the reasons why. Working and nonworking women are equally likely to be misled by their emotions. Delving into feelings that are below the surface can bring potentially dangerous motivations for wanting a second child to light.

Wrong Reason 1: Outdated ideals.

Certainly most of us used to believe that two are better than one. Harboring the belief that one is not a family and/or conforming to our parents' model could make you miserable. Be cautious not to let what was once important in *everyone's* life lead you to the maternity ward or adoption agency more times than you want to be there.

Wrong Reason 2: One for him; one for her.

One of the most common and subtle motivations to increase your family is created by the strong bonds parents have with their firstborn. Each parent is possessive and "wants" the baby to relate best to him or her. The obvious solution, although rarely declared or understood, seems to be to have another baby so there will be one for him, one for her. Or it may be a desire to have a child of the opposite sex from the one you have to "fill out" your family, a girl to "dress up," or a boy to play catch with. Perhaps you should first consider playing ball with your daughter or checking out the adorable fashions for boys.

Wrong Reason 3: The need for attention.

If either of you has the slightest inclination toward having another, gather your strength when someone close to you has her baby. On the announcement of the birth of a friend's, neighbor's, or especially a relative's offspring, attention immediately focuses on those parents and child. Wistfully, you may recall your turn as the stars. As you admire the radiant new family, you may not know what you are feeling, but you're feeling something. It may be an emptiness, even jealousy, but if it's not "thank goodness it's them and not us," be on the alert. Save your major decision until the novelty of the new arrival has worn off and you have some distance on the jolt you experienced.

Wrong Reason 4: The lure of motherhood.

Because being a mother is one of the most rewarding and satisfying experiences a woman can have, it is natural and easy to "lose yourself to motherhood."

Some women relish pregnancy and flourish during it. They like the physical feeling of carrying a child and the attention it garners. They feel more sensual and attractive than in a nonpregnant state. Husbands, friends, and relatives are solicitous; there is a certain reverence accorded pregnant women. To some, this is a huge impetus to bear children. Think about it. The glow lasts a short time, followed by the daily realities of motherhood.

Wrong Reason 5: An excuse to stay home.

The Supermom image looms large and a woman can fall victim to feelings of inadequacy and inability to perform successfully in the worlds of work and family. She may give up her job to have a second child.

Consciously she thinks that two children justify staying home. She can juggle one child and a job, but not two. Home is where she is most needed. A second baby allows her to walk away from the business world gracefully and stop tearing herself apart attempting to meet the demands of a family and a boss.

But under the surface, other things may be going on. It could be she hates her job . . . or thinks she does. Unhappiness at work can translate into a strong desire for a second child. Before making another lifetime commitment, explore ways to correct problems at the office. Talk to your employer; talk to your co-workers. Consider delegating some of your authority or reducing your responsibilities at the office. Ask about a shorter workday or workweek with a compensatory cut in salary. Consider looking for another job, finding something closer to home, possibly changing fields entirely. Any of these alternatives should be explored in order to rule out the birth of a second child as a remedy for work-related problems.

In other cases, a woman may simply want to quiet "the nesting instinct." Columnist Anna Quindlen writes that this cannot be accomplished by adding a second child. Ms. Quindlen states that the desire to be a homemaker (which "we think of as a 1950s phenomenon"), to bake cakes, to go off on afternoon shopping trips, or to curl up and do whatever you want is "barely tolerated by men and by women, too" in our current society. A second child, she states, could be the "hole in the bottom of your career boat, plunging you into the depths of domesticity."[10] And it may not be what you are actually looking for. In short, the urge to nest is multi-faceted, more involved than bearing children. Take time off to figure out your true needs.

Wrong Reason 6: Loss of confidence.

A woman places undue pressure on herself to have a second and third child when she believes that her husband is the more competent of the marital pair. Such a woman gains stature from her husband's success, while sacrificing her own. Being a mother is less trouble and less frightening, for this woman, than creating an identity for herself. Home is a known—it's safe, secure, nonthreatening.

If submerged too long, she loses both the desire and the confidence to make an effort on her own behalf. It becomes simpler to busy herself with household tasks and fill time with pursuits that benefit children and husband and make them "look good."

Wrong Reason 7: Illusions of perfect childhoods.

Optimism convinces a parent that his children's lives will be happier and better than his own was. The desire to have more children can also block out the trials of one's own childhood.

Candice Crummley's husband wants another child, but Candice says, "He doesn't see that his relationship with his brother is neither here nor there. He has an immense amount of jealousy with his brother. He won't admit it or accept the fact that it's hit-or-miss with siblings."

Wrong Reason 8: "I want a baby sister/brother."

Your strong desire to have another child may actually originate with your only child and quietly work on you. "Studies in this area suggest that parents are motivated to have a first child to gain the psychological benefits of parenthood, but are motivated to have a second child primarily for the sake of their first-born child."[11] What your child thinks he wants should not be the critical factor.

When a child learns that one of his friends is getting a new sister or brother, parents will hear variations on this theme—"I want a baby, too"—as if he were asking for a new caboose for his train set. The fiercest requests are more often than not passing ones. The pleas for a sibling are concentrated during those years when an only child's friends are greeting siblings.

Constant complaints about having no one to play with and questions like "What am I going to do today?" can wear parents down. Your child may argue his point when you declare there will be no sibling. "Why not? You have plenty of room in your stomach," one insistent four-year-old told his mother.

"I'm proud of my mother," claims Cynthia Loman, a thirty-two-year-old mother of an only. "She never acquiesced to the pressure, most of which came from me. I pleaded loudly and often."

"A child who is an only child does not believe that he or she is going to be an only child until about age seven," explains child analyst Laurie Levinson. "There is always the fantasy that a sibling will be born. The fantasy may manifest itself in the child asking you for a brother or sister although he may actually want you to say no. Just to say 'I want a sibling' doesn't necessarily mean they want one."

"When I was younger," recalls thirteen-year-old Billy Pratt, "I begged for a brother or sister. I grew out of that. I'm glad my parents didn't listen to me." Some never ask.

Your only child may see a sibling as a source of immediate gratification—someone to play catch with, to be on the other side of the checkerboard, to borrow clothes from, to get him dates, to talk over family problems. Mary Kelly Selover admits her desire was not strongly highlighted. "When I was listing the things I wished for—a bike, a new outfit, whatever—a brother or sister would be on the same list."

At different ages and stages, most of us want, or at least think about having, a different name, a different neighborhood, or curly hair or straight hair. So many children want what they don't have even when they don't understand the difference or possible alterations to their lives. If friends have baby brothers and sisters, your only may want one, too. It's natural to think about what you don't have, but many parents of onlies believe a child can't miss what she doesn't know.

No matter what a child says, no matter how much he pesters, no child should make the decision about the ultimate size of the family. To help your child over the hurdles of singleness and the seemingly endless stream of younger brothers and sisters who arrive for his friends, straight talk is the most reassuring tactic. Detailed accounts of the effect a baby will have on an only child's life have changed many young minds. When they hear about nightly crying, sharing a room, less time with parents, more responsibility, and the tagalong aspects of a younger sibling, the appeal of a new baby wanes. Explain how happy you are with the family "just the way it is." Emphasize the positive aspects of singularity and give honest responses to questions your child may pose.

Wrong Reason 9: To save the marriage.

A marriage turned sour is rarely made sweet by a newborn. This ploy, though not necessarily deliberate, is used by men and women who fear losing their mate. Not only is it guaranteed to fail, it actually generates prolonged unhappiness. When a marriage is on shaky ground, an only suffers enough without the encroachment of a sibling.

In some one-child families, the child is the single common bond between husband and wife. On a superficial level, because the family seems to be flourishing, a second child is planned. Before proceeding, it is wise to look carefully at your marriage to see how sound it really is. If there were no child, would you be together? Happily? If the answer is negative, it's unwise to strain the thin thread of your relationship with a second child. No child ever solves the problems within a marriage.

Being a Family Without Being Overburdened

There is so much emphasis on female career success that it has become the standard by which many women measure themselves. For the striving woman, staying home with two or three children can be more frightening than struggling to do everything. In a society that operates on a cash basis, there is no monetary reward for overworked mothers. In this same society, to many people being a housewife and a mother has little status.

It is important for women considering a second child to project their feelings to a time when they may be without an independent income. How will it feel to have to ask your spouse for cash when you've been used to contributing your share to the financial pot? If another baby means you may have to remain home, giving up status, power, income, the fuels that feed your self-worth, think some more.

Don't let the illusion that other women are managing well with multiple children fool you. Women experience a great deal of stress when they believe that their peers are balancing home and work successfully and with ease. They are well groomed, their children immaculate. Their dinners taste divine. Yet these women, who appear to be coping, are paying a price that may not be visible. While there are no outward signs of wear and tear, they are suffering quietly. Don't delude yourself: There is no such thing as a happy Supermom.

The idea of being Supermom is neither practical nor realistic for most women, including mothers of one. The addition of a child creates a geometric progression—two are *more than* twice as difficult as one. The feat of keeping it together with one is tough enough; organizing a couple kids, a full-time job, and a partner usually breeds a mixture of unpleasant emotions—chronic guilt, mild depression, exhaustion, and desperation.

You must know yourself well—your wants, weaknesses, and capabilities—before seriously entertaining the idea of a second child in the hectic age in which we live. More men and women than ever before have considered the issues and are sure that they are not candidates for repeat parenthood for reasons that have nothing to do with age, physical condition, or economics. They have figured out who they are and what they want for themselves and what they want to give to their child.

Barbara DeMarco-Barrett and her husband have pieced together the puzzle for themselves. "My husband is very involved with our son," says Barbara. "One child makes it possible to have a happy kid, a good family life, to keep what my husband does, to keep what I do, and to keep it all going."

As you weigh the option to have another child, keep in mind the intangibles—the psychological and physical drain of a child. Parenting is more demanding than ever before. Overwhelming love and affection are not enough to do an adequate job. Few places outside the home instill a healthy moral code or provide the basic "fiber" and attitudes of mutual respect children need to develop.

In a newspaper sports column titled "Players aren't different today, it's just the world is more dangerous," veteran sportswriter and former Yankees pitcher Jim Bouton talks about hero worship and the dark side (women, alcoholism, and drug use) of our professional athletes' lives. Bouton writes, "What they [kids] see is that an athlete got suspended, ended up in jail, or died . . . Like it or not, these guys are role models for our kids. Shouldn't kids have someone to look up to?"[12]

Busy parents who abdicate teaching decency, respect for others, and a sense of personal responsibility to schools and outside care facilities will be less than pleased with the result. Schools are increasingly devoting nonacademic time to the prevention of drug use and violence. Value systems are a low priority in the face of order and life-threatening issues. The social atmosphere—beginning with our children's idolization of sports figures, musicians, and film and television celebrities who repeatedly present negative images— further underscores the need to rethink our childbearing patterns and hesitate before we proliferate beyond our desire and ability to care for and teach our offspring.

As you contemplate increasing the size of your family and withstand the pressure, think of your "limited edition" family as artwork or books. The small number makes it all the more meaningful and treasured.

future Issues
Without Siblings

"I don't see any disadvantages right now for my son as an only child, but way in the future when it comes to Christmas it may be lonely for him," envisions Debbie Diehl-Camp, mother of a toddler.

Susan Leites worries that her son will have no one who shares his history. "That is sad," she says. "I try to get him to know his cousins."

For only children, there are few people who will share memories or be able to validate them unless parents make every effort to include younger friends and relatives as often as possible. Says one grown only child, "I have memories of places I lived and experiences I had, but no one to share them with. After my aunts and uncles died, no one was left who remembered. My past is gone."

As the era of the large family disappears, parents are developing new formulas to compensate for the lack of siblings and for the sense of family and tradition that we all would like. When family size and/or logistics are such that a child's cousins and other family members are across the country or across the world, it is helpful for parents of one to nurture relationships with friends who have children or a child close in age to their own, as Steve Katz, his wife, and his twelve-year-old daughter Rhana do. The Katz family exemplifies the old large-family tradition being eclipsed by the new. "We have very close friends with a daughter two years younger than ours. We see them often so Rhana has a sense of family. These are people she can lean on; their daughter is a semisister."

"My husband and I both have such small families," states Sue Astley, "that over the years we have developed relationships with friends and neighbors to create family time for our son, especially at Christmas."

"The only thing parents of an only child can do is substitute," recommends Stacey Gibson, an only whose family is scattered around the country. "My friends are more a part of my life at this point than my family. My friends are pretty much family to me."

It is quite common these days for children—no matter what the family size—to call their parents' good friends "aunt" and "uncle." Transforming friends into relatives, if only figuratively, fills the void for an only child. Says Lori Karmazin, "Although we have no family here in Oklahoma, my son has many adults that he feels close to who have become his 'aunts' and 'uncles.'"

Invite them, as you would cousins, aunts, uncles, and grandparents, to significant family functions. You will be amazed how quickly a pattern and a dependency forms to the point that you would not consider a party or a holiday dinner without including those with whom you and your child have an ongoing relationship. In effect, you are stockpiling experiences with other children and families so they will have shared memories of their childhood as you would if your family were large and lived together, or close by, as was the case early in the last century. In this way, you make sure your child does not miss the adult fun and joy of remembering holidays and trips, funny incidents, and silly things he or the families did early in his life.

In this day and age, when relatives live great distances away, there are numerous ways to instill positive feelings, to keep family ties strong, and to build meaningful tradition. Telephone often.

Send e-mails and letters frequently and attach recent photographs, especially ones of important events such as your child's birthday parties, a fishing trip, or a new family pet.

Parental concern and expressions of affection for family members who are not in the vicinity teach the only child the value of family ties. Say to your only, "Do you think cousin Michael got into college yet? Did cousin Jeffrey win his tennis tournament? Let's call tonight." Simple statements reveal your strong attachments and make the only child truly a part of a family that is not present. For example, when your son prepares his cereal the same way his uncle does, remind him that "that's the way Uncle Gordon eats his cereal." If your daughter uses a phrase that's familiar, tell her, "That's just the way cousin Lisa would word that." Or say to a teenage only, "I like your new hairstyle. It looks a lot like Aunt Lynda's, but that outfit is definitely cousin Jolie's style."

Our society is such that houses we lived in as children are razed to make way for highways, shopping malls, or high-rises. Products we knew as children disappear: the old washing machine, the car, the radio and television set. The objects and physical reminders of those times change rapidly, but you can create a personal memory bank for your only. Take lots of photographs and videos. Include the people at each gathering and clues that pinpoint locations by writing descriptions on the backs of photos or in the computer: "This is the lake where you learned to swim; this was your first bedroom; this was our house on Water Street; this is the front of your elementary school; this is the stuffed bear that you carried on every trip until you were eight years old." Save the stuffed bear and other small memorabilia of your only's childhood.

Aside from the issue of shared memory, concern may rise around the belief that, as adults, siblings provide bonding and support, especially in times of family crisis. Rita Graham, the second in a four-generation chain of onlies, says, "Family love and support is very important. You miss knowing you can call a brother or sister and you miss being involved with their marriages and the birth of their babies. There is no love and loyalty of the kind there is in a sibling relationship."

But don't many of us have a friend we call before we call a sibling? A compassionate friend whose presence in our life is more germane than our sister's or brother's? Siblings don't always fill the bill. How many sibling relationships do you know that are completely devoid of conflict and tension? How many brothers and sisters do you know who when "put to the test" have disappointed—even enraged—one another? Think how often you hear of siblings who haven't spoken to each other for years or have argued intensely on a continuing basis. In the final analysis, rare are the adult siblings who "are there" for one another under both the most pleasant and adverse circumstances. One cannot assume siblings would be wonderful and cooperative, especially when decisions must be made about upsetting emotional, financial, or health issues.

In spite of what we know about sibling interaction and how negative it often is, idealism reigns. Admits Lynn Murphy, the forty-year-old parent of one, "I worry about my health and I've always been healthy. If there are brothers and sisters, they can take care of each other. I make an effort to build a relationship with my son's older cousins so that they will view him as a brother. I talk to them openly about my concern."

As our population of only children continues to rise, singletons and their parents will be forced to lean on friends more and more. Bonds between friends will ultimately be (and many already are) as substantial and as loyal as the most solid sibling attachments.

Safeguarding Your Only

There is a grim but practical benefit to having only one. Should anything happen to you, relatives or close friends are more apt to accept the guardianship of one than that of a flock. Erin Masters, mother of three, is not satisfied with her arrangement. "We could not come up with anyone who was thrilled with the idea of rearing our children if anything happened to both of us. I asked one friend and she looked at me as if I were crazy. 'I'm flattered that you asked me, but I would not feel comfortable and don't think I could handle it.' That was a polite way of saying, 'Raise three more kids? No way.' "

Cecily Schafly, on the other hand, had a different experience seeking a guardian for her only. "We had no trouble finding people willing to raise Whitney. It's a big thing to ask of friends or even relatives, but we felt it was essential to know that there was someone who could carry on for us. Actually, we have three couples who were delighted at the prospect. Well, as delighted as you can be when you're discussing something as serious as your own demise."

Although it is unlikely that both parents will die before their child reaches adulthood, such a situation is not beyond the realm of possibility, in light of the increase in the number of older parents. Therefore, if you have a minor child, you should have a will—no matter what your age—and you should appoint a legal guardian.

Attorneys advise against leaving such an important decision to chance. "Appoint a guardian by will," explains trust and estate attorney Myrna Blume. "It is as important as anything else you are going to do in terms of the disposition of your assets. If no appointment is made in the will, there is the possibility of conflicting claims of guardianship by uncles, aunts, grandparents, whomever. In the absence of a designation in the will, you cannot guarantee who the court will ultimately appoint as guardian of your minor child."

In other words, to ensure that your child remains with the people you feel most suitable, arrangements must be by court appointment, according to explicit instructions in your will. Keep in mind that the person you appoint as guardian may not be able to serve. Therefore, you should also name an alternate or successor guardian in your will. A letter outlining your wishes might be persuasive to a judge, admits Blume, but she warns that "a letter is no assurance that the person you want to raise your only child will be the one who does it. A long, often ugly, battle over your child can be avoided by simply adding a guardian's name to your will." If you elect a friend rather than a relative, or if there is animosity among your relatives, be absolutely sure your preference is stipulated in this way.

Too many parents live under the false assumption that family ties bind. A child's guardian does not have to be a family member. If aunts and uncles are too old, or have grown children, or you don't feel good about them for whatever reason, a better choice might be friends who have children or a child close in age to your only. Choose a family your child would enjoy and be sure to ask before you make it official. Don't assume someone wants the responsibility.

Fredda Bruckner-Gordon would choose friends over family. "Our daughter has one cousin," she explains, "and we work to keep them interested in each other, but it's hard. They are growing up in totally different environments. We get together five or six times a year. We have friends with whom we have set up a very overt system. We actually say, 'If we were not around, we would want you to raise Emily.' "

It is reassuring to know that, should your child be without you, she will be with people whose values, lifestyle, and interests are closely aligned to your own. Because circumstances and people change, it is wise to reassess your chosen guardians every few years. If doubts or questions arise that make you feel uncomfortable with your original selection, elect a new guardian. Don't hesitate to make a switch and don't delay making the change legal by incorporating it into your will. The only child has no sibling buffer, so it is important to be sure she is somewhere she will be as happy as possible.

Cultivating a Support System

The major drawback to being an only child comes late in life when the adult child is faced with aging or sickly parents. Before you panic about leaving your only child "holding the bag" in this respect, think about the tales of siblings who disappear when they are most needed. No one, including you, can predict how brothers and sisters will act toward each other or toward you once they are independent.

In her book *The Mother Dance,* Harriet Lerner writes about her own sibling support. "It never occurred to Susan [her sister] or me that one of us would end up as their primary support system in their [parents'] old age, especially because our mother, Rose, had two sisters living near her home in Phoenix . . .

". . . [T]here were times when I felt totally abandoned by Susan. I feared she had emotionally jumped ship and would disappear if I didn't keep after her and insist that she pay attention to our parents . . .

". . . I can still feel overwhelmed that Steve [Lerner's husband] and I are the only family members on the scene."[1]

"I think a support system for only children is wonderful, but you can't automatically assume that family members are going to be congenial people who can give support," argues Bill Sheehan. "If you've got a bunch of idiots in that support system, the best thing to do is get rid of them. I like to see people that I like and that I have something in common with. If I had to depend on my family for emotional support, I would die.

"I see others hoping that they can get emotional support from people who are incapable of giving it and the reason they think they will get the support is because the people are family members. I don't think family guarantees anything."

Dr. Sylvia Saltzstein expands Sheehan's thinking. "In the past, families stayed together with lots of stress and strain because they felt they had to. What's happening is that people realize that they can choose the people they can be intimate with. You don't have to rely solely on bloodlines."

Having siblings doesn't guarantee that the responsibilities will be divided. Parents of only children worry that their child will have no one to rely on as their parents age or die. In addition to the support systems parents build, children become adults and build their own support systems with best friends, spouses, or partners. If you're thinking a sibling will be a ready-made, absolute support for your child, you must factor in that he or she may have a partner who can and often will exert a powerful influence on the type and amount of support a sibling can give when it's needed.

The lion's share of responsibility usually falls to the *one child* who can deal with it best emotionally and financially or who is geographically closest. Dale Schlein restates this painful truth: "I don't think it would make any difference if I had a sibling. I don't know that everyone is responsible and will assume their share of the load. Someone—a spouse, a friend—can share the emotional turmoil."

Only child Katie Crosby is inclined to agree. "My mother was ill almost all of my life and very ill during the last ten years of hers. I don't know that a brother or sister would have helped. I felt responsible because I was a responsible daughter. I shared my feelings with my husband a lot."

"I see a difference in the intensity of my feelings of responsibility as opposed to those who have brothers and sisters to share the responsibility," remarks Kathryn Joyce. "I always knew I was the only one responsible. There is no other family member; I accepted that as a given."

Those with siblings, like Renee Larsen, are frequently in the position of an only. "I'm the youngest of three girls, but my husband and I know when my father is ill, we will be caring for him and paying all the bills. My one sister is thirty-nine and still trying to find herself, whatever that means, and my oldest sister disappeared about ten years ago. My sisters will be no help; if anything, should they be around, they'll just make things more difficult."

Bernadette Girardi, an adult only who has buried both parents, adds, "In a crisis like a parent's illness or death, I think siblings spend more time arguing over who did more—or less—and worrying about who will get what from the estate. I never felt caring for Mother after my dad died was a burden. In a way, I was relieved that I didn't have to deal with siblings who had differing ideas on what we should do with our mother."

"Close friends are a good emotional support system," offers Evelyn Wolff, "but it's still up to me to do everything and make the decisions."

Like Evelyn Wolff, your only child will bear the burden of decision making when you grow old, but she can have a strong network of emotional support. You can lay the groundwork now for that future support system. Seek out family beyond the obvious immediate relatives. Strike up links with second and third cousins, aunts, uncles, and cousins of stepparents. A remarriage can provide additional supportive connections for the only child. Encourage ties with stepbrothers and stepsisters who live with the other parent. All are potential sources of aid beyond a partner on which your only may be able to draw in the years ahead.

For the Long Haul

Only children eventually have responsibility in some way for their parents' well-being. This fact occurs fleetingly to the child and it too frequently fails to occur to her parents either, especially when the network of caring friends and relatives is large. Parents of only children should think about and plan for their later years while they are still able.

Many, like Tina Nukkom, do. "I don't want to be a burden and I don't want him to feel as if he always has to be around to help us out . . . or live close by. I don't want my son to feel guilty if he's not around. I want him to have his independence, to be able to go forth and have his own life and not feel as if he has to be checking in."

At this stage of your life this may seem like a lot of premature fuss, morbid and unnecessary, but vital concerns should be addressed now and their solutions filed away for the future. Your child, when faced with the sadness and stress of your illness or death, will be thankful that you handled the difficult decisions and details.

In the long run, you'll feel better knowing matters are being handled as you wished. As soon as you can, set money aside to defray possible late-in-life medical expenses or housing costs. You might look into the types of places you would like to live when you are older.

Consider appointing someone to act on your behalf for both health and financial decisions. This person is your legal agent. When your child becomes an adult, you may want to turn that responsibility over to him or her. Keep your finances in order as you advance in years and discuss them with your child or the person you have designated to act for you.

It is imperative to provide for your own needs, however distant they may seem. "There is no responsibility on the part of a child to care for a parent in the United States," warns Myrna Blume. Offspring cannot be forced by law to assume an aging parent's debts or to provide care no matter what the financial condition of parent or child."

Blume advises her clients not to be overly generous in giving a child monies that they may need one day for themselves. Your child will not be required to return this money if you find yourself strapped for dollars to pay for essential health care.

Ease eventual duties any way you can and long before they threaten to become issues. It's a good idea to alert an adult only child to any special wishes you have concerning extraordinary medical assistance to keep you alive. Prepare a Living Will, which stipulates how you want your medical treatment handled should you become incompetent to make such decisions. This document must be legally and properly executed according to individual state law.

Living Will information and forms can be requested or filled out online.[2] A Health-Care Power of Attorney, similar to a Living Will and also a legal document, gives someone the power to make decisions about your medical treatment if you cannot. Both the Living Will and Health-Care Power of Attorney ensure your medical wishes are carried out if there is no hope of recovery and you are unable to speak for yourself. All fifty states honor either type of advance-care directive and your directive can be accessed online from the hospital providing your care.

Your child should also be aware of where and how you would like to be buried and what kind of funeral services you prefer. If talking about this is not possible for you, put your thoughts and directions in a letter to be opened on your death.

"My son [in his early twenties] doesn't like to discuss this subject," says attorney Howard Vogel, "but he has been told what we would like him to do should anything happen to us."

"My mother sat me down when I was a young teenager," Judy Lynn Prince recalls. "She told me what I had to do, what she had, and where it was. Even now, in her seventies, whenever she takes a trip, she reminds me that she charged her airline ticket on a credit card that provides extra insurance if the flight crashes."

Although not legally responsible, most only children will want to or try to care for and/or supervise their parents' financial matters. As a parent, you do not want to leave your only child in the position this adult only finds herself—over the last seven years her father has become progressively ill with Alzheimer's disease: "I panic because there's only me; my mother refuses to recognize his condition. I ask them to explain their financial situation because my dad can't write a check anymore. What happens if my mother has a heart attack? They don't want to deal with the reality. I need to find out about their bank accounts, if and where they have certificates of deposit, what kind of insurance coverage they have, and so forth. I ask; they don't answer." Only children can adapt more readily to increasing parental needs if finances are in order and care parameters are defined.

People are certainly more aware of the aging process today. As the parent of an only child, the skew of the population age curve is in your favor. The older population has more money, lives longer, and is in better health than in earlier generations.

By the time your only is in the position of caring for you, she will also have corporate help and possibly city, state, and government support. Services exist throughout the country to counsel adult children who work and live away from their parents. Because the problems can become so complex, ranging from nursing care to mental and emotional support, corporations have realized that care demands can gravely effect employees' performance on the job. Like cities, many companies have implemented programs to advise and direct employees who need assistance caring for elderly parents.

What companies don't supply in the way of assistance can be found on the Internet. Enter your state, region, and city in online senior-care directories to find nearby senior centers, nursing homes, home-care resources, hospices, assisted living facilities, even care managers who can help you assess a parent's needs and make arrangements long distance.

Moreover, group homes for the elderly are multiplying rapidly. In such homes, older people who, for financial or health reasons, are unable to live alone but do not require medical attention or constant supervision live together to have companionship and to eliminate the fear of being alone. As few as two and as many as twenty-five adults live together; arrangements vary in the amount of supervision, cooking, cleaning, and health care services provided.

As our population of only children increases, online and off-line support groups will flourish and many of the seemingly insurmountable problems will be resolved. In short, there will be ample ways for onlies of the forthcoming generation to care for their elderly parents and find adequate and comfortable living arrangements for them. The major drawback of having an only child will be well eased and simplified by the time your only might have to care for you.

Most adult only children have a good perspective and will do what they have to do. Dr. Toni Falbo feels that "to some extent it might be a benefit to have one child because she can't pass the buck."

Lisa Denne Reilly had no intentions of shirking her responsibilities. "Since my father died, I talk to my mother every day just to make sure she's okay for the day. Before that, I spoke to both of them once or twice a week. She's twenty miles from family, but that's all she requires for now. When she needs more, I will fly down and make proper arrangements for her care."

Judith Miller faces the future calmly. "It doesn't bother me that I will have to make decisions for my mother, such as putting her in a nursing home. I am very clear-thinking about other people."

A few, like Ellen Stern, harbor grave doubts. "I have a lot of fears about my parents; I will be the only person they will turn to. It's a big factor in whether or not I have a third child. If something happens to either of my two, the other will have to cope with what I've had to cope with. It will be more of a shock because they will not have been used to living as an only child."

Of cases like Ellen Stern, Dr. Deborah Matro explains that "she is exhibiting a tremendous incapacity to separate her own experience from what her children's experiences or another only child's experiences might be. Her fears have nothing to do with her own children and everything to do with her own history."

Unlike Stern, Gail Duncan is pragmatic about her only child's future responsibilities. "The burden of having to care for her parents will be on her. Not to sound callous, but she'll have to deal with that. I can't give her everything to get through life. If our old age is going to be the bane of her existence, then it will be. Up until that point she is going to be fine."

Without realizing it, you are setting an example by how you treat your own parents and older family members. Your concern for a friend's well-being or the comforting assistance you give those around you—including your child and your spouse—will greatly influence your only child's attitudes decades from now.

Parents with one child have more money later in life and are better able to care for themselves. The best precaution parents can take to spare an only is advanced thought and preparation. Dollars aside, if you've raised your only well—and you will—she will be responsible, well adjusted, and equipped to deal with any difficulties.

"I often say to myself," muses Ruth Hague, " 'What if Jeffrey marries someone who wants nothing to do with me; what if he's living in Anchorage, Alaska, and I'm in Louisiana?' Then I think, because we have a good relationship and care about each other, he'll be there if I need him."

Adult only Denise Montgomery is ready. "When my parents get sick, I am going to be the only one dealing with death and dying. I will lean on my extended family and use the resources available. I really can't say that being an only child has had a major impact on my life."

Mother of an only daughter, Barbara O'Connor still worries about the time "when my husband and I get older and we will be a burden. I worry that she will be angry at us for not giving her a sibling. At least now, for her, with so many onlies, it won't be so different."

12

An Only—the
Only Way to Go

Presently unmarried at the age of thirty-four, Barbara Friedman typifies the predominant American outlook on family. She thinks and feels as do many of the women and men who will raise our future babies. "One would be terrific, two less so because I think life is crowded enough. Furthermore, I'm getting too old to have children and space them properly."

In his book *Maybe One,* an environmental argument for having smaller families, Bill McKibben writes, "No decision any of us makes will have more effect on the world (and on our lives) than whether to bear another child. No decision, then, should be made with more care."[1] The enormous and steady increase in the number of only children is convincing proof that after weighing their personal situations, factoring in the pressures parents face in raising children, and considering what they want for themselves and for their offspring, more and more people decide a single child may be the only way to go.

Master Plan for Minor Pitfalls

As we have seen, raising a single child is not without glitches. Here are some final pointers to sharpen your "only" parenting skills:

When you are busy with outside responsibilities and not particularly bogged down by parental chores, it's very easy to become lax about praising the only child. Remember to say "Great job," and to realize that your child has put forth a special effort that should be acknowledged. Be sure your child knows and believes that his endeavors are appreciated.

On the other hand, minimize the gloating to friends who have children in the same age group. Although you'll often be proud of your offspring's achievements, bragging affects how other parents react toward your child.

Take extra time (you will have it) to be with your child, doing and sharing activities he likes, but give him space and the time to be with friends or alone if he so chooses. Let him engage in children's pursuits, not sedentary grown-up projects.

Be as involved as your schedule permits. Volunteer for school activities—if only to bake cookies for the school sale or to work a booth at a weekend carnival. Attend weekend sporting events, cheering on the sidelines with other parents. Your participation will encourage friendships that can grow into long-term relationships for your child. Your contact with parents of other children helps make your child feel part of a larger, more encompassing unit than the small one at home.

Above all, don't shelter your only child. Separate yourself, something well-adjusted adults want to do anyway. "When you become obsessive, overly concerned about the productivity, well-being and, survival of a child," warns Dr. Frank Main, "you are probably worrying more about yourself than about the child."

Don't be intrusive. It's an easy thing to do when you are interested and concerned. If your six-year-old daughter decides not to tell you what happened in ballet class, allow her some breathing room. Don't make her feel as if she lives in a fish bowl. The inclination to pry, even when your motives are positive, robs an only child of his private self. Unless you feel a facet of his life is going poorly, respect his independence. Most young children, only or not, spill out the information when they are ready.

Don't make your only child your only project. Foster independence and encourage peer interaction. Avoid fighting your child's battles and being overprotective.

Don't be too critical. Find out what movies, books, and magazines other children are absorbed in. Be as tolerant as possible of the music they prefer and the clothing they insist on putting on their backs. Look around to see what other kids are wearing before you forbid tattered shirts or plastic fruit earrings.

Be aware of the fact that in a twosome or threesome it's very easy to smother or spoil your child. On the same note, because your family unit is so closely interwoven, compromise helps to keep each member content. Imagine a curfew is the issue. The mother wants her teenage daughter in at 10 P.M., the father, at 11 P.M., but the daughter is pushing for midnight, her close friends' curfew. Discuss where she is going and find a reasonable time on which the three parties agree. "When there's only one child it's very easy to be democratic. Parents might give in a little more to the child because her wishes are generally pretty reasonable," points out Dr. Sharon Ramey.

Compromise on expectations, too. Expect less and be surprised. Don't be picky; allow mistakes. Demanding perfection may strain your only and lead to serious psychological problems. Adjust your expectations so that they are realistic, an alteration that may automatically put reins on your desires for perfection.

Avoid lecturing the only child who isn't up to snuff—your snuff. The only child knows well when he is failing to meet his parents' goals. A lecture—or series of them—makes him feel worse . . . and/or defeated.

Be sure there are sibling substitutes and one or several other adults with whom your child relates well and to whom he can talk openly about feelings and problems that may be impossible to bring up with a parent. The only child needs a safety valve, other than one of his parents, to release emotions openly without fear of being criticized or judged.

Keep in mind that having one child doesn't mean you have to

parent better because you are not dividing your time, energy, and resources. No one hands out report cards on your parenting skills; you don't have to be any more or less successful than parents who have more children.

Nicholas D'Elia (Age Five): Profile of an Only

It was Anna D'Elia's first parent-teacher conference. Ms. Paul, her son's kindergarten teacher, tapped Nicholas's file with the eraser end of her pencil. Anna was momentarily disarmed; she had not considered the possibility of any serious problems. She thought Nick was doing well.

"Let me start by saying that Nicholas is the very reason I teach school. He's the reason I worry about everything I say in class. His memory is incredible; he absorbs and processes every morsel of information. One day when his 'bytes' are crammed, I don't want him to think back and say, 'My kindergarten teacher cluttered my brain with useless facts.' Believe me, he'll remember."

"What about friends? With whom does he get along?"

Ms. Paul laughed. "Everyone. The other children adore him. They seek him out. Every girl in the class is in love with him; every boy wants to be his best friend. That's an area you certainly don't have to worry about."

Holding up Nicholas's bear drawing, she explained how each child had developed a story around the bear. "Nicholas's story is advanced. He tries very hard. You can see it in his face when I'm talking. He's always ready for more.

"His disposition is sunny. His teachers will love him throughout school. And he's terribly funny. Really, Mrs. D'Elia, whatever you are doing, keep it up."

Nicholas D'Elia is an only child. Not every parent of an only child will be fortunate enough to get such a glowing kindergarten report. But when planning your family, deciding whether or not to keep your firstborn an only, think about Nicholas. He is not fictitious. He is a very real little boy who is adored, but not pampered, by his parents.

Only Children Have Their Say

Unquestionably, the D'Elias provide a nourishing environment for their son—Nicholas is thriving. He is not alone.

When asked, "What don't you like about being an only child?" Crystal Harper, a seventeen-year-old Texan responds, "*Nothing!* My parents and I talk together like friends and any disadvantage is blocked out by all the advantages."

Jamie Morton, who at the age of eleven wants to be exactly like her peers, is completely unhampered by her lack of a sibling. "I'm an only child and I don't mind it one bit. No diapers to change and there's no one around to bug me or take my stuff. If I had a younger brother or sister, I wouldn't be able to spend as much time with my friends because I would have to baby-sit. If I had an older brother or sister, he or she would always be yelling at me. So I'm happy being an only child."

Victoria Howe, a twelve-year-old Louisiana only, professed to being neutral. "I enjoy being an only child sometimes. Sometimes, I'd like to have brothers or sisters." Then she jotted down what she perceived as the advantages and disadvantages of being an only. Advantages (5): The house is always quiet when I want to read, study, etc. I never have to wait for a brother or sister to get out of the bathroom. I have my own room. I never have to argue with anyone about what *I* want to watch on TV. I'm never being compared to a brother or sister. Disadvantages (1): Being an only child *can* be boring. There's never a brother or sister to do anything with.

High school freshman Samantha Ingram adds to the plus column. "My friends complain about the teasing they get from their siblings. I don't miss that. I don't have to worry about a sibling listening in on my phone conversations or borrowing my clothes. One of my friends has assigned computer time because her mother couldn't stand the arguing. Mostly, my friends say, 'You're so lucky, you don't have siblings,' and I feel that way, too."

A mature Victor Smythe, age eighteen, reviews his formative years and draws his own positive conclusion. "I would not trade what I have gained for a little company from or intimacy with siblings. It has been easier to find those things elsewhere or to do without them."

John Armour, fifteen, voices the opinion of many teenage boys and girls. "I like not fighting and not being pestered constantly. I feel I have more freedom than my friends with siblings."

Seventeen-year-old Peter McNally sees a definite drawback to a houseful of children. "My parents treat me like an individual with his own life. They talk to me as an adult. If they had had more children, they probably would have labeled us 'a toddler, a teenager, a child, or preteen,' and paid more attention to our ages than to who we are."

When you listen to this generation of only children, it is apparent that the need for siblings is overrated. It is important to realize that the strong preference—or at the very least, contentment—with being an only child, was not uniformly the case among only children of past generations. An adult only may have an extreme tale similar to this one: "I wanted a sibling so badly that my best friend and I wrote a letter to an orphanage, signed my parents' names, and started the process of adoption. When my parents were called for an interview at the agency, my plan was uncovered," recalls Felice Roberts, a writer whose creativity was evident as a young teen. To this day, Felice, who is approaching fifty, yearns for a sibling.

Such stories must be kept in the perspective of the times and should not influence you or be confused with how only children feel today. The world is a very different place.

There is a smattering of young onlies who complain about wanting a sibling. Only children who express this desire fancy that the sibling will be their best friend. They idealize a condition that almost never is that way in real life. As only children mature, they realize that the brother or sister they dreamed about probably would never have measured up.

Moreover, to the extent that onlies do wish for siblings, their grievances are more age-related than long-term influences on their lives: "I don't have anyone to look up to," laments twelve-year-old Lucy Parent. "You don't have anyone to share your clothes with," complains Melinda West, age thirteen. Penny Rand, also thirteen, wishes "I had an older brother so that I could meet his friends." Ten-year-old Jolie Miles says, "When I get grounded, there is no one else who gets grounded with me."

When the going gets tough, everyone wants company. Only children are no exception. Under adverse circumstances, siblings look appealing. "In a way, life's fun without a brother or sister, but my parents are getting divorced," Mariette Didiere, age thirteen, sighs. "If I had a brother or sister, we could compare our feelings."

Being an Only Is a Huge Break

On balance, the consensus among only children is that being an only is "a huge break." A child without siblings will view his singleness as a problem *only if* you see it that way.

The only child has full access to the financial, intellectual, and emotional resources of his parents plus he is more likely to take on adult responsibilities sooner. "I was aware early on—around thirteen or fourteen—that I had money at my disposal and that it put me at an advantage," claims adult only Ross Yearwood.

At tender ages, only children know. "At eight, my son is well aware of how great it is not to have to share attention or resources. He has no illusions about what life is like with a sibling," notes Dr. Leiblum.

Because only children are treated as special, they feel they are special. "The attention I got worked to my benefit. It gave me a better education and more exposure to the world," assesses Ann Luther, who is in her thirties.

On the occasion of her bat mitzvah, a ceremony that marks a Jewish girl's crossing the threshold into womanhood, Sarah Kramer, then thirteen, elected to speak of the significance of being an only child: "I have had to take on responsibilities which would not have been mine if I had an older sibling. These little responsibilities have made me ready to handle the bigger one of taking care of myself and being my own person. I also think only children are more mature. If you have a younger sibling, you stay a kid longer. When you are an only child, more time is spent with adults and you get a head start in growing up."

Only children balk fiercely at "name tags," the stereotypes that are often imposed on them. "People, especially my friends," announces Penny Rand, "think because I am an only child, I get everything I want. That's a definite untruth! My parents do let me do things that some of my friends' parents won't let them do, but it's all within a range."

Says Barbara Friedman, "People say onlies are spoiled and demanding and it's really quite the opposite. Only children are trying to please people all the time because they are reacting to everyone as if each person were a parent."

Only-borns, like those with siblings, are a composite group. Consider the self-appraisals you've read. Like the rest of the population, onlies differ vastly in their personal traits and cannot simply be assigned uniform labels.

The only-child choice works and it works very well. Crystal Harper is further proof. When asked what she felt was the single biggest advantage to being an only child, she replied, "Being able to handle time alone. I cherish my time," Crystal openly explains. "I love kids, but not a brother or sister. I wouldn't want the bother. You make your own fun and develop creativity. You also learn to really know and love yourself."

"When I discover my five-year-old doing something alone, it's almost always creative," remarks Dr. Bonnie Markham, herself an only child. "David is comfortable with himself as I was and am and he does interesting things. He's self-directed and that trait has to be helpful forever and forever."

"Being there" for your child—something parents of one find a much simpler task—boosts a child's performance. "My parents were supportive in everything I did," muses twenty-three-year-old Justin Norcross, who actively participated in team sports from eighth grade through high school. "They attended every baseball game and football game I played. Their presence in the stands gave me great confidence in myself."

Only children realize early that there are also extreme emotional advantages to the strong bonding that takes place in only-child families. At thirteen, Missy Licatta reinforces how only children feel about their parents. "If I had a brother or sister, I wouldn't get as much love as I do now."

Such feelings are long-lasting. Adult only child Theresa Galinsky often thinks her parents are "the only people in the world who speak the same language. There are things I can only say to my mother; I have friends that I'm very close to, but I'm closest to my parents."

"Too much is made of being an only child," insists Duff Badgley. "You're born into a situation, so go ahead and make the best of it."

There will always be the child who feels her problems were created because she didn't have siblings. That feeling is caused by a society that has not fully shed the belief that siblings are a necessary part of normal development.[2] Similarly, there will always be the child who feels her problems were created by her siblings. Many more subscribe to the latter group.

Gone are the days when parents need to apologize for having an only child. Only children no longer feel set apart or different in negative ways. Rather, as Jennifer Walsh states, "Only children have to stand out in one way or another. Every only child I know is unique in some way." If only in attitude and approach to life . . .

"Every now and then I wonder how my life would change if I

had a brother or sister," admits eleven-year-old Jackie McGowen. "Then I remember I have the two greatest parents in the world. So I have stopped wondering and started living the way I've always been, alone and wonderful."

The Myth Was . . . The Reality Is . . .

The idea of "putting all your eggs in one basket" is appealing and should be. The only child is no longer in disrepute. Parents are making the determination that only children easily do as well as if not better than children with siblings. Within the last two decades only children have been evaluated around the world—in Scotland, the Netherlands, and other European countries, in China, Korea, and America—and from unique perspectives. Studies have looked at congressmen, psychiatrists, preschoolers, grade-school-age children, teenagers, young adults, and those older, to discover attitude or behavior differences. Throughout this book you've heard from hundreds of onlies and their parents. What we know from all these investigations is that the only child is no different from children with siblings and that he or she is, in many ways, advantaged. Onlies have slightly higher levels of self-esteem and education. Their intellectual ability and achievement edge are linked to the close parent-child interaction in the single-child family.[3]

When parents do opt for a second child, their reasoning is not what it used to be, states Dr. Sylvia Saltzstein. "It is not so much that they don't want an only child, but rather they want more children."

Given the current family climate, Richard Dewhurst notes that "it is more important to have a family unit than to have brothers and sisters. In Los Angeles it's a miracle to have two functioning parents without worrying about how many children you are going to have."

The belief, if ever true, that siblings play together for concentrated periods of time has given way to a practice of fragmented child rearing in which siblings in any given family are separated by age, school grade, and their elected sports and other activities. Most preschool classes are divided by age and as siblings get older, one child is off to soccer, while his sister goes to gymnastics. Because of crowded schedules in families with multiple siblings, on average, the children tend to interact with and spend more time with their parents one-on-one than with their siblings, further underscoring that a child needs caring parents far more than he needs siblings to insure his positive development, and further undermining the myth that a child needs siblings.

China, as a result of legally imposed childbearing restrictions between 1979 and 1999, has more than 50 million only children. Psychology professor Mao Yuyan of the Chinese Academy of Sciences in Beijing found that only children are "faring better than those with siblings" on an intellectual level.

Professor Yuyan told *Time* magazine that children with siblings can be more difficult, and concludes that "the decisive factor is not whether one is a single child. It is a question of parental attitude and education . . . We ask mothers to offer a childhood that is more than just chocolate plus toys, to teach the child to be courteous, collective-oriented, and self-reliant. That way, they [only children] will not become little emperors."[4]

Whether studying Chinese or American only children, the results are quite similar. Whether looking at levels of maturity, cooperativeness, self-esteem, self-control, social participation, anxiety, autonomy, leadership, generosity, or so many of the other traits on which old stereotypes are based, only children scored similar to and, in the case of self-esteem and achievement motivation, slightly better than, children with siblings.[5] The parenting perspective Dr. Yuyan was promoting almost twenty years ago worked effectively on both continents.

The extraordinary power of the myths about the only child is finally dissipating, as is the way we generally define family. Family once had a very limited definition and the majority of people simply responded to that definition by marrying and having the requisite two or more children. Family planning has become much more thoughtful, taking into account parents' ability to provide for their child or children as well as their own hopes, dreams, and preferences; an approach once considered selfish is viewed today as wise.

Conventional parenting as we knew it—Mom at home with two children, Dad at work—is ancient history. And we know that sibling interaction is simply not required to raise a happy, involved, well-adjusted, and productive child. The dominant attitude today is that it's far better to raise one child well than to have a larger family that you simply can't—or don't want to—handle financially or psychologically. One mother sums up the prevailing thinking: "One child gives parents the time to be well-balanced people and that allows them to be better parents."

A new breed of parent has evolved. It clearly prefers the only child for a variety of valid reasons, making the choice to have one more the rule than the exception. Lucas Saunders is one of this generation's confident parents. He is an only child who has an only child. "My being an only child absolutely influenced the fact that I have an only child. It made me a person who enjoys his own privacy so much that having more children would interfere with that privacy. My son's onliness was motivated for my sake, not so much for his. There were times I remember feeling my friends had nice relationships with older siblings, but I also knew that I had a lot more for myself."

Only child Harry Mitchum, who grew up in the era of the large family, advises those in a quandary to "limit your family to one child and count your *only* blessing."

As time goes on, more families resemble the Grazels. "I asked my parents not to give me a sibling," recalls twenty-nine-year-old Liza Grazel. "Being an only was what I knew and I liked the way things were in our house. My daughter will be an only. I have four cousins who are all only children and they each have one child. My mother was an only, too."

Roger Clemens, like many, has a wife who thrives on working.

"I was in my twenties when my son was born," explains Clemens, age forty. "Shortly after his birth we decided we didn't want any more children. My wife felt she was a career person."

"We decided when our daughter was about three not to have another," remarks Joe Michalcewicz. "It wasn't an issue of career for my wife; she stayed home during our daughter's formative years. We liked the closeness and interaction of our small family."

Attorney Richard Cooper and his wife, Claire, a biochemist, had other reasons. "We had Emily and talked about having another, but felt we would be spreading ourselves too thin. Our jobs and social demands would have been in constant conflict with our desire to give our children good parental guidance and time."

Gail Duncan is able to offer her four-year-old love and support ungrudgingly. "I have the time to give her yet I don't feel I *have to* give her the time. I want to. She gets 'everything' I've got and I don't have to split up my free hours."

Increased interaction with adults is one of the notable benefits of being an only child. Frank Owens has a formula that stimulates his eight-year-old son without suffocating him. "I talk to him about everything I know instead of running around worrying whether a houseful of children have had baths. I talk to him as an equal, giving him a lot of information without being overbearing and without talking down to him." Owens, like multitudes of others, including those in the fields of psychology and sociology, is convinced "that's why only children do better intellectually."

"The only child has more chances to become almost anything," remarks educator Deejay Schwartz. "She has a wider knowledge of roles from her increased exposure and can imagine herself as part of almost any kind of future."

Only children born today are chosen, and the choice is an enlightened one. In comparing parenting today with parenting in the 1950s, Dr. Brazelton pinpoints why so many are stopping at one. "The changes have been so great, and the new stresses on families so real and so apparent. What hasn't changed is the passion that parents have for doing a good job in raising their children."[6]

Every one of us wants to be recognized, to be the center of attention, maybe not constantly, but more often than not. Center stage in moderate doses is a supreme luxury. Why not let your only—or planned only—soar to his or her greatest heights with every benefit the singleton status provides?

One child opens vistas not possible in the multichild family. Parents can fulfill their own personal dreams while raising, educating, and enjoying a child who will be loved, secure, and privileged and *feel* loved, secure, and privileged. Are there any better feelings for a child to carry throughout life?

Notes

CHAPTER ONE

1. Smith, Tom W., "The Emerging 21ˢᵗ Century Family." *National Opinion Research Center,* University of Chicago, Dec. 2, 1999, GSS Social Change Report 42.

2. Scarr, Sandra. *Mother Care/Other Care.* New York: Basic Books, 1984, p. 19.

3. Crossette, Barbara. "How to Fix a Crowded World: Add People." *New York Times,* Nov. 2, 1997, Sec. 4, pp. 1, 3.

4. Smith, Tom W. op. cit.

5. Barnett, Rosalind and Rivers, Caryl. *She Works/He Works: How Two-Income Families are Happier, Healthier, and Better-Off.* New York: HarperSanFrancisco, 1996.

6. Crossette, op. cit.

7. Sims, Calvin. "Japan's Employers Are Giving Bonuses for Having Babies." *New York Times,* May 30, 2000, pp. A1, A8.

8. Tripp, Maggie, ed. *Woman in the year 2000.* New York: Arbor House, 1974, p. 57.

9. Eckel, Sara. "Single Mothers." *American Demographics,* Vol. 21, May 5, 1999, pp. 62–66.

10. McClain, Dylan Loeb. "A Growing Gender Gap." *New York Times,* June 14, 2000, p. G1.

11. Wilkie, Janet Riblett. "The Decline in Men's Labor Force Participation and Income and the Changing Structure of Family Economic Support." *Journal of Marriage and the Family.* Vol. 53, Feb. 1991.

12. Merser, C. *"Grown-Ups": A Generation in Search of Adulthood.* New York: Putnam, 1987, p. 24.

13. Schmitt, Eric. "For the First Time, Nuclear Families Drop Below Twenty-five percent of Households." *New York Times,* May 15, 2001, p. A1, A20; National Vital Statistics. "Births: Final Data for 1998." National Center for Health Statistics, 48:3, March 28, 2000.

14. Steinhauer, Jennifer. "In State of Wedlock, Declining Number of Arrivals From New York." *New York Times,* Jan. 9, 2000, pp. 21, 25.

15. Brown, Patricia Leigh. "Studying the Seasons of a Woman's Life." *New York Times,* Sept. 14, 1987, p. B17.

16. Smith, Tom W., op. cit.

17. National Vital Statistics. "Births: Final Data for 1998," op. cit.

18. Marin, Rick. "As a Bachelor's Biological Clock Ticks Away." *New York Times,* Feb. 13, 2000, p. 1.

19. Schreck, L. "Men and women have similar fertility intentions, and many of reproductive age postpone childbearing." *Family Planning Perspectives* 31:5 p. 254 (1999).

20. Wasserstein, Wendy. "Annals of Motherhood: Complications." *The New Yorker,* 75th Anniversary Issue, Feb. 21–28, 2000, pp. 87–109.

21. Nolan, Jim. "The New Age of Matchmaking: More Women Bank on Sperm Donors' Genetic Perfection." *Philadelphia Daily News,* Jul. 20, 1998, p. 33.

22. Wolff, Jana. *Secret Thoughts of an Adoptive Mother.* 2nd Edition, Honolulu: Vista Communications, 2000, p. 64.

23. Lang, Anne Adams. "When Parents Adopt a Child and a Whole Other Culture." *New York Times,* Mar. 8, 2000, p. 9.

24. Mueller, Karla Ann and Yoder, Janice D. "Gendered Norms for Family Size, Employment, and Occupation: Are There Personal Costs for Violating Them?" *Sex Roles,* Vol. 36, Issue 3/4 (1997), pp. 207–20.

CHAPTER TWO

1. Brazelton, T. Berry. *To Listen to a Child.* Reading, MA.: Addison-Wesley, 1984, p. 69.
2. Dovidio, John F.; Brigham, John C.; Johnson, Blair T. and Gaertner, Samuel L. *Stereotyping, Prejudice, and Discrimination.* New York: The Guilford Press, 1996, pp. 276–319.
3. Sulloway, Frank. *Born to Rebel: Birth Order, Family Dynamics and Creative Lives.* New York: Pantheon, 1996, pp. 204, 234.
4. Blake, Judith. "The Only Child in America: Prejudice versus Performance." *Population and Development Review 7,* No. 1, March 1981, p. 43.
5. Fenton, Norman. "The Only Child." *Journal of Genetic Psychology,* Vol. 35, 1928, p. 547.
6. Bohannon, E. W. "The Only Child in a Family." *Journal of Genetic Psychology,* Vol. 5, 1898, pp. 475 ff.
7. Chen, Xinyin; Rubin, Kenneth and Li, Bo-shu. "Only Children and Sibling Children in Urban China: A Re-Examination." *International Journal of Behavioral Development,* Vol. 17, Issue 3, 1994, pp. 413–21.
8. Doh, Hyun-Sim and Falbo, Toni. "Social Competence, Maternal Attentiveness and Overprotectiveness: Only Children in Korea." *International Journal of Behavioral Development,* Vol. 23, Issue 1, 1999, pp. 149–62.
9. Kagan, J.; Reznick, J. S.; and Snidman, N. "Biological Bases of Childhood Shyness." *Science,* Vol. 240 Apr. 8, 1998, pp. 167–71.
10. Blake, Judith. "Family Size and Quality of Children." *Demography,* Vol. 18, 1981, pp. 421–42.

11. Blake, Judith. *Family Size and Achievement.* Berkley, University of California Press, 1989, p. 231.

12. Blake, Judith. "The Only Child in America: Prejudice versus Performance." *Population and Development Review 7,* No. 1, Mar. 1981, p. 47.

13. Blake, Judith, ibid., p. 47.

14. Taylor, Marjorie. *Imaginary Companions and the Children Who Create Them.* New York: Oxford University Press, 1999, p. 66, 42–43.

15. Singer, Dorothy G. and Singer, Jerome L. *The House of Make-Believe: Children's Play and the Developing Imagination.* Cambridge, MA: Harvard University Press, 1990, pp. 3, 107.

16. McCormick, Patricia. "She's There, But You Just Can't See Her." *Parents,* Vol. 68, Issue 7, July 1993, p. 94.

17. Shen, Jianping and Yuan, Bao-Jane. "Moral Values of Only and Sibling Children in Mainland China." *Journal of Psychology,* Vol. 133, Issue 1 (1999), pp. 115–24.

18. Chen, Xinyin; Rubin, Kenneth and Li, Bo-shu. op. cit.

19. Falbo, Toni. "Social Norms and the One-Child Family: Clinical and Policy Implications." *Children's Sibling Relationships: Developmental and Clinical Issues,* Ed. Boer, Frits and Dunn, Judy. Hillsdale, NJ: Lawrence Erlbaum Associates, 1992, pp. 71–82.

20. Balter, Lawrence, with Shreve, Anita. *Dr. Balter's Child Sense.* New York: Poseidon Press, 1985, p. 87.

21. Falbo, Toni. "Social Norms and the One-Child Family: Clinical and Policy Implications." *Children's Sibling Relationships: Developmental and Clinical Issues,* op. cit.

22. Falbo, Toni. "The Only Child: A review." *Journal of Individual Psychology,* 1977, pp. 53–54.

23. Polit, Denise. "The Only Child in Single-Parent Families." *The Single-Child Family.* Ed. Toni Falbo. New York: Guilford Press, 1984, pp. 178–209.

24. Main, Frank. *Perfect Parenting & Other Myths.* Minneapolis: CompCare Publication, 1986, pp. 31–44.

25. Sulloway, Frank. op. cit.

26. Claudy, J. G., Farrell, W. S., and Dayton, C. W. "The Consequences of Being an Only Child: An Analysis of Project Talent Data." Palo Alto, Calif.: American Institutes for Research, 1979, pp. 33 ff.

27. Haas, Nancy. "We are a family: Mom, Dad and Just Me." *New York Times,* Oct. 24, 1999.

28. Blake, Judith. *Family Size and Achievement.* Berkley, University of California Press, 1989, p. 231.

29. Groat, H. Theodore, Wicks, Jerry W., and Neal, Arthur G. "Differential Consequences of Having Been an Only Versus a Sibling Child." Final Report: Contract NIH-NO1-HD-92806. Center for Population Research-NICHD. National Institutes of Health, April 1980, pp. 67–89, 173.

30. Claudy, J. G. et al., op. cit., pp. 166–77.

31. Blake, Judith. "The Only Child in America," op. cit., p. 51.

CHAPTER THREE

1. Bernard, Jessie. *The Future of Motherhood.* New York: Dial Press, 1974, p. 53.

2. Bulatao, Rodolpho A. "Values and Disvalues of Children in Successive Childbearing Decisions." *Demography* 18.1 (1981): 16–17.

3. Cardozo, Arlene Rossen. *Woman at Home.* Garden City, NY: Doubleday, 1976, pp. 104–5.

4. Galinski, Ellen. *Ask the Children: What America's Children Really Think About. Working Parents.* New York: William Morrow, 1999.

5. Sauerwein, Kristina. "Companies are buying into benefit of being friendly to families." *Post-Dispatch* 13 Dec. 1998, p. A1.

6. Lardner, James. "World-Class Workaholics: Are Crazy Hours and Take Out Dinners the Elixir of America's Success?" *U.S. News & World Report* 127.24 (1999): 42–53.

7. Lague, Louise. "The Singular Pleasure of a Second Child." *Mothers Today,* March/April 1988, p. 22.

8. Brazelton, T. Berry. *To Listen to a Child*. Reading, MA: Addison-Wesley, 1984, p. 69.

9. Moses, Kate. *I Love You Both Unequally*. 1997. http://www.salon.com/june97/mothers/twokids.

10. Moses, Kate, ibid.

11. Sulloway, Frank. *Born to Rebel: Birth Order, Family Dynamics and Creative Lives*. New York: Pantheon, 1996, p. 79.

12. Bedford, Victoria. "Memories of Parental Favoritism and the Quality of Parent-Child Ties in Adulthood." *Journal of Gerontology* 47 (1992): 149–55.

13. Rinzler, Jane. *Teens Speak Out*. New York: Donald I. Fine, 1985, pp. 15–16.

14. Longman, Phillip J., "The Cost of Children." *U.S. News & World Report* 30 March 1998. http://www.usnews/issue/980330/30chil.htm.

15. Steelye, Katherine Q. "Gore Proposing Ways to Improve Child Care." *New York Times*. 2 June 2000: A28.

16. Longman, Phillip J., op. cit.

17. MSN Money Central. "Cost of Raising Kids." U.S. Department of Labor, Expenditure Survey, 2000. http://www.MSN.com.

18. Longman, Phillip J., op. cit.

19. Schmidt, Peter. "Boom in Savings Plans is Changing the Way Families Pay for College." *The Chronicle of Higher Education* 46.32 (2000): A42–A43.
Wang, Penelope. "Pay for College." *Money Magazine*. 29.4 (2000): 90–94.

20. National Association of Realtors. "Existing-Home Sales by Metro, State, and Regional Areas." *Real Estate Outlook: Market Trends and Insights,* 2000. http://nar.realtor.com/databank/link.htm.

21. Families and Work Institute. "Reframing the Business Case for Work-Life Initiatives." *Families and Work Institute,* 1998. http://www.familiesandworkinst.org.

22. Olson, Elizabeth. "U.N. Surveys Paid Leave for Mothers." *New York Times*. 26 Feb. 1998: A5.

23. Netherlands Interdisciplinary Demographic Institute Flemish

Population and Family Study Center. "Parental Leave in Europe." *U.S. News & World Report,* 12 July 2000.

24. Jordan, Laura. "Background Information of European and Canadian Parental Leave Laws." *OLR Research,* Rep. No. 99-R-1214, Dec. 3, 1999.

25. Belkin, Lisa. "Tony Blair's Baby: Some Decisions Last Longer." *New York Times* 12 April 2000: G1.

26. Orenstein, Peggy. *Flux: Women on Sex, Work, Kids, Love and Life in a Half Changed World.* New York: Doubleday, 2000, pp. 165–207; 285–86.

27. Anonymous. "Career Prospects May Be Dimmer for Unpaid Leave Takers." *HR Focus* 77.4 (2000): 8–9.
Lyness, Karen S., Cynthia A. Thompson, Anne Marie Francesco and Michael K. Judiesch. "Work and pregnancy: Individual and organizational factors influencing organizational commitment, timing of maternity leave, and return to work." *Sex Roles* 41 (1999): 485–508.

28. Kingson, Jennifer A. "Women in the Law Say Path Is Limited by 'Mommy Track.' " *New York Times* 8 Aug. 1988: 1, A15.

29. Jacobs, Deborah. "Back From the Mommy Track." *New York Times* 9 Oct. 1994: sec. 3: 1 ff.

30. Hertz, Rosanna. "Working to Place Family at the Center of Life: Dual-Earner and Single-Parent Strategies." *Journal of Marriage and the Family* 61 (1999): 557–87.

31. O'Hanlon, Ann. "When One Child Is Just Enough: Couple Opting for Freedom, Economy of Small Family." *Washington Post* 21 November 1999, p. A1.

32. Peterson, Karen S. "Working Hours Are Longer, But Workplaces Seem Nicer." *USA Today* 15 April 1998, p. 1D.

CHAPTER FOUR

1. Manning, W. D. and Smock, P. J., "Children's Living Arrangements in Unmarried Mother Families." *Journal of Family Issues* 18 (1997): 526–44.

2. Heath, D. Terri and Dennis K. Orthner. "Stress and adaptation among male and female single parents." *Journal of Family Issues* 20 (1999): 557–87.

3. Smith, Tom W. "The Emerging 21st Century Family." National Opinion Research Center, University of Chicago, Dec. 2, 1999, GSS Social Change Report 4, p. 4.

4. U.S. Census Bureau. "Population Profile of the United States." *U.S. Bureau of Census,* 2000, 1998, series P23–194.

5. Downey, D. B. "Sex of Parent and Children's Well-Being in Single-Parent Households." *Journal of Marriage and the Family* 60 (1998): 878–93.

6. Cherlin, Andrew. "Going to Extremes, Family Structure, Children's Well-Being, and Social Science." *Demographics* 36 (1999): 421–28.

7. Shireman, Joan M. "Adoptions By Single Parents." *Single Parent Families: Diversity, Myths and Realities.* The Haworth Press, Inc., 1995, pp. 367–88.

8. Ricciuti, Henry R. "Single Parenthood and School Readiness in White, Black and Hispanic Six and Seven Year Olds." *Journal of Family Psychology* 13 (1999): 450–65.

9. Curran, Dolores. Traits of a Healthy Family: Fifteen Traits Commonly Found in Healthy Families by Those Who Work with Them. Minneapolis, Minn.: Winston Press, c. 1983.

10. Eckel, Sarah. "Single Mothers." *American Demographics* 21.5 (1999): 62–66.

11. Mannis, Valerie. "Single Mothers By Choice." *Family Relations* 48 (1999): 121–28.

12. Shea, Jill. "Mother of One." *Wanting a Child.* Eds. Jill Bialosky and Helen Schulman. New York: Farrar, Straus and Giroux, 1998, pp. 195–99.

13. Blomstrom, Jennifer. "A Different Reproductive Choice." *Off Our Backs,* vol. 29, Issue 2, February 1999, p. 6.

14. Heath, Terri and Dennis K. Orthner, op. cit.

15. Ellison, Shiela. *The Courage to be a Single Mother: Becoming Whole Again After the Divorce.* San Francisco: HarperSanFrancisco, 2000, p. 80.

16. Edy, Carolyn. "Single Motherhood Is a Joy, Not a Disaster." *Newsweek.* 10 May 1999: 12.

CHAPTER FIVE

1. Bossard, James H. S., and Eleanor S. Boll. *Family Situations: An Introduction to the Study of Child Behavior.* Philadelphia: University of Pennsylvania Press, 1941.

2. Talbot, Kay. "Mothers Now Childless: Survival After the Death of an Only Child." *Omega,* Vol. 34, Issue 3, 1996–1997, pp. 177–89.

3. Matthews, Stanford, J. *The Motherhood Maze.* Garden City, NY: Doubleday, 1982, p. 9.

CHAPTER SEVEN

1. Hofferth, Sandra. *Healthy Environments, Healthy Children: Children in Families.* Ann Arbor, MI: University of Michigan, 1998. http://www.isr.umich.edu/src/child-development/fullrep.html.

2. Hofferth, Sandra, ibid.

3. Ginott, Haim G. *Between Parent & Teenager.* New York: Macmillan, 1969, p. 132.

4. Schurr, Stephen. "Too Much Pressure on Too Many Kids." *The Wall Street Journal* 6 March 1998: sports section.

5. Schurr, Stephen, ibid.

6. Lebowitz, Fran. *Social Studies.* New York: Random House, 1981, pp. 20–21.

7. Elkind, David. *Miseducation: Preschoolers at Risk*. New York: Alfred A. Knopf, 1987, p. 40.

8. Wilgoren, Jodi and Steinberg, Jacques. "Even For Sixth Graders, College Looms." *New York Times* 3 July 2000: A1, A12.

9. Relic, Peter. "Kids in the Pressure Cooker." Jan. 2000. http://www.nais.org/inform/press/pdrpressure.html.

10. Bohannon, E. W. "The Only Child in a Family." *Journal of Genetic Psychology* 5 (1898): 495.

11. Reiss, Stephen. *Who Am I? The 18 Basic Desires That Motivate Our Actions and Define Our Personalities*. New York: Jeremy P. Tarcher/Putnam, 2000, p. 196.

CHAPTER EIGHT

1. Thompson, Michael G. "Peer Pleasure, Peer Pain: Understanding the Social Lives of Children." *Independent School Magazine* 57.1, Fall 1997.

2. DeHart, Ganie B. "Conflict and Averted Conflict in Preschoolers' Interactions with Siblings and Friends." *Relationships as Developmental Contexts*. Eds. Andrew W. Collins and Brett Laursen. Mahwah, NJ: Lawrence Erlbaum Associates, 1999, pp. 281–303.

3. Thompson, Michael G. op. cit.

4. Morris, Monica. *Last Chance Children: Growing Up with Older Parents*. New York: Columbia University Press, 1988, pp. viii, 54.

CHAPTER NINE

1. Polit-O'Hara, Denise and Judith Berman. *Just the Right Size: A Guide to Family-Size Planning*. New York: Praeger, 1984, p. 11.

2. Richards, Hillary and Robert Goodman. "Are Only Children Different? A Study of Child Psychiatric Referrals: A Research

Note." *Journal of Child Psychology & Psychiatry & Allies Disciplines* 37 (1996): 753–57.

3. Brazelton, T. Berry. *To Listen to a Child.* Reading, MA: Addison-Wesley, 1984, pp. 69–70.

4. Smith, Tom W. "The Emerging 21ˢᵗ Century Family." National Opinion Research Center, University of Chicago, Dec. 2, 1999, GSS Social Change Report 4.

5. Brazelton, op. cit., p. 69.

6. Faber, A., and E. Mazlish. *Siblings Without Rivalry.* New York: Norton, 1987, p. 24.

7. Cicirelli, Victor G. *Sibling Relationships Across the Life Span.* New York: Plenum Press, 1995, p. 151.

8. Falbo, Toni. "Social Norms and the One-Child Family: Clinical and Policy Implications." *Children's Sibling Relationships: Developmental and Clinical Issues.* Eds. Frits Boer and Judy Dunn. Hillsdale, NJ: Lawrence Erlbaum Associates, 1992, pp. 71–82.

9. DeHart, Ganie B. "Conflict and Averted Conflict in Preschoolers' Interactions With Siblings and Friends." *Relationships as Developmental Contexts.* Eds. Andrew W. Collins and Brett Laursen. Mahwah, NJ: Lawrence Erlbaum Associates, 1999, pp. 281–303.

10. Newcomb, Andrew F. and Catherine, L. Bagwell. "The Developmental Significance of Children's Friendship Relationships." *The Company They Keep: Friendship in Childhood and Adolescence.* Eds. William M. Bukowski, Andrew F. Newcomb and Willard W. Hartup. Cambridge, MA: Cambridge University Press, 1996, pp. 289–321.

11. Berndt, Thomas J. "Exploring the Effects of Friendship Quality on Social Development." *The Company They Keep: Friendship in Childhood and Adolescence.* Eds. William M. Bukowski, Andrew F. Newcomb and Willard W. Hartup. Cambridge, MA: Cambridge University Press, 1996, pp. 346–65.

12. Bernard, Jesse. *The Future of Motherhood.* New York: Dial Press, 1974, p. 116.

13. Martin, Joyce A. and Melissa A. Park. "Trends in Twins and Triplet Births: 1980–1997." *U.S. Department of Health and*

Human Services National Center for Health Statistics. National Vital Statistics Report. 47.24 (1999).

14. Cicirelli, Victor G. *Sibling Relationships Across the Life Span,* op. cit., p. 151.

15. Wilson, Carol D. & Fromuth, Mary Ellen. "Childhood Sibling Abuse Common, But Most Adults Don't Remember It That Way." *The Monitor.* American Psychological Association, August 1997. http://www.apa.org/releases/sibling.htm.

16. Bedford, Victoria H. "Sibling Relationship Troubles and Well-Being in Middle and Old Age." *Family Relations: Interdiciplinary Journal of Applied Family Studies* 47, 4 (1998): 369–76.

17. Garey, Sinika Sade. *Long-term Effects of Sibling Emotional and Physical Abuse On Adult Self-concept and the Associated Guilt and Shame.* Diss. United States International University. U.S. International University: San Diego: 1998.

CHAPTER TEN

1. Coltrane, Scott. "Fathers' Role at Home Is Under Negotiation." *The Chronicle of Higher Education* 45.6 (1998): B8.

2. Risman, Barbara J. and Danette Johnson-Summerford. "Doing It Fairly: A Study of Postgender Marriages." *Journal of Marriage and the Family* 60.1 (1998): 23–40.

3. Deutsch, Francine M. *Halving It All: How Equally Shared Parenting Works.* Cambridge, MA: Harvard University Press, 1999, pp. 73–84.

4. Deutsch, Francine M. "The 50/50 Myth: Why Even Good Husbands Fail to Do Enough." *Redbook* 192.5 (March 1999): 100–103.

5. Deutsch, Francine M., ibid.

6. Spock, Benjamin. *The Common Sense Book of Baby and Child Care.* New York: Duell, Sloan and Pearce, 1945, p. 15.

7. Lundberg, Shelly and Elaina Rose. *The Effect of Sons and*

Daughters on Men's Labor Supply and Wages. University of Washington, Oct. 1999, pp. 1–43.
http://www.econ.washington.edu/wkg_papers_name.asp.

8. DeMeis, Debra and H. Wesley Perkins. " 'Supermoms' of the Nineties: Homemaker and Employed Mothers' Performance and Perceptions of the Motherhood Role." *Journal of Family Issues* 17, 6 (1996): 776–92.

9. Axinn, William G., Jennifer S. Barber and Arland Thornton. "The Long-term Impact of Childbearing Decisions on Children's Self-Esteem." *Demography* 35,4 (1998): 435–44.

10. Quindlen, Anna. "Life in the 30s." *New York Times* 27 January 1988: sect. C.

11. Polit-O'Hara, Denise and Judith Berman. *Just the Right Size: A Guide to Family-Size Planning.* New York: Praeger, 1984, p. 11.

12. Bouton, Jim. "Players Aren't Different Today, It's Just the World Is More Dangerous." *New York Daily News* 26 Feb. 1989, p. 76.

CHAPTER ELEVEN

1. Lerner, Harriet. *The Mother Dance: How Children Change Your Life.* New York: Harper Collins, 1998, p. 222.

2. Living Will Registry. http://www.uslivingwillregistry.com.

CHAPTER TWELVE

1. McKibben, Bill. *Maybe One: A Personal and Environmental Argument for Single-Child Families.* New York: Simon & Schuster, 1998, p. 208.

2. Falbo, Toni. "Social Norms and the One-Child Family: Clinical and Policy Implications." *Children's Sibling Relationships: Developmental and Clinical Issues.* Eds. Frits Boer and Judy Dunn. Hillsdale, NJ: Lawrence Erlbaum Associates, 1992, pp. 71–82.

3. Polit, Denise and Toni Falbo. "The Intellectual Achievement of Only Children." *Journal of Biosocial Science* 20:3 (1998): 275–85.

4. Chua-Eoan, Howard G. "China: Bringing Up Baby, One by One." *Time* 7 Dec. 1987, p. 38.

5. Falbo, Toni, op. cit.

6. Brazelton, T. Berry. "Working Parents." *Newsweek* 13 Feb. 1989, p. 66.

Resources

GENERAL PARENTING

ABC's of Parenting hosts its own discussion boards on general parenting topics and pregnancy in addition to acting as a search engine for other parenting sites on the web.
www.abcparenting.com

ClubMom serves mothers by giving them a place to share, communicate, and celebrate the joys and emotions of being a mom. Informative articles change frequently and are archived. Members receive a free e-mail account and can register to receive special discounts.
www.clubmom.com

College Savings Plans Network is an affiliate of the National Association of State Treasurers. Its web page links to your state's program and provides information about state college savings plans. The frequently asked questions section discusses the different types of plans and how each one can be used.
www.collegesavings.org

Families and Work Institute, a non-profit organization, addresses the changing nature of work and family life. It is committed to finding research-based work-life solutions that foster mutually supportive connections among workplaces, families, and communities.

www.familiesandworkinst.org

Family.com is easy to navigate. Divided into categories from activities to travel, the site offers expert advice on health, child development, and family issues. Family.com features message boards pertaining to family, individual needs, and pastimes for children.

www.family.com

Family Education, the Learning Network, focuses on various aspects of education and includes information by age and grade, school resources, expert advice, and idea exchange in the form of bulletin boards and assorted grade-related online newsletters.

www.familyeducation.com

Librarians' Index to the Internet is a comprehensive index with links to family and children resources.

www.lii.org

Moms Online is a virtual community of mothers who collaboratively create a friendly site in cyberspace. Their definition of "mom" is far reaching and includes anyone engaged in nurturing the next generation—stay-at-home moms, working moms, married moms, single moms, teen moms, dads, and grandparents. Tips and discussions range from pregnancy issues to family outings.

www.momsonline.com

Only Child, a website and newsletter published quarterly, is devoted to one of the fastest-growing segments of our society—only children. The creators' mission is to work with only children, parents, relatives, friends, community organizations, and educational institutions to provide support and information on the only child, from child care to elder care.

www.onlychild.com

Parenthood Web features discussion boards by parenting topic and chats with a large section devoted to pregnancy. The site offers news stories, recent product recalls, and an online newsletter to order.

www.parenthoodweb.com

Parenting-L is an Internet discussion group on topics related to parenting children (including child development, education, and care) from birth through adolescence. Discussion ranges from family leave and parental rights issues to parents as partners in their children's education, and is carried on by e-mail.
http://ericeece.org/listserv/parent-l.html

Parent News in the form of articles, product alerts, health care tips and more can be accessed from this site. Sign up for their e-mail newsletter to receive up-to-date information.
www.parent.net

Parent Soup offers advice on the stages and concerns of parenting be they pre-natal, medical, developmental, or educational. Parents can submit questions to professionals in selected fields. The resources section links to fun things such as games, a pregnancy calendar, and a baby name finder. A Careguide provides national directories for child or senior care. Thousands of message boards including a "Parents of only children" board let parents interact and share ideas.
www.parentsoup.com

ParentsPlace gives information on fertility, pregnancy, health, financial calculators, family, and much more. It provides a forum for people interested in parenting through chat rooms, message boards (with one called "Only Child"), newsletters, and relevant articles.
www.parentsplace.com

SavingForCollege.com's goal is to provide you—the parent/investor or professional advisor—with the most comprehensive, current, and objective information available regarding qualified state tuition programs ("529 Plans"). This site covers in-depth information on college savings plans and offers state-by-state comparisons, relevant articles, a newsletter, and a message board.
www.savingforcollege.com

U.S. Living Will Registry, a free service, gives you the tools to set up and register an advanced directive. An advanced directive allows a person to make health-care choices known in the case of an incapacitating illness. By registering with the Living Will Registry you grant permission to release your directive to hospitals.

www.uslivingwillregistry.com Also see: www.partnershipforcaring.org

Work & Family Life Newsletter is a monthly newsletter with information and practical solutions on a wide range of family, job, and health issues in an effort to reduce stress and find pleasure and satisfaction in parents' roles at work, at home, and in their communities. Call (800) 278-2579 for a sample copy or to order.

Books

Deutsch, Francine M. *Halving It All: How Equally Shared Parenting Works.* Cambridge, MA: Harvard University Press, 1999.

Orenstein, Peggy. *Flux: Women on Sex, Work, Kids, Love and Life in a Half Changed World.* New York: Doubleday, 2000.

SINGLE PARENTING

Father's World celebrates fatherhood as a leading source of information, resources, support, and education for all types of fathers and their families. Father's World posts articles and provides discussion groups for single fathers where they can share experiences, ask questions, and voice concerns.

www.fathersworld.com

Parents Without Partners is the largest international, non-profit, educational organization devoted to the interests of single parents and their children. Founded in 1957, Parents Without Partners provides discussions, study groups, publications, and social activities for families and adults. Included on the web site are a newsletter, resources, and facts about single-parent families.

www.parentswithoutpartners.org

Single and Custodial Father's Network is an international, member-supported, non-profit organization dedicated to helping fathers meet the challenge of being parents. The network lends support to both custodial and noncustodial fathers. While visiting the site you can peruse the cookbook, send postcards, chat, browse the bookstore, and join the listserv. Topics range from debate to humor.

www.scfn.org

Single Father's Lighthouse is an effective guide for single dads, but moms are also welcome. The webmaster gives helpful comments on resources and books for single parenting, and provides links to legal assistance regarding custody and visitation. A unique aspect of the Single Father's Lighthouse is the section on inspiration and humor. The site provides a listserv for single dads.

http://users.qnet.com/~rlewis3/

Single Mothers by Choice is a unique support system for single women who have chosen or are considering single motherhood. Members form friendships and share information on national and local levels. Membership includes a quarterly newsletter and a private e-mail listserv.

www.singlemothersbychoice.com

Single Parents Association, an international nonprofit organization, provides educational opportunities and fun family activities via a network of chapters throughout the United States with an online virtual chapter to join if there is no chapter in your area. Its online site, also open to regular chapter members, features book reviews, an e-mail discussion forum, chat room, parenting tips, and a section on continuing education for single parents.

www.singleparents.org

Single Parents Support Group is a community of single parents sharing ideas, concerns, and advice.

www.singleparents.net

SingleParenting on About.com is a comprehensive web site containing features, discussion rooms, and newsletters. This site provides single-parent statistics and other web resources. Information also focuses on financial matters for single parents.

http://singleparents.about.com

Books

Brott, Armin A. *The Single Father: A Dad's Guide to Parenting Without a Partner.* New York: Abbeville Press, 1999.

Ellison, Shiela. *The Courage to be a Single Mother: Becoming Whole Again After the Divorce.* San Francisco: HarperSanFrancisco, 2000.

Klatte, William C. *Live-Away Dads: Staying a Part of Your Children's Lives When They Aren't a Part of Your Home.* New York: Penguin USA, 1999.

Lamott, Anne. *Operating Instructions: A Journal of My Son's First Year.* New York: Fawcett Books, 1994.

Mattes, Jane. *Single Mothers by Choice: A Guidebook for Single Women Who Are Considering or Have Chosen Motherhood.* New York: Times Books, 1997.

ADOPTION

Adopt: Assistance Information Support is an informative site for those looking to adopt, adoptees, and adopting professionals. Support boards deal with topics ranging from general, gay and lesbian adoption to surrogate issues. The site details a search for finding birth parents. A unique aspect is the list of famous adoptees and adoptive parents.
www.adopting.org/ar.html

Adopt Vietnam is a guide to adoptions from Vietnam that provides adoption, travel, and parenting information in conjunction with a companion site, **Families with Children from Vietnam** (FCV). These sites are effective because they educate on aspects of Vietnamese culture and offer travel hints. The FCV site contains photographs, e-mail addresses, and personal adoption stories, while Adopt Vietnam gives parenting pointers and recommends books.
www.adoptvietnam.org and www.fcvn.org

Adopted Child has information, support, and counseling advice for parents and professionals about adopted children of all ages, including such topics as how children understand adoption. www.raisingadoptedchildren.com

Adopting.com has the largest adoption resources index on the web. In addition to general resources, the site provides monthly feature sites. Adopting.com also provides access to waiting child photo listings from adoption agencies, facilitators, and attorneys. www.adopting.com

Adopting from Korea is a prospective parents guide to Korean adoption with comprehensive information regarding benefits of Korean adoption, requirements, restrictions, and a waiting child photo listing. The site furnishes Korean and other international adoption related web sites, listservs, and books. www.adoptkorea.com

American Academy of Adoption Attorneys is a national nonprofit association of 300 attorneys throughout the United States and Canada who are experts in the complexities of adoption law. The Academy, the largest and most accessible source for finding an adoption attorney, provides information on why to hire an adoption attorney and tips for choosing the right one. www.adoptionattorneys.org

Evan B. Donaldson Adoption Institute sources adoption professionals and others interested in adoption research policy and practice with current adoption information. The institute offers comprehensive statistics on national and international adoption. As a site for professionals, the institute lists current studies and books on issues related to adoptions, such as prenatal alcohol exposure and surveys of adult adoptees. www.adoptioninstitute.org

Families with Children from China, an organization of families who have adopted children from China, offers a network of support for families who have adopted in China as well as information for prospective parents. The site has been put together by the families to make it easier for future parents to consider adoption from

China. It is especially effective because it offers current statistics and a frequently asked questions section covering questions of adoption cost, ages, and travel advice. FWCC also has an on-line resource guide for adoptive parents.
www.fwcc.org

National Council for Single Adoptive Parents is a non-profit organization that helps children find families. The Council publishes "News for Single Adoptive Parents," which lists sources of adoptable children, support groups, and information for singles who want to be parents, plus other adoption resources.
www.adopting.org/ncsap.html

Books

DellaVecchio, Andrea. *The Unofficial Guide to Adopting a Child.* Foster City, CA: IDG Books Worldwide, 2000.

Varon, Lee. *Adopting on Your Own: The Complete Guide to Adoption for Single Parents.* New York: Farrar, Straus & Giroux, 2000.

Wolff, Jana. *Secret Thoughts of an Adoptive Mother.* Honolulu: Vista Communications, 1999.

Wheeler, Kathleen and Werner, Doug. *Adopting in China: A Practical Guide/An Emotional Journey.* Chula Vista, CA: Tracks Publishing, 1999.

INFERTILITY

Child of My Dreams is designed to help people become parents and to demonstrate that with information, support, and determination, you really can have the child of your dreams. Visitors gain support and advice from other members on both infertility and adoption, in addition to accessing an impressive panel of experts, who provide medical, psychological, legal, and financial advice.

Message boards, chat rooms, and live "guest speakers" swap information on myriad infertility topics.

www.childofmydreams.com

Fertile Thoughts supports infertile couples and couples seeking adoption as well as couples and single parents in various stages of parenthood. The site was created with one purpose in mind: providing relief for the site's visitors. Much of the site's materials are created and contributed by their enthusiastic online community.

www.fertilethoughts.net

Fertilitext is operated by a national pharmacy provider specializing in infertility. The goal is to provide information about infertility and reproductive issues to those pursuing fertility treatment. Fertilitext offers fertility news, education, information about medications and supplies and links to fertility services such as directories of fertility specialists, sperm/tissue banks, and listings of books and articles. Visitors can sign up for the bi-monthly newsletter and receive important updates on fertility treatment.

www.fertilitext.org

Fertility Network specializes in providing information for reproduction scientists. However, it also includes a section devoted to providing information for fertility patients. You can find or become a fertility penpal, search the Internet for fertility links, and browse the IVF Bookstore for books on fertility procedures and coping.

www.ivf.net

InterNational Council on Infertility Information Dissemination (INCIID—pronounced "inside") is a nonprofit, consumer advocacy organization dedicated to helping couples explore their family-building options. This site highlights current reproductive news and research, related bulletin boards, chat rooms, an infertility glossary, a recommended reading list, and web links. In addition, they post a series of frequently asked questions sheets related to infertility.

www.inciid.org

Books

Bialosky, Jill and Schulman, Helen, Eds. *Wanting a Child.* New York: Farrar, Straus and Giroux, 1999.

Marrs, Richard, Lisa Friedman Bloch and Kathy Kirtland Silverman. *Dr. Richard Marrs' Fertility Book: America's Leading Infertility Expert Tells You Everything You Need to Know about Getting Pregnant.* New York: Dell, 1998.

Peoples, Debby and Harriette Rovner Ferguson. *Experiencing Infertility: An Essential Resource.* New York: Norton, 1999.

Resolve Staff. *Resolving Infertility: Understanding the Options and Choosing Solutions When You Want to Have a Baby.* New York: HarperCollins, 1999.

Simons, Harriet F. and Julia Litwintschik Ellis. *Wanting Another Child: Coping with Secondary Infertility.* San Francisco: Jossey-Bass Inc., 1998.

Book Mark

The text of this book was composed in
the typeface Adobe Garamond
with display typography in Ojaio
by Berryville Graphics,
Berryville, Virginia

This book was printed
by Berryville Graphics,
Berryville, Virginia

Book Design
by Ellen Cipriano

ABOUT THE AUTHOR

Social psychologist Susan Newman, Ph.D., an authority on only children and herself the mother of an only child, specializes in issues that affect children and family life. She teaches at Rutgers University in New Jersey and is the author of eleven books including the bestselling *Little Things Long Remembered: Making Your Children Feel Special Every Day, Little Things Mean A Lot: Creating Happy Memories with Your Grandchildren,* and *Never Say Yes to a Stranger. Parenting an Only Child* has been featured on *NBC Nightly News,* CNN, ABC, and Fox News, as well as in the *New York Times,* the *Los Angeles Times, USA Today,* and the *Boston Globe.* Several of her books have also become award-winning educational videos. Newman is often a featured speaker and workshop leader on parenting topics. Visit her web site at: www.susannewmanphd.com